ECONOMIC EXPANSION
AND SOCIAL CHANGE:
ENGLAND 1500–1700

Volume I
People, land and towns

ECONOMIC EXPANSION AND SOCIAL CHANGE: ENGLAND 1500–1700

Volume I
People, land and towns

C.G.A. CLAY

Reader in Economic History, University of Bristol

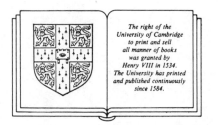

The right of the
University of Cambridge
to print and sell
all manner of books
was granted by
Henry VIII in 1534.
The University has printed
and published continuously
since 1584.

CAMBRIDGE UNIVERSITY PRESS

Cambridge

London   New York   New Rochelle
Melbourne   Sydney

Published by the Press Syndicate of the University of Cambridge
The Pitt Building, Trumpington Street, Cambridge CB2 1RP
32 East 57th Street, New York, NY 10022, USA
296 Beaconsfield Parade, Middle Park, Melbourne 3206, Australia

First published 1984

Printed in Great Britain at the University Press, Cambridge

Library of Congress catalogue card number: 83–23221

British Library Cataloguing in Publication Data

Clay, C.G.A.
Economic expansion and social change.
Vol. I, People, land and towns
1. England–Social conditions
I. Title
942.05   NH 385

ISBN 0 521 25942 8 hard covers
ISBN 0 521 27768 X paperback

TM

CONTENTS

VOLUME I

v

VOLUME II

TABLES

FIGURES

MAPS

PREFACE

More than a quarter of a century ago Professor F.J. Fisher, in a most memorable phrase, referred to the sixteenth and seventeenth centuries as the 'dark ages' of English economic history. Since he wrote an entire generation of research has thrown a flood of light onto many matters that were then almost entirely obscure. New methodologies have been developed, new sources of evidence exploited, and the frontiers of historical understanding rolled back uncovering in the process a wide range of developments whose existence was entirely unsuspected in 1956. Some old controversies may have been laid to rest, but new ones aplenty have sprung to life, and both student and teacher are now faced with an awe inspiring mass of literature to master if they are to come properly to grips with the subject. There are several short introductory books available which give an excellent overview of the economic and social history of the period, and a number of useful pamphlets by acknowledged authorities devoted to particular aspects of it. However, there has not hitherto been one which provided a substantial amount of information about all major aspects, set firmly in an interpretative context. What follows is an attempt to fill that gap.

The work is explicitly designed as a text-book. This does not mean that only those studying for examinations will find it interesting, but that its purpose is to provide a synthesis of present understanding, organized in such a way that the reader may easily locate the discussion of any particular matter in which he is interested. It is not concerned to advance a particular thesis or interpretation of the sixteenth and seventeenth centuries as a whole. Rather it examines the principal subject areas into which the economic and social history of the period has been conventionally divided, considers the main issues which their study has thrown up, relates them to one another either by discussion in the text or by cross-reference, and attempts to reconcile the conflicting view points of historians rather than to take sides between them. And as in another economic history text-book, albeit one devoted to a later century, 'isms'

xi

have been eschewed as far as possible. So have the dreadful jargon derived from sociology and the chilling abstractions of economic theory, both of which have begun to disfigure some historical writing. Phrases like 'probated decedents' and 'negative externalities' may have their uses in other disciplines, but the Muse of History should speak with a voice that all may understand.

The period has been treated thematically rather than chronologically in order to stress its underlying unity, although in certain chapters where this procedure was likely to cause confusion some chronological sub-divisions have been introduced. Despite its length the book cannot pretend to be a complete treatment of *all* aspects of the economy and society. There is something, but not a great deal, about transport and the conduct of internal trade. There are no chapters devoted specifically to living standards or economic fluctuations, although a good deal is written about both in various contexts; nor are the economic and social origins of the Civil War separately discussed, although at various points its consequences are duely emphasized. But had I covered absolutely everything the book would have extended into three volumes rather than two, and it seemed worth treating the most important subject areas fully even at the expense of omitting others.

In many ways this book may be compared to a voyage undertaken by one of the Elizabethan privateers chronicled by K.R. Andrews, not because I have loosed off salvoes of shots at every historian whose works I have encountered, but because I have ruthlessly plundered them for facts and ideas. This is inevitable in a work of synthesis, and I hope none of the numerous scholars involved will find their views misrepresented or reproduced unacknowledged, though over the years of reading I have inevitably absorbed ideas of whose origin I am no longer aware. As far as possible I have indicated by means of the bibliographical references inserted into the text the sources upon which I have drawn, although some passages, such as the first two sections of Chapter 3, will be found to have few of these because the argument draws so widely that it would have been impracticable to cite all the works that might have been cited, and invidious or misleading to mention only a few. The references are, however, intended to fulfil a dual function for they are also a guide to further reading on each aspect of the subject matter, and some items are therefore also included for their general relevance to the argument in question.

A considerable number of people have assisted me in one way or another during the preparation of the book. My wife has given much needed encouragement and listened with patience to my frequent lamentations at ever having got involved in doing it. William Ashworth,

Joan Thirsk and Bob Malcolmson read certain chapters in draft, while Joe Bettey, Bernard Alford, John Moore, Patrick McGrath, John Guy, Bob Machin, Mike Costen, John Holman and Raine Morgan helped by discussion and correspondence to clear areas of doubt, provided bibliographical references and furnished missing pieces of factual information. Errors of fact and judgement no doubt remain, but they are the fewer for their efforts. I would also like to thank Anne Griffiths and Rosemary Graham who between them typed the whole of the very lengthy manuscript at least once, some parts twice, and a few obstinate passages several times.

Finally I am grateful to Patricia Williams, formerly of the Cambridge University Press, for commissioning this book in the first place, and to her and to Stephen Barr for the patience displayed as its completion date was postponed again and again, and its predicted length grew greater and greater.

Bristol, April 1983.

ABBREVIATIONS

Ag.H.R.	*Agricultural History Review*
A.H.	*Agricultural History*
A.H.E.W.	*Agrarian History of England and Wales* (8 vols. Cambridge, 1967, continuing)
B.H.R.	*Business History Review*
B.I.H.R.	*Bulletin of the Institute of Historical Research*
Carus-Wilson	*Essays in Economic History*, ed. E.M. Carus-Wilson (3 vols., London, 1954, 1962)
C.E.H.E.	*Cambridge Economic History of Europe* (6 vols., Cambridge, 1942–77)
E.H.R.	*English Historical Review*
Ec.H.R.	*Economic History Review*
H.L.Q.	*Huntingdon Library Quarterly*
J.B.S.	*Journal of British Studies*
J.E.Ec.H.	*Journal of European Economic History*
J.E.H.	*Journal of Economic History*
J.I.H.	*Journal of Interdisciplinary History*
Minchinton	*Essays in Agrarian History*, ed. W.E. Minchinton (2 vols., Newton Abbot, 1968) vol. I
N.H.	*Northern History*
N.S.	New Series
P. & P.	*Past and Present*
R.E.H.	*Research in Economic History*
R.O.	Record Office
Ser.	Series
T.E.D.	*Tudor Economic Documents*, ed. R.H. Tawney and E. Power (3 vols. London, 1924 and later impressions)
T.R.H.S.	*Transactions of the Royal Historical Society*
U.B.H.J.	*University of Birmingham Historical Journal*
V.C.H.	*Victoria County History*

I

POPULATION

i Introduction

The population of England at the beginning of the sixteenth century was something, although not a very great deal, over two million. Most of these people lived in the countryside in villages and smaller settlements, and probably little more than 10 per cent of them lived in towns of any size. It is also likely that as many as three quarters lived south and east of a line drawn from the Severn to the Humber, for it was the southerly part of the country which contained the main areas of arable farming, of rural industry, and most of the important towns. The six northern counties contained some limited areas of fairly densely populated arable farming, especially in the Vales of York and Cleveland and the coastal plains of Northumberland and Durham; and there were a handful of substantial towns, notably York, Hull and Newcastle. But there were huge areas of mountain, fell and moorland, where settlement was exceedingly sparse and virtually confined to the more hospitable valleys, and where towns were very few and often hardly worth the name. Up to a point comparable conditions prevailed along the Welsh border and in parts of the West Midlands, although the environment was nowhere quite so hostile as in the far North and a larger proportion of the land was suitable for settlement.

Within the more densely populated half of the country, the Home Counties and Suffolk, and parts of Gloucestershire, Somerset and South Devon, especially those where the manufacture of woollen cloth was carried on, probably had the thickest concentration of people. Coastal areas were often more heavily populated than their hinterlands, but districts of rich and productive soil devoted to arable farming carried large populations everywhere (Sheail, 1972). However, even in the South distribution of population was very uneven and there were stretches of countryside which were very sparsely inhabited. In some cases this was because of poor soils, as in the case of the Norfolk Brecklands or the

I

moorlands of Devonshire. In others subjection to forest law in the interests of preserving game for medieval sovereigns had limited the extent of penetration by settlers, as in the case of the forests of Rockingham, Salcey and Whittlewood in otherwise well peopled Northamptonshire. In fact over the previous century and a half there had been little movement into these relatively empty districts. Indeed, there had been some drift away from many of them, as part of a tendency for population to concentrate in the most favoured areas, illustrated by the fact that from all parts of the country there is evidence of villages, usually small ones on marginal soils or in otherwise unpromising situations, being abandoned altogether in the later Middle Ages. (See also below p. 67.) This was a development which had taken place in the context of a heavy drop in the population since the mid fourteenth century, which had affected all areas but whose consequences, because of currents of internal migration, were very much more dramatic in some than in others.

Certainly even southern England in 1500 was lightly populated compared with the situation which had prevailed in 1300. Thus a Venetian traveller, visiting England just before the end of the fifteenth century, remarked: 'The population of this island does not appear to me to bear any proportion to her fertility and riches. I rode ... from Dover to London and from London to Oxford ... and it seemed to me to be very thinly inhabited', and his enquiries confirmed that things were no different in either the North or the South West. It is believed by historians of the Middle Ages that around the beginning of the fourteenth century the population reached a peak, which may have been as high as 5 or even 6 million, before a series of natural disasters, of which the famine

Table 1 *English population, 1541–1701: estimated totals at decennial intervals*

1541	2,774,000	1631	4,893,000
1551	3,011,000	1641	5,092,000
1561	2,985,000	1651	5,228,000
1571	3,271,000	1661	5,141,000
1581	3,598,000	1671	4,983,000
1591	3,899,000	1681	4,930,000
1601	4,100,000	1691	4,931,000
1611	4,416,000	1701	5,058,000
1621	4,693,000		

Source: E.A. Wrigley and R.S. Schofield, 1981, Table 7.8, pp. 208–9.

of 1315–17 and the Black Death of 1348–9 were the worst, precipitated a prolonged period of decline. By 1377, when the returns to the Poll Tax provide a reasonably sound basis for an estimate, the people of England seem to have numbered no more than 2.5 or 3 million. By the mid fifteenth century there had been yet further decline and the population may have dropped as low as a mere 2 million, but at this level it seems to have stabilized until some point in the second half of the century when recovery at last began (Hatcher, 1977, pp. 13–14, 63–6, 68–9). At first growth was extremely slow, may have been discontinuous and confined to some areas only, and not until after the turn of the sixteenth century, perhaps 1510, did the upward movement become pronounced. Even in the early 1520s the population seems to have no more than 2.3 million (Cornwall, 1970). However, as is indicated by Table 1 and Figure 1, by the early 1550s it had probably reached 3 million, and soon after, if not before, the end of the century had passed 4 million. By the early seventeenth century the rate of increase was slowing down, and although 5 million was probably reached in the 1630s, there seems to have been little or no overall growth between the 1640s and the 1680s, and indeed at times some slight decline. Renewed upward movement in the last decade or so of the century brought the population of England in 1701 back to just over 5 million. It must be said that estimates of the total size of the population at particular moments in time are fraught with difficulty especially for the fourteenth, fifteenth and early sixteenth centuries, and the results are necessarily subject to a considerable margin of error. However, the recent publication of a monumental work of demographic reconstruction by the Cambridge Group for the History of Population and Social Structure has provided a credible series of figures for the later sixteenth and seventeenth centuries (Wrigley and Schofield, 1981, pp. 208–9). At any rate it is safe to say that during the sixteenth century the population increased by at least 75 per cent and may have practically doubled, whereas during the seventeenth century, although the additions were quite large in absolute terms, they amounted to no more than 25 per cent in proportionate terms. Every part of Europe, it should be said, experienced a similar upward movement in population, although its extent and timing differed somewhat from one country to another.

Why the population moved as it did, when it did, is, however, difficult to establish. Reliable conclusions require a great deal of detailed information about birth rates and death rates, not only for the population in general but for each age group within it, about age at marriage, how large a proportion of the population did in fact get married, and so on. They also require knowledge about many aspects of the economy at large, and the social structure, in order to provide a context within which such

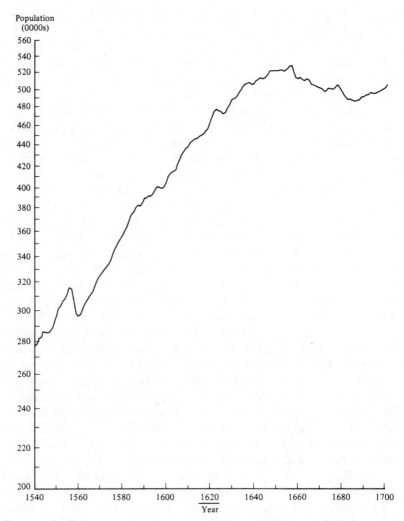

Figure 1 English population, 1541–1701. (Source: Wrigley and Schofield, 1981, Appendix 3 Table 3.)

changes can be interpreted. Until very recently virtually none of the necessary demographic information was available, and historians were only
able to speculate in the most general way about what they thought must
have occurred. A growing interest in population history has, however, led
to an intensive assault upon those contemporary sources which can be
made to yield appropriate data. For the late Middle Ages and the earlier
part of the sixteenth century the most promising source is wills. These

were made only by those who owned at least some property, but they were left by a numerous enough group to provide a substantial, if socially biased, sample of the population, and their analysis is beginning to throw light on some previously extremely obscure problems.

After the mid sixteenth century, however, a much better source, in the form of the registers of baptisms, marriages and burials, which a government order of 1538 directed should be maintained in every parish church, becomes available. Now it can never be assumed that registers record all the 'vital events' which took place in a parish. Some of them were carelessly kept, and even if the incumbent was conscientious some members of his flock may have been very irregular in their attendance in church, so that they did not bother to have their children baptized, whilst the rise of Non-Conformity in the seventeenth century meant that others kept away for a different reason. Nevertheless, in the hands of researchers who are aware of their shortcomings as historical evidence, parish registers can provide a substitute for the civil registration of births, marriages and deaths, which did not begin until the nineteenth century. Subjected to the laborious process of 'family reconstitution' they can provide the basis for exceedingly detailed and informative studies of population in particular communities, whilst even less intensive methods can yield interesting results if several or many parishes are studied together as a group.[1] In the last twenty years or so the population history of a growing number of localities has been at least partially unravelled in this way, and with the completion of the Cambridge Group's study of several hundred parishes widely distributed throughout the country, there is at last a set of findings which can claim to reveal something about the mechanics of national population movements. However, before we turn to the conclusions suggested by all this work, some parts of which are, alas, intimidatingly technical, let us consider in a general way some of the factors that will be involved.

ii Influences affecting population movements

Throughout the period we are discussing English society experienced what were, by the standards of recent times, relatively high birth rates and death rates.[2] These rates certainly varied over time, from place to place, and between different groups in the community, but averaged out over the period and the population as a whole fell within the range of

---

[1] For family reconstitution, and other methods of recovering historical evidence about population, see Hollingsworth, 1969
[2] They were *not*, however, as high as those of many under-developed countries in the twentieth century.

30–40 and 22–32 per 1000 of the population per year, respectively, compared to a birth rate of 13.7 per 1000 and a death rate of 11.9 per 1000 for England and Wales in 1973. The high death rate meant an expectation of life at birth which rarely exceeded forty years but which equally rarely dropped below thirty-two, compared to sixty-nine for men and seventy-five for women in 1973. However, since infant mortality was so very heavy, with anything up to a fifth of all children born dying before their first birthday, and many more in the few years following, those who survived the dangerous early years and reached a fifth or tenth birthday had good prospects of surviving into their fifties or even beyond (Schofield and Wrigley, 1979. Wrigley and Schofield, 1981, pp. 230, 311, 528).

The main reason for the high death rate was the prevalence of infectious disease. From the demographic point of view this appeared in two forms: diseases that were endemic, that is always present and claiming a substantial number of victims every year, such as tuberculosis or pneumonia, and those which occurred as epidemics and caused heavy mortalities only at irregular intervals, such as plague, typhus, smallpox or influenza.[3] It was the former which ensured that even in a normal year the death rate was well above the modern level, but on their own they would have been unable to maintain it at the high average which characterized the sixteenth and seventeenth centuries. It was the occasional epidemics, which every now and then drove the death rate far above normal, which ensured that the average rate over a period of time was considerably higher than the rate prevailing in the typical year. In any one place there might be no serious outbreak of epidemic disease for ten years, for a generation, or even a longer period, during which time there would probably be a continuous increase in population, but eventually plague or some other killer would strike and drive numbers abruptly downwards. Thus the movement of population in any given town or rural area tended to be somewhat irregular, whether the underlying trend was upwards, downwards or stable. However, because epidemics tended to appear somewhere every year, whilst hardly ever in this period affecting the whole country simultaneously,[4] the course of national population change was a very much smoother one.

There was clearly a connection between the high death rate and prevailing economic conditions, although the relationship certainly

[3] Strictly speaking this distinction is a great over-simplification. Disease such as plague were endemic over long periods so that they too caused a steady trickle of deaths every year, but this mortality paled into insignificance compared with that in an epidemic outbreak.
[4] The influenza of 1556–8 was the major exception to this generalization, and the epidemics of 1679–86 perhaps another. Before about 1480, by contrast, nationwide epidemics of plague occurred on several occasions. See below pp. 12–13.

cannot explain everything. Poverty, with its concomitants of an inadequate diet, insufficient warmth in winter and poor housing conditions, was certainly the main reason for the ravages of endemic disease. When living standards improved there is every reason to think that mortality from them abated somewhat, and that when they deteriorated, as in years when food was unusually dear, it increased. It has been discovered that the poorest classes in the community had smaller families than the well-to-do and the rich, and there is little doubt that the higher infant mortality they suffered was one of the main reasons for this (Chambers, 1972, pp. 67–9). Yet the low living standard of the mass of the people was not the only reason for the high death rate. Even the richest and most powerful group of all, the aristocracy, had a relatively low expectation of life and one which was falling in the second half of our period (Hollingsworth, 1964), although they lived in dry and solidly built houses, could afford all the food and fuel they wanted, and could escape epidemics by prompt flight. They, together with everyone else, paid the penalty of ignorance; ignorance of the importance of well balanced diets, of personal cleanliness, of maintaing hygienic conditions during childbirth and in the nursery, and so on. Medical skills, such as they were, could do nothing to reduce the number of deaths from disease in this period, whilst lack of knowledge of the mechanisms of infection meant that such public health measures as the authorities took to try to check the spread of epidemics were usually ineffective[5] and sometimes positively harmful. The shutting up of houses in which a case of plague had occurred, for instance, frequently condemned the other inmates to catch the disease, but did nothing to protect the rest of the community, thus increasing rather than reducing the number of deaths.[6]

Epidemics themselves, and the mortality they caused, were thus uncontrolled and uncontrollable, which is well illustrated by the fact that on a number of occasions in the sixteenth and seventeenth centuries certain English towns, including London in 1563, Norwich in 1579 and York in 1604, lost approaching a third of their inhabitants from plague in a few months. The outbreak of plague in London in 1665 was not the worst in terms of the proportion of the population killed, but it left more than 70,000 people dead before the onset of winter weather brought about a spontaneous end to the epidemic (Shrewsbury, 1970. Sutherland,

[5] At the national level, however, quarantine regulations at the ports were eventually successful in preventing epidemics of plague from being imported from abroad, and thus in eliminating the disease from England altogether (Flinn, 1979. Slack, 1981). See also below p. 22.
[6] This was because bubonic plague is not infectious between humans, but is transmitted by fleas, usually those parasitic upon rats rather than upon humans themselves. Rats were thus, usually, if not invariably, the carriers of the disease.

1972. Palliser, 1973 (1). Slack, 1979, pp. 40–3). Poverty and squalor had much to do with the havoc wrought on such occasions; and, especially in the case of plague, whose destructive power no other disease could equal, the largest number of deaths tended to be in the poorest slum districts. Some other diseases, however, were less class conscious. Smallpox appeared in the households of the rich as frequently as in those of the poor, whilst the sweating-sickness of the first half of the sixteenth century seems also to have been extremely common amongst the well-to-do.

Nor is it clear how far, if at all, changes in the frequency and severity of epidemics in general can be related to improvement and deterioration in standards of living. Epidemics were sometimes associated with years of unusually high food prices, but not all years of scarcity saw epidemics, and many broke out when there was no particular shortage of food. Contemporaries believed that widespread hunger was likely to be followed by pestilence, and especially in the early part of the period there is some evidence that it frequently was. Certainly the consequences of harvest failure could be very serious, especially for those who relied in whole or in part upon wages to feed their families. Even at the best of times there were many whose earnings left little margin above the costs of subsistence, and employers did not normally increase wage rates to take account of short term increases in the price of essentials. Indeed many workers, especially perhaps those in the countryside who were partly engaged in small scale pastoral farming and partly in the manufacture of consumer goods such as cloth, would find that their wage earnings decreased or even dried up altogether in times of unusually high food prices. This was because dearer food cut purchasing power for non-essentials in the country at large, and the reaction of employers thus faced with a decline in demand for their products was to reduce production, or even stop it altogether for a while, by the simple expedient of ceasing to put out raw materials to some or all of those who worked for them, beginning with those who lived furthest from their base of operations. As for small peasant farmers who relied upon the grain they raised on their own holdings to feed their families, seriously deficient yields might mean that they simply did not have enough to last them throughout the year. They would have to realize any savings they had to buy food, and if all their resources were exhausted before the next harvest, then they too would be in a parlous way.

Some deaths from starvation probably occurred almost everywhere in the years of the worst harvests, although the majority of victims are likely to have been economically marginal individuals, such as wandering paupers, elderly widows and orphaned children; and many more are likely to have succumbed to famine related diseases, such as dysentery and typhus. In some districts, even over considerable regions, the direct and indirect effects of hunger forced death rates very high indeed in crisis years. But the findings of the Cambridge Group indicate that even in the mid and later sixteenth century, whatever their *local* effects, neither famine itself, nor epidemics precipitated by famine, were a major influence upon the *national* death rate. In particular there is little evidence by this stage of any connection between harvest failure and plague. Certainly the great London plague of 1563 came immediately after a very bad harvest, but the other major outbreaks (1603, 1625, 1636, 1665, for instance) were at times when food was relatively abundant, whilst the appalling harvests of the mid and later 1590s saw little plague anywhere in England. Indeed in the case of London a detailed comparison between bread prices and fluctuations in mortality from all the main killing diseases, in so far as these are recorded in the contemporary 'Bills of Mortality', indicates that there was little correlation between them (Wrigley and Schofield, 1981, pp. 320–32. Slack 1979, pp. 53–5. Appleby, 1975).

Whatever happened in particular places at particular times, short term variations in overall death rates thus appear to have been largely unrelated to economic conditions: disease, especially epidemic disease, was the key factor in determining national mortality levels, and it seems to have been for the most part a random or 'autonomous' one. Nor does it seem at all probable that periods when epidemics were more than usually active can be safely explained by medium or long term alterations in the material prosperity of the population. A new disease, or fresh strains of an old disease, introduced to the country from abroad will often have been the cause of a new wave of epidemics: the sweating-sickness definitely had a foreign origin, and each of the major series of plague outbreaks probably derived from the importation of a new and virulent form of the virus through the port of London (Shrewsbury, 1970). Furthermore it is a well established fact of medical science, although one which historians have only recently come to accept, that the infectivity and virulence of the micro-organisms which cause disease alter over time, sometimes to a striking degree, so that illnesses which are often fatal at one period may turn into relatively mild complaints at another, or vice versa. Factors such as these are thus of very great importance in determining changes in levels of mortality.

If we turn to fertility and the birth rate, however, we shall find that economic conditions exerted a greater influence. In the short run, periods of heightened mortality were often accompanied by a drop both in the number of conceptions and of marriages, which was reflected by a smaller crop of births than usual in the months following. However, after a slightly longer interval a sudden upsurge in the number of births is frequently found to have occurred. This was partly because of a revival in fertility amongst couples already married, partly because there was an unusually large crop of marriages as those which had been postponed were carried through, and partly because improved economic conditions for the survivors meant large numbers of marriages between people who had previously not been in a position to afford setting up house on their own. This well attested phenomenon of a compensatory upsurge in births meant that much of the loss of population caused by an epidemic or a serious dearth was repaired within a remarkably short period, and the demographic effect of epidemics tended to be much less devastating than might have been supposed.[7] In the longer run important factors in determining the birth rate included the proportion of adults who never married at all, since if this was high it would, unless off-set by a rise in illegitimate births, clearly bring down the rate for the population as a whole; and the age at which they got married. Changes in the female age at marriage had much more effect than changes in the male age, because of the shorter period during which a women is fertile. The longer she delayed marriage the fewer children she was likely to have, an effect which was the more marked because of the tendency of female fertility to decline with advancing age.

The average age at marriage was certainly affected by economic conditions, since people tended to delay matrimony until they felt that they would be able to maintain a family at the standard of living they, or their parents, regarded as acceptable. They would therefore be influenced by such things as the availability of agricultural holdings, employment and housing. If land was abundant and men did not have to wait for a parent to die before they could get a farm of their own, or if wages were high and cottages at low rents easy to come by, then people were likely to marry younger than if the opposite conditions prevailed. However, in practice the age at marriage was not sufficiently sensitive to changes in these respects to ensure that population and resources remained in balance, and thus that living standards remained more or less stable. Once a particular pattern had become established it tended to persist for a considerable time. No doubt this was in part because of the strength of convention in determining such matters in a traditional society, and in part because it might be several decades before the permanence of some forms of changes in economic conditions, the level of real wages for instance, could be clearly perceived by contemporaries and distinguished

[7] The rapidity of the recovery was also aided by the fact that after a period unusually heavy morality the death rate would drop markedly for a few years, since many of the deaths which would have taken place in the normal course of events had been anticipated.

from the continuous short run fluctuations which afflicted the centuries with which we are concerned. Thus if for any reason economic conditions improved, this process might continue for a considerable time before the age of marriage dropped far enough for higher living standards to be eroded by an increase in the birth rate. Contrariwise if the population was increasing faster than economic opportunities, so that living standards were falling, they were likely to drop a considerable distance before the age of marriage rose to the level necessary to bring the process to a halt.

A third regulator of the birth rate which certainly operated in the seventeenth century and probably at some earlier periods too, was the deliberate limitation of family size by married couples, either by some method of preventing conceptions, or by the procuring of abortions, or by some form of infanticide. Even if family size was not deliberately restricted before the mid seventeenth century something was keeping the average number of children per family well below the biological maximum which would have resulted if marital fertility had been completely uncontrolled. Other possible explanations for this would include 'social' controls on the possibility of conception, for instance prolonged breast-feeding combined with a taboo against intercourse during that period. Like age at marriage such customs would prove persistent, but would eventually change under economic pressure: the length of time an infant was breast-fed was likely to be determined in part by the ease with which the parents could afford to provide it with other food, and thus by their standard of living. But if both age of marriage and the various types of behaviour within marriage which limited fertility were normally slow to change, there is some evidence that when change finally did come, at any rate within particular communities, it could be quite sudden, especially in cases where some particularly acute mortality crisis administered a severe psychological shock.[8]

Finally it needs to be said that death rates invariably fluctuated much more widely in the short term than did birth rates, and the high peaks in mortality found in parish registers in crisis years were undoubtedly the most dramatic demographic phenomenon of the sixteenth and seventeenth centuries. Yet this does not mean that mortality was necessarily the more important influence upon population movements in the long run, for over extended periods the average level of fertility could register as great or greater changes than the average level of mortality (Wrigley and Schofield, 1981, pp. 236–45). Besides, other things being equal, changes in fertility will have greater long term consequences, because unless alterations in the death rate are highly age-specific, it is the

[8] For the example of Colyton, Devonshire, in the mid seventeenth century, see Wrigley, 1966, and below p. 23.

former which will have a greater impact upon the age structure and thus upon the number of potential parents in the next generation. Yet in the conditions prevailing in this period a rise in fertility was less likely to be the principal cause of population *growth* than was a fall in the death rate. This was because of the importance of infectious disease as a cause of deaths, and the high incidence of infant and child mortality. It is a fact, well established from other periods, that the larger families suffer the heaviest child mortality, and increased fertility would mean more large families and thus a rise in the death rate amongst children. In other words, unless a rise in fertility was accompanied by a simultaneous reduction in the incidence of disease it would be largely cancelled out by a corresponding increase in child deaths. A drop in the death rate, however, especially if it mainly affected the young, would eventually produce a corresponding rise in the birth rate because the age structure of the population would gradually be altered in such a way that the proportion of it who were potential parents would be increased. A fall in the death rate would thus have a built-in accelerator effect. A slowing down or reversal of population growth, however, could equally well be the consequence of either a rise in the death rate, or a decline in the birth rate. The former would probably mean a disproportionate increase in infant and child deaths, and by altering the age structure so as to reduce the proportion of those able to act as parents in the future, would in due course have an adverse effect on the size of the next generation. But a fall in the birth rate would, of course, bring about the same result more directly.

iii The origins of sixteenth century population growth

Let us now return to the movement of the population between 1500 and 1700, and bearing these general considerations in mind see how far it is possible to explain it. For the origins of the rapid growth of the sixteenth century, however, we must go back to the fifteenth, and the first problem which confronts us is when and why the prolonged decline in numbers, which had characterized most of the later Middle Ages, was finally halted and reversed. For eastern England, at any rate, the answer seems to be not until between 1470 and 1490, although whether growth was continuous even from that time onwards is uncertain. The historical record leaves little room for doubt that the main reason why decline continued so long was the exceptional prevalence of disease in the fifteenth century, and in particular the prevalence of plague. Ever since since the Black Death of 1349 the country had rarely been free of this most dreadful of all the killing diseases for any length of time, and between 1430 and 1480 there were at least seven widespread outbreaks, besides a large number of more localized ones. On average there was a major epidemic somewhere in England once every four years. The towns, and above all London, were invariably badly afflicted, but contrary to what has often been asserted, plague was not a primarily urban disease in the fifteenth century, and the countryside also suffered severely from it (Gottfried, 1977; 1978, chs. II and VII).

Nevertheless it is clear that the demographic effects of plague were compounded by the fact that fertility was remarkably low. Remarkably, because, plague apart, economic and social conditions were in many ways favourable to a *high* birth rate. This was because of the very low level to which numbers had fallen in relation to available resources, especially of cultivable land. In consequence the average size of the peasant farm was much larger than it had been a hundred years before, and for the ambitious, or the man with sons to provide for, an additional holding was relatively easy to come by. The level of rents and other financial obligations owed by manorial tenants to their lords was low, and thus the bulk of what the peasants produced was available for their own consumption, or to provide them with a money income. Finally only a small proportion of countrymen were unable to find land to farm, and for those few employment was plentiful and real wages were at an historically high level, in the case of building workers having just about doubled since the early fourteenth century (Phelps Brown and Hopkins, 1981, ch. 2). There is no doubt that, because of the great drop in population since the latter period, the survivors were enjoying a higher level of material well-being than had been known by their ancestors, or indeed was to be enjoyed by their successors of the sixteenth century.

This, it might have been expected, would have encouraged earlier marriages and larger families, but it appears that for a long time it did not do so. In a large sample of those sufficiently well off to leave a will, but including many relatively humble people both rural and urban, for the whole period 1430–80, nearly a quarter (24.2 per cent) of all males died unmarried, whilst nearly a half (49 per cent) of those who did marry died without a male heir. Altogether, and including those who did not marry, over half (54.4 per cent) of the entire will-making population left no child of either sex to succeed them, and only 18 per cent had at least one of each alive at the time of their death. This is a situation which must reflect a combination of a high death rate, especially amongst children, and certain social factors, notably a disinclination amongst men to assume the responsibilities of marriage at an early age or even at all (Gottfried, 1978, pp. 177, 191, 221. Thrupp, 1965). Now it seems likely, although some obscurity surrounds the issue, that it was during the later fourteenth and fifteenth centuries that English society adopted the characteristically West European marriage pattern, in which couples normally delayed marriage at least until their mid twenties. By contrast at the time of the 1377 Poll Tax, women generally married in their mid or late teens, as they did in Eastern Europe until recent times and still continue to do in Asia, Africa and elsewhere in the world. Analogy with subsequent historical episodes suggests the probability that the recurrent plagues of the mid and later fourteenth century had administered a psychological shock to the population which induced this change in marriage pattern, and perhaps changes in behaviour within marriage which resulted in lower marital fertility, and that once established these new patterns persisted long after the conditions which had given rise to them had passed away (Hajnal, 1965. Chambers, 1972, p. 71. Smith, 1979).

At any rate it is virtually certain that the fall in population in the later Middle Ages was not due just to an increased death rate, whether caused by the appearance of a new and lethal epidemic disease (i.e. plague) on its own, or by a combination of plague and the increased severity of other scourges, but was also due to a decline in fertility. And it was, according to the most recent study, an improvement in fertility which finally brought the long downward movement to an end. The evidence, which is drawn entirely from wills, particularly the numbers of children referred to as surviving the testators, is difficult to handle, and cannot be pushed too far. However it does seem to reveal that in the 1470s, for the first time in the fifteenth century, the population was at least maintaining itself and that the reason was that more children were being born per family, most probably because of a fall in the age of marriage. By the 1480s there are also signs of an increase in the proportion of the population who got married, and this too must have contributed something to increasing the overall birth rate. Why fertility should have begun to increase *when* it did is difficult to explain, although most probably it was the result of the gradual erosion, after several decades of considerable prosperity for the peasantry, of the customs and conventions which had previously kept it low, and which first began to show perceptible results at the particular time.

However, if fertility began to rise in the later fifteenth century, from the 1480s onwards mortality began to fall, as, after the great epidemic of 1479–80, outbreaks of plague became very much less frequent. Of course there were still plenty of other epidemic diseases about, and indeed the 1480s itself saw the advent of a new one, the sweating-sickness, perhaps a form of influenza, which caused much consternation at the time.[9] But whilst 'the sweat' was certainly lethal, the evidence

[9] It struck five times between 1485 and 1551, and then disappeared.

shows conclusively that it did not cause nearly as many deaths as the alarmist reports of contemporaries would suggest, and their obsession with it would seem to have been a reflection of its novelty rather than its killing power. Nor were any of the other afflictions of the time capable of carrying off such numbers as was plague: on some occasions in the sixteenth century it pushed burials up to ten or even twelve times their normal level, whereas mortality 'crises' arising from any other cause rarely involved an increase of more than three or four fold. Besides, not only was plague less frequent, it also tended to spread less widely when it did appear, and as the sixteenth century wore on it increasingly confined itself to the towns. As late as 1546–7 it swept through the rural areas of Devonshire, visiting even quite small villages, but this had probably for some time been the exception rather than the rule, and in the second half of the sixteenth century the countryside usually escaped almost entirely. Since only a very small proportion of the population lived in the towns, perhaps not much more than 10 per cent in 1500, this change was of the greatest importance. What brought it about, however, we can only speculate: slight changes in climate which rendered a rural environment less congenial to the warmth loving rat fleas which carried the disease may very well have been responsible (Gottfried, 1977; 1978, chs. VII–VIII. Slack, 1979).

Whatever the underlying cause, the evidence at present available strongly suggests that the reduction in plague mortality was the single most important factor in the recovery of population from the low level to which it had fallen in the fifteenth century. Especially will this have been so if contemporary observers of the later Middle Ages were right in their repeated assertions that a disproportionately large number of the victims of plague were children and young adults, for in that case it will have reinforced the effects of rising fertility in progressively changing the age structure in such a way as to bring about a steady increase in birth rate. There may also have been some diminution in the frequency of other epidemics, for by the 1530s it was being remarked that the times were less unhealthy than formerly, but in any event as time went on the growth of population, which was clearly very gradual and perhaps not continuous at first, began to accelerate. Indeed by the 1540s and early 1550s, when the first parish registers become available, the birth rate was very high, higher that it was to be again before the end of the eighteenth century; the death rate was apparently on a falling trend; and the population growing at a compound rate of around 1 per cent a year (Hatcher, 1977, pp. 57–62, 65–6. Wrigley and Schofield, 1981, pp. 528–9).

iv The end of the upward movement: the rôle of the death rate

The upward movement of numbers in Tudor England seems to have received at least one major set-back in mid course. The harvests of 1555 and 1556 were among the worst of the whole period with which this book deals, and in terms of their effect on prices perhaps *the* worst. After the second failure wheat prices rose to twice their normal level and other grains by almost as much, so that the cost of living of building workers is reckoned to have increased by about two-thirds above the average of the previous decade (Hoskins, 1964. Harrison, 1971. Phelps Brown and Hopkins, 1981, ch. 2). Then beginning in 1556, and lasting through the two or three years following, influenza accompanied by a variety of other diseases probably including typhus, began to work its way through the hunger weakened communities, taking a heavy toll in lives, and continued to do so even when food was once more reasonably abundant. Indeed the heaviest mortality seems to have come after the worst of the dearth was over, but between them famine and disease combined to create both the most prolonged and the most acute mortality crisis of the entire period. There were, however, considerable regional variations in its severity, and whereas in some places burials rose to four times their normal level for two or even three years in succession, other districts escaped almost entirely. Total mortality was thus probably not so high as has sometimes been suggested, but combined with a sharp albeit temporary drop in fertility when food prices were at their highest, it was enough to bring about a reduction of at least 6 per cent in the country's population (Fisher, 1965. Slack, 1979, pp. 27–32. Wrigley and Schofield, 1981, pp. 310, 333, 664–6, 670–1).

Once the crisis was over recovery and renewed growth seem to have begun again immediately, and during the 1560s, 1570s and much of the 1580s proceeded as rapidly as ever, with compound rates once more a little below or above 1 per cent per annum. This was a period remarkably free of either serious epidemics or harvest failures, during which the expectation of life, as calculated by the Cambridge Group, reached its highest level in the whole of the sixteenth and seventeenth centuries, exceeding forty years at birth in the late 1570s and early 1580s. Nor were contemporaries unaware of their good fortune as compared to earlier generations. In 1584, for instance, Hakluyt attributed the country's visibly increasing numbers to the long period of peace and 'seldom sickness'. However the last fifteen years of the century saw an end to this halcyon interlude. Mortality crises returned, and as the seventeenth century wore on there is no doubt that the rate of population increase and the expectation of life were both falling. By the middle of the seventeenth century, according to the Cambridge Group, the compound growth rate was no more than 0.2 per cent a year, and in the 1660s, 1670s and early 1680s the population was actually declining, with life expectancy down to only $28\frac{1}{2}$ years at the worst point (Wrigley and Schofield, 1981, pp. 234–6, 528). Now it is sometimes stated or implied that the underlying cause of this was that numbers had risen so far that they were pressing on the resources available to support them (for instance *A.H.E.W.* IV, 1967, pp. 605–6, 621). The period from about 1590 onwards is thus interpreted as one of Malthusian crisis, in which the economic conditions of the mass of the people had deteriorated to the point where increased mortality from famine and disease gradually brought the upsurge in population to an end. Certainly the sixteenth and early seventeenth century rise in rents and fines had involved a redistribution of income from the small farmers to their landlords. (See below Ch. 3 sec. vi.) Certainly also the proportion of the population without sufficient land to support a family, and thus wholly or largely dependent on wages, had greatly increased, whilst the relatively slower growth in employment opportunities had produced a long term fall in real wages so that the purchasing power of the wages both of building craftsmen and of agricultural labourers in the early seventeenth century was less than half of what it had been in the late fifteenth (Phelps Brown and Hopkins, 1981, ch. 2).[10] Another indication that employment was hard to find was the number of vagrants who wandered around the country, driven from their place of origin by its inability to furnish them with a living. (See below Ch. 7 sec. i.) It is also true that contemporaries were conscious that the country's population was too large and economic opportunities too limited, as is demonstrated by their interest in the establishment of settlements overseas as a means to draw off some of the excess, and the frequency with which schemes 'to set the poor on work' were advocated. However it does not necessarily follow that the deteriorating economic situation directly accounts for the cessation of population growth, and the thesis of a Malthusian crisis requires closer consideration.

   To start with it is clear beyond any question that in the late sixteenth and early seventeenth centuries there *was* a series of acute dearths, or 'subsistence crises' as some historians euphemistically describe them, when bad harvests drove grain prices so high that the poorest members of the community could no longer buy enough food. The harvest failure of 1586 caused substantial increases in mortality in a number of places, especially in the far North West where typhus, the classic companion of

---

[10] See also below Table VI and Fig 4 in Ch. 7 sec. i.

famine, spreading in the wake of widespread malnutrition, seems to have been the principal factor. Then in the 1590s there was a still more severe crisis. The years 1594–7 saw the longest run of bad harvests of the century, and after each of them grain prices rose well above normal. The first two years were not disastrous in themselves, but they left many poor people without further savings or reserves of any sort: then the catastrophic harvest of 1596 drove prices up to over 80 per cent above their usual level, and that of 1597 brought little respite. The registers of parishes in the North West, the West Riding of Yorkshire, Shropshire, Staffordshire and Devonshire all reveal a pattern of heightened mortality which leaves no room for doubt that the very poor were dying of hunger, from the effects of eating unsuitable or contaminated food, and from diseases closely connected with famine such as dysentery and typhus. Literary evidence tells of the same thing happening in the city of Newcastle and the town of Nantwich in Cheshire. In the former, for instance, corporation records for the autumn of 1597 tell of the burial at municipal expense of twenty-five 'poor folks who died for want in the streets'. A quarter of a century later these conditions were repeated when, in 1622–3, a less dramatic rise in the price of grain coincided with a severe depression in the cloth industry, owing to a drop in exports, so that unemployment in the manufacturing districts was high and many people had no money to buy food at any price. Once again there is clear evidence of deaths from starvation, especially of vagrants, elderly widows and pauper children, from places as far apart as Greystoke in Cumberland, Ashton-under-Lyne in Lancashire and Brewood in Staffordshire. At the first of these places the parish registers actually attribute some of the deaths specifically to hunger: thus in March 1623 there was buried 'a poor hungerstarved beggar child' and in May 'a poor man destitute of means to live' (Drake, 1962. Appleby, 1978, chs. 7–9, esp. pp. 113, 126. Palliser, 1974. Slack, 1979).

Now it is clear that the South and East did not altogether escape some increase in deaths in these periods of crisis, especially that of the mid 1590s, when the burials in a number of towns, notably Salisbury, Exeter and Bristol, and some rural areas including parts of Suffolk, Essex and Kent, also increased sharply. In 1622–3 these parts of the country were less acutely affected, although there was undoubtedly much hardship: indeed a Lincolnshire landowner wrote that in his district the situation was such that 'Dog's flesh is a dainty dish, and found upon search in many houses ... And the other day one stole a sheep who for mere hunger tore a leg out, and did eat it raw' (Slack, 1979. Wrigley and Schofield, 1981, pp. 672–3. Thirsk and Cooper, 1972, p. 24). There must have been some deaths, but no instances of dramatic increases in mortality which can be directly attributed to scarcity of food have yet been found for any place in the lowland zone in the seventeenth century. Indeed even in the later sixteenth the impact of these episodes was very much more apparent in the highland zone, particularly in the North West, where the agricultural economy was mainly pastoral, and large numbers of small farmers did not raise enough cereals to support themselves, but depended on income from the sale of livestock or wool, supplemented by industrial earnings, to buy what they needed. The South and East, and most of the Midlands, where much the larger fraction of the population lived, was by contrast already largely free of the most serious effects of dearth, thanks to improvements in the marketing and distribution of food-stuffs, and the scale upon which the merchants of London and the other large ports were able to bring in grain imports when need arose. There are signs that some districts may have experienced subsistence crises after 1623, in 1638 for instance, but by the middle of the century famine seems to have become a thing of the past almost everywhere (Appleby, 1978, pp. 136, 191). Bad harvests continued to occur at irregular intervals, and to cause high food prices as before, but they no longer caused starvation, at least on any scale, or the outbreak of starvation-induced epidemics.[11] There was a run of very bad harvests in the later 1640s, in the years 1657–61, on two separate occasions in the 1670s and above all in the 1690s, yet there is no evidence that any of these periods of dear food resulted in an exceptionally heavy mortality, although people starved in both Scotland and France in the last of them. There were some years, such as 1661–2, when food was very expensive and the death rate somewhat higher than usual, but it is far from certain that the two things were connected. Contrariwise there were several occasions, 1657–8 for instance, and 1665–6, when mortality rose sharply, even though grain was at very moderate prices, and the longest period of higher than average death rates during the whole of the seventeenth century, 1678–9 to 1684–5, certainly did not see consistently high prices (Wrigley and Schofield, 1981, pp. 320–35).

It is of course possible that, even without the help of subsistence crises, worsening economic conditions and high food prices could have caused the decline in the expectation of life which occurred in the seventeenth century, by so weakening large sections of the population that there was a general rise in the death rate from endemic disease and, perhaps, from epidemics not directly connected with shortage of food.[12] This is very

---

[11] The increasing effectiveness of organized poor relief must have had something to do with this: see also below Ch. 7 sec. ii.

[12] It is not certain, however, that malnutrition does increase human susceptibility to epidemic diseases, nor that it renders people more likely to die from such diseases if they contract them.

likely to have occurred, and yet the fact that the fall affected not only the population at large but also the landed aristocracy, suggests that poverty and malnutrition were not the only or even the main factors behind it. The health of the aristocrats would hardly have been affected by changes in the price of goods which were of small account in comparison with their huge incomes. Another fact which suggests equally strongly that levels of material well-being did not by themselves determine the trend of the death rate is that, whilst the living standards of the wage earners reached their nadir in the first quarter of the seventeenth century, and had recovered perceptibly by the last quarter, the expectation of life was at its lowest between the early 1660s and early 1680s (Hollingsworth, 1964. Phelps Brown and Hopkins, 1981, ch. 2. Wrigley and Schofield, 1981, pp. 414, 528).

In fact there does seem to have been an increase in the incidence of disease but this is more satisfactorily explained as a consequence of the growth in the size of towns, and of changes in the virulence of the infective organisms themselves, than by an attempt to link it to living standards. London had grown continuously and prodigiously from about 60,000 people in the 1520s to at least 200,000 by 1600; had doubled again to 400,000 by the 1650s; and then expanded more slowly to reach about 575,000 by 1700. (For London, see also below Ch. 6 sec. vi.) None of the other English cities approached the capital in size, and in most cases they grew very much more slowly during the sixteenth century. In the seventeenth century, however, their rate of growth accelerated. In the case of East Anglia the urban population grew by 50 per cent between 1603 and 1670, whilst the total population of the area rose only by 11 per cent, and the largest towns grew fastest of all: Norwich, with perhaps 12,000 people in 1600, had 30,000 by 1700. Taking the country as a whole the proportion of those living in towns rose from around 10 per cent at the end of the Middle Ages to 22–23 per cent by the late seventeenth century (see also below Ch. 6 sec. i), but in Norfolk and Suffolk the proportion was as high as one third (Patten, 1978, pp. 121, 286. Corfield, 1972). Increases in urban population, however, did not mean proportionate increases in either the built-up area or the facilities available to their inhabitants. In the case of sixteenth century York, indeed, a 45 per cent increase in numbers took place without there being any significant net additions to the housing stock (Palliser, 1973(1)). At any rate as towns grew, so problems of overcrowding, bad housing, water supply, sewerage and waste disposal, became steadily more acute, and any alleviation of them was completely beyond the municipal authorities of the period. Living conditions in the towns thus deteriorated, to some extent for all classes, but especially for the poor in the squalid slum suburbs where most of the additions to the urban populations were concentrated, and which constituted an ideal breeding ground for disease. Virtually every house was infested by rats which were the carriers of plague; gross over-crowding provided the basic conditions for the spread of louse-borne typhus and highly infectious diseases such as smallpox; polluted wells meant that water-borne diseases like typhoid were an ever-present danger; the piles of filth and garbage in the streets, and the numerous stinking outdoor privies, encouraged the flies which transmitted the gastro-enteritis so fatal to infants. Not only was an increasing proportion of the whole population exposed to these health hazards, but (and this was probably more important) each town was more and more a reservoir of infection from which epidemics might spread to other towns and the surrounding country areas. Places remote from the main trade routes might rarely contract infections of urban origin, and so suffer few epidemics at all, but those on the main roads, especially in the South and East which was the most highly urbanized and had the best communications network, caught them all too often.

Above all London, because of its huge size and its close commercial links with all other regions, acted as a purveyor of disease to the kingdom as a whole, frequently passing on what it had itself received from abroad. Each of the major outbreaks of plague in London during this period, in 1563, 1593, 1603, 1625, 1636 and 1665, was followed by a crop of outbreaks in provincial towns large and small which on several of these occasions were so widespread as to amount almost to a national epidemic. Thus in 1603 or 1604 Norwich, Bristol, York, Hull, Newcastle, Chester, Oxford, Northampton and Salisbury, all experienced major epidemics, many other important towns had limited ones, and scores of smaller places suffered in varying degrees (Shrewsbury, 1970). Indeed, increasingly in the early seventeenth century, the records tell of heavy losses from plague in little market towns, even villages, as well as in the larger towns. Probably this was partly because they too had become very congested during the long period of population increase. Where good agricultural land was too scare to be sacrificed for building the larger numbers could not be accommodated by laying out new streets, and so had somehow to be housed within the confines of the old site. So existing dwellings were sub-divided, gardens built over, new cottages crammed into the spaces between the old or onto the edge of the village green. Higher population densities inevitably meant less wholesome living conditions, and a greater likelihood that infection would spread from one house to another.

Plague, however, was not the only disease to be disseminated from the towns along the corridors of trade and travel in this way, although it is the most thoroughly documented one. Typhus was also important in this respect, at least in the 1640s, when the Civil War set armies marching and counter-marching across the kingdom, and there were plenty of others. Indeed the whole pattern of epidemic disease underwent a considerable change during the second half of the century, which provides a striking example of the unpredictable way in which the relative importance of the various scourges of mankind can alter over time. Plague disappeared suddenly and completely from England after the later 1660s, as it did from the other countries of Western Europe at much the same time, a development which has long mystified historians, but which is probably accounted for by the successful enforcement of quarantine regulations, and the rigorous exclusion from English ports of ships from ports where the disease was known to be present (Slack, 1981). However, despite the extremely heavy mortalities which it had caused during the first two thirds of the seventeenth century, its disappearance after the 1660s was not followed by any upsurge in the population. This was partly because the elimination of a single disease in a society in which many others are prevalent, and also causing many deaths, will simply mean that those saved from the one will fall victim to another. Besides the disappearance of plague roughly coincided with the rise of smallpox as a major killer. The latter was not completely new to England, but it apparently had not made a major contribution to the death rate before the seventeenth century. Mainly a childhood affliction, it never caused as many deaths as plague in a single year, but it flared up more often and in London and other large towns took a substantial toll roughly every third year, so that over a period of twenty to thirty years the total mortality from it was almost comparable. There was also, seemingly, over much the same period, an increase in the incidence of influenza and various 'fevers' of uncertain identification, which likewise tended to strike at much shorter intervals than plague, whilst amongst the endemic diseases tuberculosis was also becoming more common, at least in London where, according to the Bills of Mortality, it was the single most important cause of death in the later seventeenth century (Appleby, 1975). If the final disappearance of subsistence crisis mortality and, above all, of plague, accounted for the less extreme year to year fluctuations which the Cambridge Group found to characterize the death rate as the seventeenth century wore on, it must have been these other diseases which caused it to stabilize at a higher over-all level (Wrigley and Schofield, 1981, pp. 316–18). Certainly smallpox, influenza and 'fevers' seem to have been the principal components of the widespread epidemics, affecting both town and country in the late 1670s and early 1680s, and which postponed any sustained renewal of population growth until after the very end of the century.

v The end of the upward movement: the rôle of the birth rate

A rise in the death rate and a fall in the expectation of life were not the only reasons for the slowing down of the growth of the population from the end of the sixteenth century onwards. There was also a marked fall in the birth rate, and according to the Cambridge Group this was actually a *more* important factor in what occurred. The fall was apparently brought about by a general rise in the age at which women got married, accompanied by an increase in the proportion of those who never married, and at least in some places and amongst some social groups, a decline in fertility within marriage which was probably due to deliberate efforts by couples to limit the size of their families. At the Devonshire village of Colyton, for instance, a family reconstitution exercise has shown that the average age at marriage for women rose from 27 years in the period 1560 to 1646 as a whole to 29.6 years in that between 1647 and 1719, which was enough to reduce family size by about one child per family. In the latter period only 4 per cent of women got married in their teens, and as many as 40 per cent were still unmarried at the age of thirty. A larger sample of parish studies suggests, however, that nationally the upward movement in age at marriage was less striking, with correspondingly fewer demographic implications, and that it was the growing number of those who eschewed matrimony altogether that accounted for most of the decline in fertility. In the later sixteenth century few people who lived a full span of years remained single, certainly less than one in ten, perhaps only one in twenty, but after about 1600 this became increasingly common. It is impossible to establish exactly how common, but it seems that during most of the seventeenth century the proportion was not much less than one fifth, and at some periods it may have been as high as one quarter, which meant a return to the situation prevailing in the mid fifteenth century (Wrigley, 1966. Wrigley and Schofield, 1981, pp. 229–32, 240–5, 253–65).

This fall in fertility, the origins of which the Cambridge Group have traced well back into the sixteenth century, before the rate of population growth began to decline, bears all the hallmarks of a response to economic pressure, by a society faced with worsening living standards and taking steps to limit its own increase in order to ensure that numbers did not outrun the resources available to support it. The shortage of small farms which had developed in many mixed farming areas, the economic difficulties to which the high level of rents and fines had reduced many of those who did have land (see also below Ch. 3 secs. vi and vii) and the inexorable decline in real wages, which was affecting a steadily increasing proportion of the total population, all combined to make it more and more difficult for young couples to set up new households. So much so, indeed, that the relatively slight increase in the age of marriage detected by the Cambridge Group in their twelve-parish family reconstitution study, suggests that amongst those *most* poorly off, pauperization was tending rather to lower age at marriage, as people felt that they had nothing to gain by waiting, thus in part off-setting a greater increase on the part of those who still felt it to be worthwhile.[13] It is true that fertility continued to decline for half a century after real wages reached their lowest point in the 1610s, and only began to recover significantly in the last twenty years of the century after they had been rising again for more than two full generations (Wrigley and Schofield, 1981, pp. 255–6, 418–19, 430–5). However this delayed response to demographic change need cause no surprise: we have seen that in the fifteenth century an improvement in fertility was long delayed, even though economic conditions had ostensibly been very favourable to it for many decades.

And yet it must be admitted that there are problems in the way of accepting this interpretation. The aristocracy did not experience a deterioration in the basic conditions of life, and to the extent that their fertility also declined in response to a rise in the average age of marriage and a reduced propensity to get married at all, it throws some doubt on the accuracy of the diagnosis for other social groups (Hollingsworth, 1964). But in fact, as we shall see, they and the landowning class in general were subject to pressures at this time, albeit of a rather different type, which are quite likely to have brought about these alterations in behaviour.[14] At Colyton the changes in question did not come about gradually, as one would perhaps have expected if economic stringency were the cause of them, but quite suddenly in the aftermath of a lethal plague in 1646 which must, at least temporarily, have improved the economic prospects of those who survived. The timing of the changes at Colyton, indeed,

[13] A relevant factor here may have been the increasing reluctance of farmers to hire young people as living-in farm servants, since part of the considerable costs of providing them with board and lodging could be saved by employing labourers who had their own cottages and fed themselves out of their wages. Living-in servants had to remain unmarried to retain their employment, so that a decrease in the incidence of living-in almost certainly led to earlier marriages amongst the children of cottagers and small farmers. Contrariwise, a revival in the practice of living-in from the mid seventeenth century onwards, apparently because a return of conditions of relative labour scarcity, made it necessary if employers were to secure the workers they needed, may have led to a reversal of this trend (Kussmaul, 1981, ch. 6).

[14] Particularly the increasing cost of making financial provision for daughters. See below pp. 147–8.

suggests that at least the proximate cause was the psychological shock which the survivors of a close-knit community had received from the dreadful experience of living through the plague year, but there is every reason to think that the underlying reason why the villagers adopted new conventions in respect of the age at which it was appropriate to get married, and new modes of behaviour within marriage, was the pressure on living standards which the steady rise in numbers over the previous century had exerted. For final proof of the assumption that economic stringency brought down the birth rate we shall have to await local studies which deal with both population history and economic history, but although such proof is at present wanting it is difficult to see that any other explanation is likely. It has been suggested that the psychological effects of epidemics on their own could have been responsible, but some areas such as Staffordshire which had suffered severely from plague continued to register an excess of baptisms over burials, indicating that regionally fertility remained high, and local variations of this sort are more likely to be explained by differing economic conditions than by differing psychological reactions to extreme stress (Wrigley, 1966. Chambers, 1972, p. 71. Palliser, 1974).

Besides, there is one factor that was both a response to economic pressure and probably of considerable importance in lowering fertility through its impact upon the incidence of marriage, which remains to be mentioned – emigration. In the two centuries with which we are concerned there was both immigration and emigration. The principal groups of immigrants were protestant refugees from the Low Countries in the later sixteenth century; Scots after the union of the crowns in 1603; and French Huguenots in the later seventeenth century. Their numbers are unknown but none of the groups can have exceeded a few tens of thousands and, whatever the importance of the first and last for the introduction of new industrial skills, their demographic impact was negligible. There was little emigration in the sixteenth century, but much more in the seventeenth, both to Ireland and to the new colonies in North America and the West Indies. Especially in the 1630s, 1640s and 1650s, the outflow to the New World was on a substantial scale, perhaps approaching 70,000 a decade, although the numbers declined steeply towards the end of the century. It has been estimated that 378,000 people left the British Isles for the Americas between 1630 and 1699, and though part of this total was from outside England this is probably balanced by the movement of English people to Ireland. There was thus undoubtedly a net loss from international migration during the century as a whole, and though the numbers leaving were not large in relation to the total population, they consisted overwhelmingly of young men, who thus ceased to be available as husbands for a corresponding number of women. And in any event the flow abroad reached its height when the rate of natural increase had already declined to an exceedingly low level. The fact that population actually *declined* for a time in the second half of the century was thus in significant measure due to emigration (Gemery, 1980. Wrigley and Schofield, 1981, pp. 185–6, 223–8, 232–3).

Our examination of the thesis of a Malthusian crisis in the late sixteenth and seventeenth centuries has shown that, on the basis of the evidence now available, the rise in mortality was not, in most parts of the country, a direct consequence of the pressure of population on resources, but that the fall in fertility almost certainly was. It thus seems safe to conclude that the demographic developments of the seventeenth century represent not a Malthusian crisis, in which 'positive checks' cut the population back to keep it in line with resources, but the forestalling of such a crisis, partly by the intervention of a spontaneous increase in the death rate owing to an increased incidence of epidemics, but mainly by the operation of 'preventative checks' operating principally through the age of marriage and the incidence of marriage.

vi *Regional variation and internal migration*

Discussion of the movement of the population of the country as a whole tends to obscure the fact that there were regional and local variations in the extent and timing of the developments we have noticed. For instance it has been estimated that the population of Leicestershire rose by 31 per cent between 1524 and 1563, 58 per cent between 1563 and 1603, and a further 5 per cent by 1670, whilst in Cambridgeshire population actually fell by 6 per cent in the first of these periods and in the hundred years after 1563 rose by only 34 per cent. For Staffordshire no estimate is available for the early sixteenth century, but between 1563 and 1665 the population apparently increased by about 130 per cent. And if the national population actually declined for a time in the later seventeenth century, it certainly did not do so in all districts (*V.C.H. Leics*, III, pp. 137–44. Spufford, 1974, pp. 14–16. Palliser, 1974). Moreover even figures for single counties conceal wide differences between one district and another. To begin with there probably were some geographical differences in birth rates and death rates. For instance the latter may have been higher than average in some marshy areas where malaria was endemic; and likewise in the far North, where the climate was harsh and an inability to grow sufficient food grains to feed its population without reliance on outside sources of supply was made especially dangerous by more than usually inadequate transport facilities. Likewise the fact that in some districts it was easier for labourers to get cottages than it was in others, and thus easier for them to marry and start families, must have led to higher birth rates in those places.

However the most important reason for differential rates of population growth was undoubtedly internal migration, the movement of people out of areas where economic opportunities were relatively limited into areas where they were more abundant, which drained off part, or even all, of the natural increase of some districts into others. There were two principal currents of internal migration in the centuries with which we are concerned: from the countryside in general to London and the other large towns, and from the densely populated arable farming regions in particular to those more sparsely inhabited pastoral districts where the existence of either ample common land or employment opportunities in rural industries, or both, offered a better chance of making a living. The flow of people into London was the most powerful of these currents, for the high death rate and the relatively low birth rate in a city where servants and apprentices made up so large a part of the community that up to two thirds of the population were unmarried, meant that without a constant influx of fresh immigrants numbers would not even have been maintained, let alone increased at the rapid rate which in fact they did. At times, indeed, the flow must have become a torrent: a well-informed contemporary, Graunt, noted that the enormous losses which London suffered in the seventeenth century plagues were made good by the second year after an outbreak. For the post-plague period of the later seventeenth century it has been calculated that as many as one sixth of all those born in the whole country in each year must have eventually found their way to the capital, which implies an inflow of nearly 30,000 persons a year (Sutherland, 1972. Wrigley, 1967). Other cities were no less dependent on immigration for their growth and though the numbers they attracted were individually much smaller, in aggregate they must have been almost as numerous. However, whereas London drew in at least some from almost every part of the country the provincial towns had a geographically much more limited catchment area. (See also below Ch. 6 sec. iv and, for London, the latter part of sec. vi.)

As for the movement of people from one type of rural area to another this will be discussed more fully later on. (See below Ch. 3 sec. viii; and Ch. 6 sec. iv.) Most of it was over relatively short distances, but the net effect was to make the distribution of population by 1700 considerably more even than it had been in 1500, since many areas of forest, marshland and waste which had been relatively empty at the end of the Middle Ages now had large populations. This was true, for instance, of the Weald of Kent and Sussex, and fens of Cambridgeshire and the adjacent counties,

the royal forests (or former forests) of Leicestershire and Northamptonshire, and many of the valleys on both sides of the Pennines where various
forms of the textile industry had come to flourish. The North and the
West Midlands were still more thinly peopled than East Anglia, the East
Midlands and the south, but the difference was less marked than it had
been two hundred years earlier. This was mainly because the two former
regions contained so many of the pastoral–industrial districts where
population growth had been especially rapid, and in some of which, such
as Staffordshire with its coal mining and metal industries, it had
continued throughout the seventeenth century. At the beginning of the
eighteenth century, therefore, the counties north of the line from the
Severn to the Humber probably contained somewhere between a third
and two fifths of the population, compared to only a quarter in 1500.

This chapter has been entirely concerned with the causes of population
movements, and nothing has yet been said about their consequences. Yet
clearly the size of the population, and its tendency to grow, or otherwise,
is one of the most important influences determining the nature of the
economy and the society. The size of the market for food-stuffs, for fuel,
for raw materials and for manufactured goods, indeed the intensity of
demand for land itself, will depend in substantial measure upon the level
of population; so too will the supply of labour for all forms of economic
activity. The economic and social results of the population trends which
we have established in the foregoing pages were thus inevitably far
reaching, but complicated as they were by the impact of a wide range of
other factors, they are too many and various to summarize at this stage.
They will, however, gradually be unravelled in the chapters that follow,
and one of the principal themes in the remaining part of this book will be
to trace the manifold direct and indirect effects of changing rates of
population growth.

2

THE MOVEMENT OF PRICES

i The determinants of changing prices

The growth of population in the sixteenth and the early part of the seventeenth centuries had extensive consequences, both direct and indirect, for society and the economy. Many of these were expressed through changes in the level of prices. Every decade a larger number of people than before required food, fuel, clothing and housing, and since such continuing increases in demand could not be fully matched by equivalent increases in supply, after a long period of comparative stability in the fifteenth century, prices necessarily rose. The extent to which they did so depended very largely on relative elasticities of demand and supply, but in part also upon changes in relative costs of production.

The demand for the most basic necessities, especially cereal food-stuffs of which the diet of the masses largely consisted, was highly inelastic and increased *pari passu* with the growth of population. Market demand for cereals, however, grew much more rapidly than the population because the growth of the latter was accompanied by a continuous increase in the proportion of those who were unable to produce their own food, either because they lived in towns or because, whilst remaining in the countryside, they had little or no land of their own and relied on wages earned in agriculture or rural industry. (See below Ch. 3 secs. vii and viii; and Ch. 6 sec. i.) Increases in supply, on the other hand, were limited by the low productivity of arable farming; because of the difficulties of expanding the arable acreage in much of the country, either because no land remained uncultivated or because the land available was not suitable for use as arable, given sixteenth century farming techniques; and because of competition for land from other branches of agriculture, particularly the raising of sheep for wool. In fact, with some help from imports in years of particular shortage, increases in total output of grain crops cannot have fallen very far short of increases in demand. However, much of the cereal production was in the hands of farmers whose first objective was to feed themselves and their families,

29

and who would always retain as much of their crop as was necessary for that purpose. The short-fall in supply was thus not shared equally by the whole community but was borne almost entirely by those who had to buy their grain for cash in the market place, and the price of cereals therefore rose very sharply indeed. Livestock and meat, too, rose in price very steeply, for without draught animals, and sheep to manure their land, the farming population could not carry on their husbandry. Besides there was almost certainly some element of 'cost push' in the upward movement in the prices of both sets of commodities. As we shall see later the rents demanded by landlords for farms, which made up the largest single element in their occupiers' outgoings, also rose very greatly down to the middle of the seventeenth century (see below Ch. 3 sec. vi), and at least on some estates did so *more* rapidly than the price even of grain crops (Kerridge, 1953). Certainly many people in the mid sixteenth century believed that the financial demands of the owners of the soil were forcing producers to pass on the additional burden to consumers.[1] As the Husbandman put it in the *Discourse of the Commonweal* (1549): 'I think it is long of your gentlemen that this dearth [i.e. dearness] grows by reason you enhance your rents to such a height as men that live thereon must needs sell dear again or else they were never able to make their rent' (Dewar, 1969, p. 39).

By contrast with the demand for grain and livestock that for less essential food-stuffs, such as dairy products, and for most manufactured goods, such as textiles, which were also less than essential, was fairly price-elastic. It did not, therefore, grow as rapidly as demand for those commodities without which life could not be sustained at all, especially as rising grain prices absorbed an increasing proportion of the purchasing power of large sections of the population. At the same time increases in output, at least of industrial goods, were relatively easy to achieve.[2] This was because labour, by far the most important factor of production in virtually every form of manufacturing, was plentiful. Besides, because it was plentiful it was also cheap, so that the upwards pressure on costs was very much less than in agriculture. Consequently the prices of such items rose much less sharply. Labour, indeed, was the one commodity which was in great over-supply in the period in question. Those obliged to rely on paid employment for their livelihood were increasing in numbers even more rapidly than the population as a whole, and certainly faster than the

---

[1] Although grain prices rose further and more rapidly than Kerridge reckoned in the article cited, nevertheless his index of 'rents on new takings' rose faster still.

[2] It has also been suggested that there may have been considerable increases in the output of animal products as a result of improvements in the management and feeding of livestock, which produced heavier and healthier animals (*A.H.E.W.* IV, 1967, p. 603).

ability of the economy to employ them.[3] The price of labour, that is wages, thus fell heavily in real terms. In terms of money, it is true, it rose, so that skilled and unskilled building workers, who were paid 6d and 4d a day respectively in the late fifteenth and early sixteenth centuries, received 18d and 12d by the mid seventeenth (Phelps Brown and Hopkins, 1981, ch. 1). But the increases in the money prices of most goods were greater, and in the case of essential food-stuffs much greater.[4] It will be seen from Tables II and III in the Appendix to this chapter that in the same period the price of food grains had risen between seven and eight fold, with barley, oats and rye, which provided the poor with their bread corn, registering a greater increase than wheat which went mainly to feed those who were better off. Livestock and meat had risen in price between six and seven fold, timber over five fold, animal products about four and a half fold, textiles and a varied sample of industrial goods around three fold.

By the middle decades of the seventeenth century the much reduced rate of population growth meant a lessening of the pressure of demand, but the end of the long upsurge in prices was also the result of alterations in the supply situation. There were important improvements in agricultural productivity, as a result of the gradual dissemination of new farming techniques, which affected both arable and livestock husbandry and, together with additions to the cultivated area, these meant a more rapid rate of increase in the output of food-stuffs and other farm products. (See below Ch. 4, *passim*.) Agricultural prices thus reached a peak in the middle third of the seventeenth century (the two series of indices reproduced in the Appendix differing as to which decade recorded the highest figure) and thereafter, for the remainder of that century and the first half of the next, fluctuated around a slightly declining trend.[5] Industry did not experience any comparable improvement in productivity at this time, and perhaps for this reason the prices of manufactures continued to rise for somewhat longer: by the 1670s, however, they too had reached a high point from which they subsequently fell back, albeit very slightly. As in the period of rising prices, so in the ensuing period of falling ones, different types of commodities followed rather different paths. (See below Tables II and IV in the Appendix to this chapter.) The inelasticity of demand for grain, which had ensured that it rose further in price than any other commodity when

[3] For some of the social consequences, see below Ch. 7 sec. i.
[4] Conclusions about consequent changes in living standards should, however, be drawn with care: see also below p. 217 and n.
[5] Except for the prices of livestock which continued to show a very slight upward trend until *c* 1700. For some possible reasons for this exception, see *A.H.E.W.* v, Part ii, 1983, pp. 11–12.

growth of supplies was failing to keep pace with the requirements of the market, also ensured that it fell further once supplies became more abundant, especially after 1700. On the other hand the greater elasticity of demand for semi-luxury food-stuffs, and for manufactures, prevented such a marked downward movement in their prices, especially as cheaper cereals and some rise in money wages (now that labour was rather more scarce) gave the mass of the population increased purchasing power for non-essential items.

The interplay of supply and demand can explain much about the long term movement of prices in the two centuries we are concerned with, but not everything. It does account for 'real' price changes, that is changes in the relative prices of different types of goods and services and of labour in general. However, it does not explain why for so much of the period the price of virtually everything rose in money terms, even those things whose real price was falling; nor why in the later seventeenth century the money price of almost everything except labour was tending to fall. There were, in fact, changes in the value of money as well as in the balance of supply and demand, and it was these two basic factors together which brought about what is sometimes called the 'Price Revolution' of the sixteenth and early seventeenth centuries, and the very different price conditions of the succeeding period.

Until twenty-five or so years ago, indeed, most historians considered that monetary inflation had been the main, if not the sole, cause of the great rise in prices down to the mid seventeenth century. They believed that the period saw very large increases in the money supply, larger than the output of goods, so that prices were inevitably driven upwards. Money in the sixteenth and seventeenth centuries, it needs to be said, consisted entirely of coins made either of gold or silver, except that from the early seventeenth century the very smallest denominations were struck from some base metal such as copper. Of the two precious metals silver was much the most important, for it was silver coins which were used for everyday transactions. Gold coins, being of very high value, were used mostly in wholesale and international commerce, and for holding wealth. Paper bank-notes were not yet in use, and although there were various forms of paper 'near-money', such as bills of exchange, they had limited uses and were not in general circulation. The money supply thus depended mainly on the quantity of silver available for coining, and during the Middle Ages both in England and in Europe as a whole, this seems to have been inadequate. Governments showed much concern about the export of bullion and repeatedly lowered the precious metal content of their coinages to make the limited supplies go further, and this relative shortage of currency was, without doubt, one of the factors responsible for the low and indeed gently declining price level which prevailed throughout much of the fifteenth century.

The underlying reason for the shortage was the fact that in the fourteenth century the output of the European silver mines had dwindled away to almost nothing. However, as silver grew scarcer its price rose, and eventually this, together with technical advances in mining, led to a renewal of production in Germany, Austria and Bohemia. From about 1460 onwards European silver output was rising again, to reach a peak in the 1520s and 1530s (Nef, 1941). There was also an increasing flow of precious metals into Europe from outside. First, in the later fifteenth century, came gold from the trading activities of the Portuguese in West Africa, then in the early sixteenth century from the plunder of the Aztec and Inca empires by the Spanish conquistadores. Moreover, once the Spanish had consolidated their conquests in the Americas, they began to undertake mining operations themselves and to send home both gold and, by the 1530s, increasingly massive quantities of silver. The shipments of American silver to Spain continued to increase in volume throughout the second half of the sixteenth century and reached their highest levels between about 1590 and 1600 (Hamilton, 1928). The Spanish government turned the bullion into coin and the money was used to support its armies abroad, and to pay for imports to Spain, so that it gradually percolated throughout the Continent, and even before the sixteenth century was out some contemporaries had begun to connect it with what was happening to prices. 'Another reason I conceive in this matter', wrote an anonymous author in 1581, is 'the great store and plenty of treasure which is walking in these parts of the world, far more in these our days than ever our forefathers have seen in times past. Who does not understand of the infinite sums of gold and silver which are gathered from the Indies . . . and so yearly transported unto these coasts' (Dewar, 1969, p. 145).

From these various sources, historians believed, the money supply of every country in Europe was increased, at first very slowly but in the sixteenth century at an accelerating pace, and as it rose so did the price level. However, as the European stock of silver grew, so progressively larger annual increments to it were required to maintain the rate at which it was being increased and these were not forthcoming indefinitely, so that by the early seventeenth century the inflationary effects were considered to be weakening. Eventually, in the middle decades of the century, the imports began actually to decline, whilst the expansion of European trade with the Far East and India, which was largely a matter of importing oriental commodities and paying for them with exports of bullion, meant that a growing proportion of the additions to the stock of precious metals was being promptly exported again. By the second half of the century, it was thought, the money supply was no longer growing fast enough to fuel inflation, and its much slower growth, combined with continued increases in commodity output, explained the slightly downward trend of prices in the last part of our period. This interpretation held the field for so long because it appeared to explain why the price rise began and ended when it did, and why prices behaved in a similar fashion all over Europe, from Spain and Italy to Scandinavia, and from England to Hungary; and since little was then known about late medieval and early modern population movements there seemed to be nothing else which could account for so universal an historical development.

However, it is now generally agreed that, on its own, it is not an adequate explanation for what occurred in Europe in general. To start with, an increase in the quantity of money in circulation alone would not cause the prices of some commodities to rise so much faster than those of others, nor explain why almost all rose faster than wages. Simple monetary inflation would tend to push up all prices more or less equally. Moreover, a greater understanding of the rôle played by money in economic systems in general has led to a realization that increases in the supply of it will not *necessarily* cause prices to rise at all. Unless there is an increase in economic activity, such as certainly accompanied the rise in population, and which required a larger money supply to support it, the result would probably be a less rapid circulation of currency and an increase in hoarding. On the other hand it is inconceivable that there could be simultaneously a large growth in population, greatly increased economic activity *and* a huge rise in prices (which is what occurred in the sixteenth and early seventeenth centuries) unless the money supply was progressively increased. It is true that if the rate at which money passes from hand to hand is speeded up, then the same quantity of money will go further and could support a somewhat higher level of economic activity, and even a somewhat higher level of prices as well. In the period we are considering, however, there were strict limits to increases in the velocity of circulation, because of the absence of a banking system and the general paucity of credit facilities. Thus any sustained increase in population and expansion of economic activity, unaccompanied by at least some increase in the quantity of currency available, would probably have caused prices to fall rather than rise,[6] since the same amount of money would have had to stretch further. An increased supply of money was thus an essential factor in making possible the great upsurge of prices, but it was not, at this time, in itself a sufficient cause of that development.

[6] And any such fall would in turn probably have brought any such economic expansion to a premature end.

There is no doubt that there was a great expansion in the English money supply during the period with which we are concerned, although its precise extent is uncertain. The total amount of precious metal in circulation, it has been plausibly estimated, is not likely to have been less than £1.67 million in 1526, whilst by 1603 it was probably at least £3.5 million. The amount of silver, however, had much more than doubled, possibly increasing as much as four and a half fold, for by the latter date the gold coinage had dwindled away to a small fraction of what it had formerly been. During the course of the seventeenth century the value of the silver coinage increased more slowly, roughly doubling to between £6 and £7 million, and whilst there was also an enormous increase in the amount of gold, because of the uses to which this was put, it had less significance for the price level (Challis, 1978, pp. 150, 236, 247. Horsefield, 1960, pp. 14, 258–60).

There has, however, been some debate as to whether much of the additional precious metal which was incorporated into the coinage had in fact come from the various sources which were adding to the general European stock of bullion. For it has been pointed out that England can only have increased her own stock at the expense of the outside world if she enjoyed a favourable balance of payments, since even if American silver was actually shipped into the country specifically to be coined, as under an agreement with the Spanish government it was for a time in the 1630s, it would not have been retained for long had the balance been chronically in deficit. For much of the period, however, the state of the balance of payments is obscure, to say the least. There were periods when the balance of visible trade seems clearly to have been favourable, notably when cloth exports were growing strongly, as at certain times in the first half of the sixteenth century and at the very beginning of the seventeenth. (See below II, Ch. 9 sec. ii.) But there were other periods when things were very different, and it has usually been assumed that throughout much of the later sixteenth century, and during the first half of the seventeenth after 1614, the balance was often adverse and that in a good many years there must have been a net outflow of bullion. Yet it has been shown that until the very end of the sixteenth century the English mint remained highly active, and had no difficulty in attracting silver without having to raise the price at which it was willing to purchase, indicating that there must have been an ample supply available within the country. And it has also been shown that at some periods at least the bulk of the silver actually being minted was of Spanish origin. It is possible that there was more often a surplus of exports over imports, and thus an inflow of bullion, than is usually believed, although this is unlikely to be the main explanation. More important, it has been suggested, were the very large imports of capital in bullion form seized by privateers and Elizabethan naval expeditions (in the most spectacular instance Sir Francis Drake brought home perhaps £600,000 worth in 1580), supplemented by lesser amounts brought over by protestant refugees from the Continent. It is true that these were in part balanced by exports of capital, such as Elizabeth's subsidies to the Dutch and her military expenditure in the Netherlands, but only, it would seem, in part.

Nevertheless it remains probable that at some periods a large proportion of the gold and silver to increase England's money supply came from within the country, and since there were no significant mines of either metal, the only possible source remains bullion not in monetary form, of which there was certainly a very great deal in the sixteenth century.[7] Thus in the 1570s William Harrison remarked how, 'In noblemen's houses it is not rare to see abundance of arras, rich hangings of tapestry, silver vessel, and so much other plate as may furnish sundry cupboards, to the sum oftentimes of £1000 or £2000 at the least... likewise in the houses of knights, gentlemen, merchantmen, and some other wealthy citizens... costly cupboards of plate, worth £500 or £600 or £1000...' (Edelen, 1968, p. 200). The Dissolution of the Monasteries put into the hands of the crown an enormous quantity of plate and religious ornaments made of precious metal which was eventually melted down and coined.[8] There was also dishoarding by private landowners who, when they needed to mobilize funds, whether to buy monastic lands in the 1540s, or to escape the financial difficulties which continuing inflation certainly brought to many of them, especially in the few decades on either side of 1600, are likely to have drawn on the reserve of capital to which Harrison referred. They could literally turn silver dishes and candlesticks into money by sending them to be coined, and many did so, although it is impossible to tell on how large a scale (Brenner, 1961; 1962. Challis, 1978, ch. 3).

By the mid seventeenth century, however, this domestic source of bullion was almost certainly becoming exhausted, especially after the

[7] Much of this bullion was gold rather than silver, but it has been suggested that for long periods it must have been profitable to export gold from England in order to finance the import of silver, since the price which the mint offered for silver was high relative to that which it offered for gold. Such a bimetallic flow (as economists call it) certainly occurred in the debasement period of the later 1540s and early 1550s, and there is little doubt that it did so at other times also, and it provided a mechanism whereby non-monetary and hoarded gold, as well as gold obtained by means of a favourable balance of payments, was converted into additions to the stocks of silver coinage (Outhwaite, 1969, pp. 52–5). At other times alternations in the relative valuations of the two precious metals, either at home, abroad, or both, led to the reverse occurrence, that is an inflow of gold financed by an outflow of silver: see below p. 47.

[8] The quantity of this particular source of bullion should not, however, be exaggerated (Challis, 1978, p. 165).

Civil War during the course of which many landowners gave plate as their contribution to the war effort of one side or the other and thousands more were plundered, legally or otherwise, of all their valuables. Moreover, there is no question that the country's balance of payments was particularly unfavourable around the middle of the century, so much so that one contemporary calculation put the value of imports at twice that of exports, and it is thus very likely that a tightening of the money supply at this time may have contributed first to bringing the price rise to an end and then to reversing it. The balance of payments, however, certainly improved in the last third of the century as the colonial and re-export trades boomed, despite the very large volume of bullion exported by the East India Company.[9] The chronic import surplus of the middle decades was thus transformed into an export surplus, able to sustain the cost of the government's military expenditure abroad, which was especially heavy in the 1690s, the Grand Tours undertaken by the wealthy, and all the other 'invisibles' of the period (Wilson, 1949). The period after 1660 also saw the rapid development of goldsmith banking in London, which must have added to the velocity of circulation since it became possible for their clients to make payments by writing what were, in effect, cheques in the modern sense. Moreover the 'notes' which these early bankers issued on the security of cash deposited with them began to add a new element to the circulating medium, and by the 1690s they may have been worth as much as £2 million, although in practice, like gold, they had a restricted range of monetary usages (Horsefield, 1960, p. 260). These factors seem to have permitted an expansion of the money supply which was sufficient to ensure that the long term trend of prices was only very gently downwards.

ii The chronology of changing prices

The detailed study of prices and price movements in the sixteenth and seventeenth centuries involves many difficulties, apart from the very considerable problem of accumulating the necessary information. To begin with, owing to the high costs of transport and the limited degree to which the various parts of the country were integrated to form a single economy, there were broad differences in price levels between regions.

[9] The development of trade with West Africa during the mid seventeenth century decades was also important because gold was one of the principal imports, and this was one of the reasons why the value of the gold coinage increased so much more rapidly than the silver in the second half of the period. The contemporary name for the part of West Africa frequented by the English, 'Guinea', came indeed to provide a name for the gold coins issued by the Mint at this time. See also below II, pp. 175–6.

The North and North Midlands were, in general, a low price region, particularly for agricultural goods, whilst in the Home Counties, which were most directly influenced by the London market, and increasingly in the South West, with its ever-growing industrial populations, prices tended to be relatively high. But not all commodities conformed to this general pattern: the comparative advantage of the South and East in the production of barley, for instance, made it cheaper there, even in London, than in some more distant areas. The extent of regional price differences, moreover, tended to alter over time as prices rose more rapidly in some districts than in others. Thus in the mid fifteenth century wheat prices in London were usually about 50 per cent above those prevailing in Oxford, but by the mid seventeenth century the margin had narrowed to less than 20 per cent (*A.H.E.W.* iv, 1967, pp. 609–16; v, Part ii, 1984, pp. 16–33). Besides in particular years local scarcity or abundance of certain types of goods could either greatly exaggerate the normal price relationships between areas, or completely reverse them. One cannot, therefore, properly write of *the* price of anything at this period: there was always a wide range of prices.

A further problem is that the prices of many goods were subject to continuous short term fluctuations. Some of these were regular and predictable because they reflected the changing seasons. Thus grain tended to be most expensive in the autumn and winter when the purchasing power of wage earners, which reached its peak in the harvest period, was still considerable, and cheapest during the following summer when their ability to buy was at its lowest. Fuel, too, tended to be dearer in winter when demand was at its height and transport difficulties restricted supply. Other fluctuations were irregular, unpredictable and sometimes extremely violent, especially those arising from variations in the yield of the grain harvest. A poor harvest, which would usually be the result of a late cold spring or an unseasonably wet summer, would force food prices sharply upwards, and a succession of bad harvests would send them soaring. Unusually good harvests would have the opposite effect. As a result wheat, barley or oats often varied in price by as much as 50 or even 100 per cent within a two or three year period. An extreme example of this is the way that the price of wheat at Exeter rose from under ten shillings a quarter in 1543–4 to over nineteen shillings two years later; fell to less than seven shillings in 1546–8; moved up again to over fifteen shillings before the end of the decade and to twenty shillings in 1551–2; then fell to ten shillings in 1553–4 before soaring to over thirty two shillings per quarter in the year 1556–7. To a lesser degree the prices of most other agricultural items, for instance hay, livestock, meat and fruit, were also affected by the weather, although not necessarily in the same way as grain. For instance a fine dry summer which led to a bumper grain crop was likely to yield relatively little hay, and dear hay might result first in cheaper meat as farmers hastened to sell off stock which they would be unable to keep over the winter and then, after flocks and herds had been reduced in numbers, in scarcity and a consequent rise in its price. The prices of non-essentials could also be affected by sudden changes in the level of demand. In a year of dear bread large sections of the population had less money to spend on anything else, so there was reduced demand for manufactures and such relative luxuries as beer and ale. This in turn meant a drop in industrial production and a consequent fall in the price of raw materials such as wool and hops. The varying fortunes of cloth exports could also have a great effect on wool prices, as is shown by their sudden rise in the years leading up to the commercial crisis of 1551 and their even more precipitate fall thereafter (*A.H.E.W.* IV, 1967, pp. 619–29; V, Part ii, 1984, pp 33–55. Hoskins, 1964).

It is these constant short term price fluctuations which make it impossible to discern the long term trend in prices if one simply compares a set of figures for one single year with those for another single year. Instead it is necessary to take periods of years during which upwards and downwards fluctuations will at least to some extent cancel each other out, and calculate an average price for the commodity in question over those periods, even though the average may not have been the price actually prevailing in any one of the years in question. These averages are usually expressed as index numbers, and a series of such index numbers for consecutive groups of years will indicate the extent and broad chronology of price trends. It will, however, be misleading in that by concealing the fluctuations it will suggest that the movements were smooth and regular, and it must never be forgotten that they were not. Price indices for various groups of commodities will be found in Tables II–IV in the Appendix to this chapter, whilst Figure 2 illustrates the extent of the annual fluctuations which lie behind the decadal averages in the case of wheat.

The great differences in the extent to which different types of product rose in price immediately raises the question how did the general price level, or the cost of living, alter. This is a very difficult question to answer satisfactorily. One reason for this is that information may be reasonably abundant for the prices of the commodities included in the tables and for a few others, but it is largely lacking for some extremely important items. Relatively little is known, for instance, about the price of bread, as opposed to the grain from which it was made, and less still about house rents, or the cost of most kinds of services. Besides, any simple answer is more likely to confuse and obscure the historical reality than to clarify it.

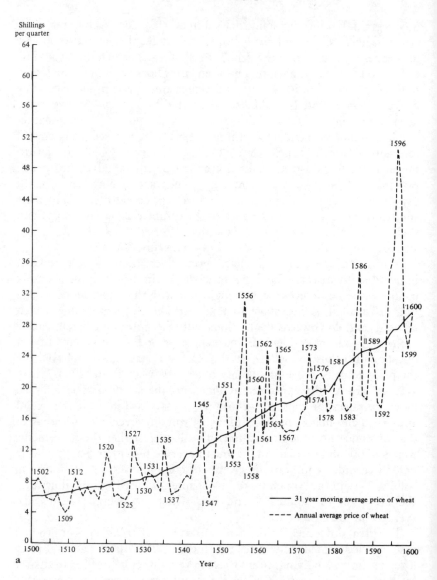

a

'Prices in general' has a different meaning for every social group
according to its pattern of expenditure, and similarly for every form of
economic undertaking according to its schedule of costs. Thus for the
poorer members of the community, who spent most of their income on
basic necessities, the cost of living would be dominated by the price of
cereal food-stuffs, fuel and shelter, whilst for wealthier people these

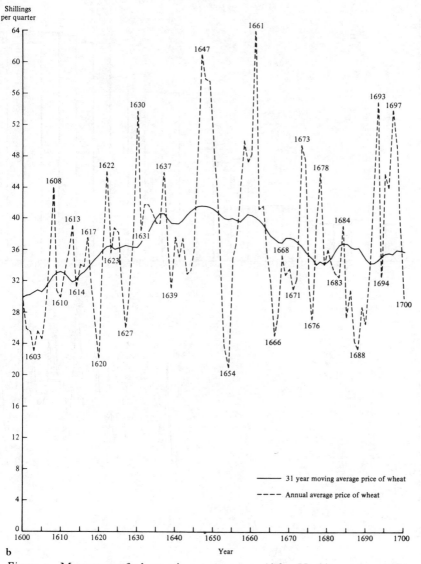

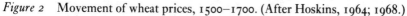

Figure 2 Movement of wheat prices, 1500–1700. (After Hoskins, 1964; 1968.)

things would bulk less large and others would be almost equally important, including meat, dairy products, good quality textiles, hardware, perhaps imported luxuries such as wine, and certainly servants' wages, all of which went up in price much less rapidly than did essentials. In fact, only for wage earners in the building trades

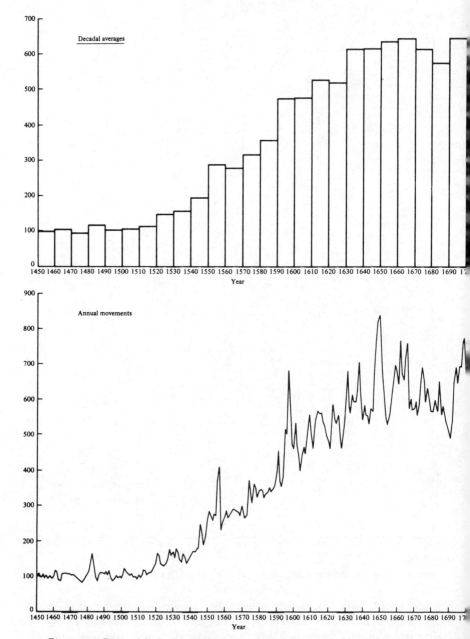

Figure 3 'Cost of living' of building craftsman, 1450–1699. Index numbers 1451–75 = 100. (Source: Phelps Brown and Hopkins, 1981, ch. 2 Appendix B.)

and in agriculture have cost-of-living indices been constructed for the sixteenth and seventeenth centuries. These are reproduced in Tables II–IV at the end of this chapter, and in Figure 3, and whilst they indicate reasonably satisfactorily how the general price level moved from the point of view of those who had to buy all their requirements of food, it does not accurately depict the experience of others. Those who could grow all or part of their own food, as many rural wage earners could, or who spent only a small proportion of their budget on cereals, would have been less affected by the huge increase in grain prices, and found that the rise in their cost of living was not nearly so great.

Let us now turn to the price indices in Tables II–IV, and see what they tell us about the chronology of the great price rise. They show clearly how throughout the second half of the fifteenth century prices of all commodities had fluctuated around a more or less level trend. Grain, and to a lesser extent some other items, had moved sharply upwards in the 1480s, but this higher level was not maintained in the 1490s. Indeed it was not until the 1520s that grain prices rose significantly above the level of the 1480s, but they then made such a large jump that the average for the decade was 50 per cent above that for the later fifteenth century as a whole. Some other agricultural products also rose steeply in the 1520s, notably other arable crops, livestock and hides, but neither dairy products, poultry, wool, timber, industrial products nor wages were yet affected much, or in some cases at all. The 1530s saw a greatly reduced rate of price increases but for no group of commodities was there any dropping back, and then later, in the 1540s and even more the 1550s, there was a fresh acceleration in the pace of inflation. This was the period when prices were rising faster than at any other time in the sixteenth and early seventeenth centuries. Grain prices in particular soared to well over three times, and those of most other agricultural products, including those which had not risen much in the 1520s, to between two and three times, what they had been in the late fifteenth century. By this time, moreover, the prices of non-agricultural commodities and wages were also going up markedly, though not at the same rate as grain prices. Once again a period of accelerated price increase was followed by a relative lull. There was a very much reduced rate of price increase in the 1560s and grains even fell back a little; then in the two following decades movement continued to be gradual until the 1590s when grain and other agricultural products took another lurch upwards, and wages which had begun to make up some of the ground they had lost down to the 1550s were once again left behind. Thus by the end of the sixteenth century grain prices were about six times, meat, livestock and animal products between three and a half and four and a half times, and industrial products rather less than two and a half times, what they had been a hundred years before. Wages, however, had little more than doubled, whilst the building worker's cost of living was approaching five times what it had been at the end of the fifteenth century, so that the purchasing power of his wage had fallen by more than half.

Agricultural prices rose more slowly in the early seventeenth century than they had done in the 1590s, with the first and third decades registering little or no increase, although the prices of industrial goods rose more rapidly, and after about 1620 wages began to move up decisively. However grain made one last sharp jump upwards in the 1630s to reach a peak of nearly 50 per cent above the level prevailing at the beginning of the century, and nearly eight times that of the decades before 1500. As already remarked all other farm products also reached their highest levels in the mid seventeenth century (see above p. 31, and below Tables II–IV in the appendix to this chapter), and thereafter until the middle of the eighteenth they fluctuated around a somewhat lower level, rising a little above it only in the 1690s. Manufactured goods taken as a whole, and the wage rates of both agricultural and building labourers, had all risen about three fold down to the 1640s, but the former continued upwards for another thirty years reaching a peak in the 1670s at roughly three and a half times the level of the late fifteenth century, whilst the latter remained unchanged during that period but began to rise again towards the end of the century.

As this outline makes clear the great rise in prices proceeded very much by fits and starts, and to some extent this must have reflected variations in the strength with which the underlying cause, population growth, was operating. For instance, it seems that the fact that after the 1550s the rate of price increase slowed down whilst money wages continued to rise, was connected with the check to population administered by famine and epidemics in the latter part of the decade (Fisher, 1965). However we shall be on safer ground when we turn to the chronological pattern of good and bad harvests. Tables II–IV show clearly that the rate at which grain prices rose differed from one decade to the next to a much greater extent than did the prices of any other group of commodities, and it was largely the importance of cereal products in the budgets of building workers which explains the extreme irregularity in the upward movement of their cost of living. Now the impact of varying harvest yields on the movement of prices was accentuated by two facts. The first was that, for reasons connected with the low yields of arable farming, good and bad harvests tended to come not singly but several in succession. When a large proportion (a fifth or even a quarter) of each year's crop had to be reserved to provide seed for the next, one bumper crop, the result of unusually favourable weather conditions, would enable farmers to sow more thickly for the following year so that another good harvest was likely, and the cycle would continue for three or four years or even longer, until unfavourable weather brought it to an end. Similarly one poor harvest tended to be succeeded by another because farmers were obliged to economize on seed. The second fact was that, perhaps as a result of fluctuations in climatic conditions, some periods got either more or less than their fair share of these runs of good and bad years, with a corresponding effect on the medium term movement of prices. All the periods when grain prices rose particularly sharply, the 1520s, the late 1540s and the 1550s, the 1590s, the 1630s and the 1690s were characterized by unusually deficient harvests. But at other times serious harvest failures were rare: there were only two between 1530 and 1548, only three between 1557 and 1589, between 1601 and 1629, and again between 1662 and 1691. Instead these periods were characterized by runs of bountiful harvests. There were for instance six good ones in a row from 1566 to 1571, and again from 1601 to 1606, which accounted for the fact that the 1560s and the 1600s were the only two decades between 1500 and 1640 when grain prices actually fell somewhat. In the later seventeenth century an even more remarkable succession of harvests with above average yields, from 1682 to 1690, explains why in the 1680s the building workers' cost of living dropped to its lowest level for over half a century (Hoskins, 1964; 1968. Harrison, 1971).

Monetary instability, that is sudden changes in the quantity and quality of the currency, also contributed something to the irregularity of price movements. The most noteworthy instance of this was the mid Tudor debasement of the coinage. In fact England suffered much less seriously from official interference with the medium of exchange than did most continental countries in this period, and there was only one such episode in the whole of the sixteenth and seventeenth centuries. In 1526 Henry VIII had made some alterations to the valuation of the gold coinage and the weight of the silver, but these were small and simply in order to keep English in line with foreign currencies, and it is improbable that they had much impact on the price level. However, in the 1540s it was a different story. The government was desperate for money to finance the wars in which Henry's foreign policy had involved the country. Heavy taxes were levied, large sums were raised by the sale of the lands confiscated from the monasteries, and amongst the other expedients resorted to was the exploitation of the financial potentialities of the royal mint. The procedure was to attract coins and uncoined bullion to the mint by offering a rather higher price for precious metal than could be obtained elsewhere, and then to turn them into a new issue of coinage in which coins of a given face value contained less precious metal than previously, either because they were lighter in weight or because their fineness had been reduced by the addition of more base alloy. By this means the crown was able to make each pound of gold and silver into a larger sum of money, in terms of face value, than before, and the difference between this on the one hand, and the cost of buying the precious metal (which was, of course, paid for in the new debased coin) and of the reminting itself, represented the royal profit. Relatively little damage was done to the gold coinage, whose fineness was reduced by less than one fifth, but by a series of reminting operations the precious metal content of silver coins was reduced from 37 parts in 40 in issues struck prior to 1542, to only one part in four in the case of those issued in the early part of 1551. At the worst point the supposedly 'silver' coins were in fact three quarters copper, and a contemporary versifier referred to this fact when he wrote of the shilling pieces known as testons blushing red for shame (*T.E.D.* II, 1924, p. 179). The face value of the coins which could be minted from a pound of silver rose from £2 8s 8d to £14 8s 0d, and the crown's total profit in these years has been calculated to have been well over £1.2 million. As far as the economy was concerned the effect was a great increase in the amount of currency in circulation: according to Dr Challis, from perhaps £1.25 million on the eve of the debasements to £2.66 million in the middle of 1551. Then Edward VI's government attempted to repair the damage done by 'calling down' the value of the debased silver coins: that is it ordered that they should henceforward pass at lower values than those at which they had been rated when issued, in order to bring their face value back into line with their intrinsic value in terms of precious metal. This had the effect of roughly halving the quantity of money over-night, and thus returning it to much the same level as in the early 1540s (Gould, 1970, esp. ch. 2. Challis, 1967; 1971; 1978, pp. 237–42, 248–57).

The most intelligent contemporary to comment upon the mid sixteenth century price rise, the author of the *Discourse of the Commonweal* written in 1549, considered that 'the alteration of the coin' was the 'first original cause' of the inflationary tide which was then engulfing English society (Dewar, 1969, p. 101). Yet, whilst prices certainly did rise during the debasement period, they did not behave as monetary theory would suggest they ought to have done. The rise was not as large as the increase in the quantity of money and not nearly proportionate to the reduction in its precious metal content, nor was the 'calling down' of 1551 followed by any significant fall in prices. Various reasons for this have been suggested, for instance that the inflationary effect of a sudden increase in the money supply was muted because before the 1540s the country had been seriously short of currency, whilst the effect of a reduction in quality was limited by the fact that most people had no means of knowing its extent and were apparently so little used to handling coins of the larger denominations that they could not easily distinguish the bad from the good (Challis, 1971). Moreover, in the case of basic food-stuffs and the cost of living of building workers, it is clear that it was not debasement but the bad harvests of 1549–51 which accounted for most of the price increases between the early 1540s and the 1550s. Nor, as we shall see, was debasement the only governmental activity which affected prices at this time, so that whilst there need be no doubt that it contributed to the general increase, it is impossible to distinguish its effects from those of other short term influences operating simultaneously.

A second occasion when temporary but acute monetary instability probably influenced the price level, but in such a way as to slow down the rate of increase, was in the later 1610s and early 1620s. The cause this time was that alterations in the relative values of the two precious metals had produced a situation where in England the official valuation of silver in terms of gold was lower than it was abroad, so that it became profitable for merchants to export silver and to import gold. There may not have been any net loss of bullion, but since it was silver coins which were used for most everyday transactions an increase in the volume of the gold currency was no real compensation for the loss of silver, and a shortage of coin began to develop. The deliberate currency manipulations of rulers in Germany and Poland after 1617 further encouraged the outflow of silver for a number of years, and the whole situation was made worse by the chronically unfavourable balance of payments at that time (Supple, 1959, ch. 8).

Another factor which may have affected price movements in the short run was large scale expenditure by the government on preparations for war. Sixteenth century sovereigns maintained very little in the way of a regular army and navy but in times of crisis, such as 1545 and 1588, they were able to mobilize very large ones running to several or even many tens of thousands of men and scores of ships. The maintenance of such forces meant large increases in government demand for food-stuffs, clothing, munitions, draught animals, transport services by land and sea, and naval stores, and in view of the relatively inelastic sources of supply this was bound to exert some upward pressure on prices. Besides, the money which the government spent on paying its soldiers and sailors and on the purchase of supplies was derived either from its own savings or raised from the subjects, either by taxation or by selling monastic lands or hereditary crown property, and much of it must have come from their past savings or have represented income they would otherwise have saved. A large amount of additional purchasing power was thus pumped into the economy, thereby further increasing demand. Extraordinary military expenditure during the 1540s was about £3.5 million, of which over £1.2 million was concentrated into the years 1544 and 1545, whilst during the long Elizabethan war against Spain it amounted to some £4 million (Williams, 1979, pp. 69, 75. Dietz, 1921, pp. 155–6). These were enormous sums at a time when the royal revenue in peace-time in the later sixteenth century was in the region of £200,000–£300,000, and even though part of the money was disbursed abroad expenditure on this scale must have had some impact on the domestic economy.

And yet it was not an influence comparable to that exerted by the harvests. Several of the main periods of war expenditure were also periods when the upward movement of prices was particularly marked, notably the 1520s, 1540s, 1590s and 1690s, but in three of these decades this seems to have been largely because war coincided with a run of bad harvests, whilst in the 1540s there was currency debasement. Moreover the decade in which war played the greatest part in the lives of Englishmen in the whole of the sixteenth and seventeenth centuries was unquestionably the 1640s, and it shows very clearly, at least as far as agricultural prices were concerned, that variations in harvest yields were a far more important cause of price fluctuations than levels of government expenditure. The Civil War period saw quite unprecedentedly large sums raised by both king and parliament, by borrowing, by taxation and by various forms of confiscation, and the money was overwhelmingly spent inside the country. Moreover, since there was at least some disruption to both agricultural and industrial production, and considerable disruption to the normal channels of marketing, it might have been expected that the inflationary effects would have been particularly marked. Yet the main period of fighting, mid 1642 to early 1646, coincided with a series of good or above average harvests and consequently the price of agricultural commodities in general showed no particular tendency to rise, and it was the poor harvests of the last years of the decade which sent them up sharply (Hoskins, 1968. *A.H.E.W.* IV, 1967, appendices). War-time conditions seem to have been a rather more important influence on the prices of industrial goods. However, on at least one of the occasions when bad harvests coincided with war, the 1590s, the greatly increased price of basic food-stuffs seems to have reduced effective demand for non-essentials enough to off-set the upward pressures engendered by large government expenditures, so that industrial prices actually rose less than in most peace-time decades.

APPENDIX TO CHAPTER 2

PRICES AND WAGES, 1450–1700

Table II *Series continuous throughout sixteenth and seventeenth centuries*
Index numbers 1451–75 = 100

	Farinaceous products	Meat	Textiles	Sample of industrial products	Building worker's 'cost of living'
1450–9	98	100	99	99	99
1460–9	104	106	103	103	104
1470–9	102	88	105	100	94
1480–9	129	126	112	103	116
1490–9	107	103	112	97	101
1500–9	116	98	112	98	104
1510–9	112	121	119	102	111
1520–9	152	165	128	110	148
1530–9	167	164	142	110	155
1540–9	169	242	155	127	192
1550–9	317	315	190	186	289
1560–9	249	315	220	218	279
1570–9	324	326	232	223	315
1580–9	426	367	231	230	357
1590–9	602	429	268	238	472
1600–9	561	478	276	256	475
1610–9	651	523	273	274	528
1620–9	595	540	276	264	519
1630–9	783	561	276	281	616
1640–9	749	603	285	306	617
1650–9	712	681	299	327	636
1660–9	795	665	305	343	646
1670–9	747	613	313	351	615
1680–9	660	631	281	310	577
1690–9	777	687	295	331	647

Sources: Derived from Phelps Brown and Hopkins, 1981, chs. 2–4.
Farinaceous products: wheat, barley, rye, peas.
Meat: beef, mutton, herrings, cod.
Textiles: woollen cloth, linen, canvas.
Industrial products: textiles (as above), candles, oil, charcoal, coal, laths, tiles, bricks, lead, solder.
Building worker's 'cost of living': mixed 'basket of consumables' appropriate to expenditure pattern of skilled building workers.

Table IIIa Series concluding in mid seventeenth century

Index numbers 1450–99 = 100

	Grains	Other arable crops	Livestock	Animal products	Average – all agricultural products	Industrial products	Timber	Agricultural labourer's wages	Agricultural labourer's 'cost of living'
1450–9	98	96	97	91	96	99	106	101	96
1460–9	99	101	102	105	102	103	98	101	101
1470–9	93	101	98	101	98	100	93	101	97
1480–9	114	99	105	107	106	103	109	95	111
1490–9	97	98	99	101	99	97	91	101	97
1500–9	112	98	111	102	106	98	85	101	104
1510–9	115	120	117	118	118	102	97	101	114
1520–9	154	132	138	105	132	110	98	106	133
1530–9	161	128	143	127	139	110	100	110	138
1540–9	187	145	185	159	169	127	115	118	167
1550–9	348	261	259	213	270	186	174	160	271
1560–9	316	294	281	236	282	218	178	177	269
1570–9	370	288	336	257	313	223	206	207	298
1580–9	454	328	352	295	357	230	247	203	354
1590–9	590	428	414	372	451	238	289	219	443
1600–9	560	454	451	387	463	256	335	219	439
1610–9	655	551	507	448	540	274	397	228	514
1620–9	642	546	524	426	535	264	450	253	511
1630–9	790	660	630	455	634	281	475	287	609
1640–9	786	664	667	458	644	306	524	304	609

Sources: Tables VII, XII and XVI, from Statistical Appendix, compiled by P. Bowden, in J. Thirsk (ed.), The Agrarian History of England and Wales, IV, 1500–1640, Cambridge, 1967.

Grains: wheat, barley, oats, rye. The figures for each of these crops are given in Table IIIb.

Other arable crops: hay, straw, peas, beans.

Livestock: sheep, cattle, horses, pigs, poultry, rabbits.

Animal products: milk, butter, cheese, eggs, wool, sheepskin and wool fells, cattle hides.

Industrial products: as in Table II above. This is reproduced again to facilitate comparisons.

Wages: daily rates for southern England (Oxford, Cambridge, Eton).

'Cost of living': weighted combination of appropriate commodities.

50

Table IIIb *Series concluding in mid seventeenth century*

Index numbers 1450–99 = 100

	Wheat	Barley	Oats	Rye	Average—all grains
1450–9	98	100	97	96	98
1460–9	99	99	100	98	99
1470–9	100	88	96	89	93
1480–9	112	118	105	118	114
1490–9	91	95	104	99	97
1500–9	109	108	107	123	112
1510–9	114	112	119	112	115
1520–9	144	136	148	195	154
1530–9	140	158	155	190	161
1540–9	171	197	191	—	187
1550–9	285	450	356	—	348
1560–9	293	338	322	338	316
1570–9	336	360	343	459	370
1580–9	385	482	457	523	454
1590–9	499	600	638	651	590
1600–9	479	583	599	600	560
1610–9	560	665	723	703	655
1620–9	564	648	630	770	642
1630–9	667	876	792	852	790
1640–9	717	796	843	—	786

Sources: *A.H.E.W.* IV, 1967, Tables VIII, XIII and XVI on pp. 857, 862, 865.

Table IV *Series commencing in mid seventeeth century*

Index numbers 1640–49 = 100

	Grains	Other arable crops	Livestock	Animal products	Average—all agricultural products	Agricultural labourer's wages	Agricultural labourer's 'cost of living'
1640–9	100	100	100	100	100	100	100
1650–9	87	103	109	94	97	100	96
1660–9	83	87	109	96	93	100	94
1670–9	81	90	111	87	91	100	92
1680–9	75	102	115	87	93	101	90
1690–9	90	104	128	98	104	102	99

Sources: derived from *A.H.E.W.* v, Part II, 1984, Tables XII and XXIX on pp. 840, 863.
Grains: wheat, barley and malt, oats, rye.
Other arable crops: beans, peas, hops, hay, straw.
Livestock: sheep, cattle, horses, pigs, poultry.
Animal products: wool, mutton, milk, butter, cheese, beef, pork, eggs.
Wages: daily rates, mainly eastern England.
'Cost of living': weighted combination of appropriate commodities.

3

RURAL SOCIETY

I AGRICULTURE AND RURAL SOCIETY IN THE
EARLY SIXTEENTH CENTURY

i English farming at the end of the Middle Ages

The great variety of soils and relief to be found in England, and the considerable differences in climate between one part of the country and another, have always ensured that many different forms of farming have been carried on. In the early part of the sixteenth century, as at other periods, even a small county like Warwickshire, let alone a large one like Lincolnshire, showed sharp contrasts between several quite distinct types of husbandry which were to be found within its borders. Each of the many farming systems of the period had its own balance between arable and pasture, between grain crops and fodder crops, and between different types of livestock, and thus produced its own unique combination of products determined by the natural endowments of the district and the accessibility or otherwise of markets. Each, too, was characterized by a distinctive social structure which was at once part cause and part consequence of the type of farming its members pursued. Even a summary description of all these systems is beyond the scope of this book and a rough classification is all that can be attempted.

The North and West of the country, often referred to as the 'highland zone', had a climate that was both wetter and cooler than elsewhere, whilst there were relatively poor soils, with only limited areas of flat land suitable for ploughing, separated by huge expanses of mountain, moor and fell. It was thus overwhelmingly a pastoral region. Grass was by far the most important crop; relatively little grain was grown; open arable fields were largely absent; hedged, fenced or walled closes the rule; and animal husbandry was the basis of the economy. What little land there was under the plough was mostly used to raise fodder crops, such as peas, beans and vetches, but it was not unusual for farmers to be entirely without arable. Specializations and degrees of emphasis, however, varied

Map 1 Highland and lowland zones.

between districts. Thus in much of Devon and Cornwall and in the Pennine counties of the North, the keeping of sheep for wool and the rearing of cattle were the main activities, but the cattle were sent elsewhere to be fattened, whereas in Shropshire and North Staffordshire both rearing and fattening were carried on. In parts of Cheshire, in the Vales of Berkeley and Gloucester in Gloucestershire, and in North and West Dorset, on the other hand, dairying was the main pursuit, whilst in some districts the rearing of horses was important. In all pastoral areas, however, the social pyramid was more broadly based than in the grain growing lowland zone, and the extremes of wealth and poverty less marked. Settlement tended to be in small hamlets and isolated farmsteads rather than in large villages, and mainly for this reason manorial organization was weak and lords of manors played a smaller rôle in the local economy than in other parts.

South and east of a line drawn, say, from the Tees to Weymouth, conditions were in most places very different. Mixed farming in which both grain and livestock were produced was the dominant form of agriculture; settlement was in nucleated villages, open fields were widespread; and there was a less even distribution of wealth so that the rich tended to be richer and the poor poorer and more numerous. Manorial control was usually much more effective, and the existence of the lord of the manor a more important factor in the lives of villagers. In the plains and vales of the Midlands, with their heavy clay soils, most of the land was arable and, owing to the population densities, relatively little could be left unploughed as pasture. Production of cereals was the main aim of the husbandman, although there were often large acreages of peas and beans which were consumed by both men and beasts. Barley, and to a lesser extent wheat, were the main grain crops on the better soils, rye and oats on the poorer ones. Elsewhere there was often a more even balance between crops and livestock. In particular on the thinner, less fertile soils of the chalk and limestone uplands, for instance the wolds of the East Riding of Yorkshire and Lincolnshire, and the downlands of the South, and in sandy districts such as parts of Norfolk and Suffolk, farmers could not produce satisfactory crops unless their land was heavily fertilized with animal manure. Consequently large flocks of sheep were kept, not so much for their wool or their meat as for their dung: they were fed on the unploughed hill pastures by day and folded on the arable by night where they deposited their precious burden.

There were, of course, some exceptions to the broad generalization of a pastoral North and West, and a South and East where mixed farming held sway. Within the highland zone there were some coastal plains and broad river valleys, such as eastern Northumberland and Durham, south central Lancashire, much of Herefordshire, the Vale of Taunton Deane and the South Hams of Devonshire. In these districts conditions had permitted the development of nucleated villages, there was much arable land often laid out as open fields, and even large areas under corn, although fodder crops tended to be more important in the North. Similarly there were enclaves in the South and East, some of them large, where pastoral farming predominated and where the patterns of settlement and social organization were nearer to those of the highland zone than of the surrounding mixed farming areas. Such were the fenlands of Cambridgeshire and neighbouring counties, where land dry enough to be used as arable was scarce but rich grazing was to be had in abundance, and the so-called 'wood-pasture' districts of Suffolk and the western edge of Wiltshire where dairying prevailed. Such also were districts like the Weald of Kent and Sussex, and the various royal forests of the Midland counties, where extensive woodlands survived to provide ample pasturage, and in general the soils did not favour arable cultivation.

Not all of the farming systems to be found in sixteenth century England had existed time out of mind, and whilst some were undoubtedly very ancient others had only evolved in the very recent past, and others still altered considerably during the centuries we are concerned with. We shall refer to some of these changes in due course (see below Ch. 4 secs. iv and v), but it may be noticed at once that they were not so extensive that the basic pattern outlined above was destroyed. There was a general trend towards greater local specialization, though not necessarily in a single product, and some areas modified their systems by adopting new elements or abandoning old ones. Some, indeed, even switched to a totally different system, with a corresponding change in social organization, as did those Midland districts where open field arable was enclosed and converted to pasture for sheep farming or fattening cattle. However, the basic facts of soil and climate set strict limits to these developments and, despite the changes, the geographical distribution of the various forms of agricultural production was not fundamentally different in 1700 from what it had been in 1500 (*A.H.E.W.* IV, 1967, ch. 1; V, Part i, 1984, *passim*).

In some other respects, however, there was a greater degree of change in these two centuries. At the end of the Middle Ages the extent of commercial farming was relatively limited because market demand was limited. The urban population was low and many of the smaller and medium sized towns were able to produce from their own fields a considerable proportion of the food they required. In the countryside the abundance of land in relation to the size of the population meant that the average size of holdings was much greater than it had been two centuries earlier, that landless labourers were few, and that consequently outside the pastoral areas most people were able to raise at least a large part of the food they required. Certainly the extent of commercial farming had diminished since the early fourteenth century, for the decline in population since that time had been accompanied by an even more rapid reduction in the number of those unable to produce their own food, and thus obliged to purchase it in the market place. The fact that perhaps two out of three markets which had existed at that period had ceased to function by the sixteenth century is a striking illustration of this shrinkage (*A.H.E.W.* IV, 1967, p. 467).

However there were a few areas where commercial farming was strong in 1500, notably those parts of East Anglia and the South East which had easy access to London by river or coastwise shipping, in the immediate environs of other important towns such as Bristol, Norwich and York, and in limited areas in the Midlands and the eastern counties where wool production had become the main preoccupation. Over most of England, however, farmers who concentrated on producing for the market were few and far between, and the proportion of the land they controlled was a small one. In the thirteenth and fourteenth centuries the great land-owners, especially the ecclesiastical ones, had often operated their manorial demesne lands as large scale commercial farms, but since the generations on either side of the year 1400 they had almost universally ceased to do so, and instead leased them out to tenants for rent. Many of the gentry, however, especially those with the smallest estates covering only a single manor, continued to exploit their own land, and where they had access to markets, to sell a large proportion of what they produced; and some of them had enlarged the scale of their operations by taking a lease of all or part of a neighbouring owner's demesne. Urban merchants and lawyers also sometimes leased demesne land in order to operate it, perhaps through a bailiff, to yield a money income, but probably the most important group amongst those who were farming for profit at the beginning of the sixteenth century were the yeomen.

Yeomen were wealthy villagers whose appearance had been one of the most significant social developments of the later Middle Ages. Frequently descended from families of men who, as manorial reeves, had managed the affairs of a manor on behalf of an absentee lord and thereby acquired more capital and business experience than the average peasant, they had taken advantage of the availability of land on easy terms in the fifteenth century to build up much larger farms than their neighbours. Sometimes they were themselves the owners of the land they tilled, sometimes they were manorial tenants, sometimes demesne lessees, or indeed all three simultaneously, but the nature of their tenure was relatively unimportant. It was the scale of their operations, and their orientation towards market production, which distinguished them from the mass of the peasantry. It is virtually impossible to generalize about the size of the typical yeoman farm because it varied so greatly according to the nature of the soil and the type of farming practised, but even in districts where the low productivity of land ensured that holdings were relatively large, anyone with more than fifty to seventy acres can be safely regarded as belonging to this class. Nor is there any satisfactory means of estimating the number of yeomen in the early sixteenth century, but they were the largest single group of those who rented demesne land and they were certainly much more numerous than the armigerous gentry. Probably most villages had one or two families who were at least approaching yeomen status, although they must have formed a very small proportion of the rural population as a whole, possibly no more than 3 or 4 per cent (Hoskins, 1957, pp. 141–2. Du Boulay, 1965).

Most agricultural producers at that time were not primarily orientated towards the market at all. Indeed in the more isolated areas even the gentry probably did not sell a very large part of their production. Rather they farmed mainly in order to supply their own households, which were often very numerous and swollen with retainers, whose function was more to add to their employer's prestige and influence than to act as servants in the modern sense; and to enable them to dispense the 'hospitality' to all comers, which late medieval convention required of the wealthy and powerful. As for the small peasant farmers who formed the overwhelming mass of the population, their concern was essentially to provide themselves and their families with food and other necessaries, and they therefore consumed most of what they produced. That the main function of a peasant holding was to provide its occupier with his subsistence is illustrated by the custom, which prevailed in some areas, of referring to them as 'livings': for instance a farm currently, or once upon a time, occupied by Hodge would be 'Hodge's living'. Few if any of them, even in the most remote areas, were truly subsistence farmers in the sense that they had no regular dealings with the market at all. However isolated they were, it was always necessary for them to sell some part of their produce because they needed money to pay their rent since the great majority of them held their land as tenants or sub-tenants and, taking the country as a whole, perhaps only one in five was a freeholder. Moreover even the minority who were independent proprietors and had no rent to pay required money to meet taxes levied by the central government, to buy essentials which they could not produce for themselves such as salt and metal goods, and to pay for the services of expert craftsmen like the wheel-wright and the village blacksmith. The amount of money they required, however, and thus the extent of their involvement in buying and selling, was not necessarily very great, especially at the beginning of the period. The rents paid by most manorial tenants were very low, and the high fines which their thirteenth and early fourteenth century forebears had had to raise at the start of a new tenancy had fallen to much lower levels, since the drop in population had so greatly reduced the demand for land. Parliamentary taxes were fairly frequent, but only occasionally, as in the mid 1520s and in the 1540s, were they at all onerous (See also below II, Ch. 11 sec. ii.) As for dependence on outside supplies and services, the peasant and his family could and did turn their hands to many things which modern farmers have long ceased to do. The peasant himself could, for instance, fashion the wooden parts of much of his agricultural equipment and such furniture as he wanted, and with the help of neighbours he could erect and repair crude farm buildings. His womenfolk could cure their own bacon, make their own butter and cheese and tallow lights, spin their own wool into thread and turn cloth into clothing, although they were less likely to attempt to weave the cloth itself. From the manorial common they could probably obtain the fuel they needed, either wood, peat or turf, and often building materials such as brick earth, stone and reed for thatching. Even in the middle of the sixteenth century, therefore, money was not something that small peasant farmers handled very much, and their probate inventories often make no mention of any cash amongst their possessions when they died.

It was in the mixed farming areas, especially in the open field villages of the Midland Plain, that peasant self-sufficiency was most marked, for there the characteristic family farm not only provided its occupants with all the cereals they required, but was also able to support a few dairy cows, some pigs and a small flock of sheep, which yielded modest quantities of protein food-stuffs such as milk, butter, cheese and bacon, as well as textile fibres (Hoskins, 1957, chs. II and VII). In some of the pastoral areas, however, especially those in the North, it was often impracticable for small farmers to grow a sufficiently large acreage of grain to supply their own needs fully, and some grew none at all, so that they were obliged to buy part or all of what they required with money obtained from the sale of livestock or animal products. Yet merely by becoming involved in a considerable degree of buying and selling a countryman did not cease to be a peasant and become a commercial farmer, for whilst there were inevitably some who fell into an intermediate category, the two groups differed profoundly in their outlook and their modes of operation. Of these it was the former which was fundamental. To the commercial farmer agriculture was a business which he carried on in order to make a profit, and which he conducted in such a way as to yield the largest possible money income. If he himself consumed any part of what he produced this was incidental to his main purpose and, particularly if he were a grain farmer, he might well prefer to take advantage of annual price fluctuations by holding the whole of his production to sell when prices were at their height, supplying his own needs by purchasing from others when prices were at their lowest. To the peasant, on the other hand, farming was a way of life, a means of supporting his family at a conventional standard of living, and one whose pattern was determined by custom and tradition rather than by the pursuit of financial gain for its own sake.

ii The nature of English peasant society

England in the early sixteenth century was thus not simply an overwhelmingly rural and agricultural society, it was also a peasant society. Now it has been recently argued that this term is inappropriate in the English context, and that even in 1500 English rural society had already for centuries been different in kind from 'true' peasant societies such as those of eastern Europe. And indeed if the absence of households in which several generations lived under the same roof, the prevalence of landholding by individuals rather than by families, and the existence of an active village land market and a considerable degree of both social and geographical mobility are incompatible with the concept of a peasantry, then English villagers were not peasants in the same sense as were many of their contemporaries elsewhere (Macfarlane, 1978, *passim*). Yet the distinctions discussed in the latter part of the preceding section were real enough, and there is no question that at the beginning of the period most countrymen in England pursued a different way of life from that lived by their successors in the eighteenth century. For want of a better word, therefore, peasant will be used to describe the subsistence orientated farmers. Even though the usage may not now receive the approval of the sociologist or anthropologist, most economic historians continue to believe that the implied parallel with the way of life of small farmers on the European continent and beyond remains appropriate.[1]

Peasant farming everywhere is invariably conducted on a family basis, but as indicated above, in the case of England the family was normally just the 'nuclear' family of parents and children only, not the 'extended' family including grandparents, aunts, uncles, cousins and so on, which historically has formed the basic economic unit in many societies outside

[1] For an interesting discussion of the economic characteristics of peasant societies, see Thorner, 1971. Longer and more complicated in its treatment is Thorner, Kerblay and Smith, 1966.

western Europe. The average size of holdings varied much from area to area, according to the type of farming practised and the local density of population, but usually they were small enough to be operated by the labour of the peasant himself and his family. In the open field Midlands the characteristic farm consisted of twenty or thirty acres of arable, with some meadow and pasture in addition, and in some areas of poor soils they were larger still. In the Lincolnshire fenland, by contrast, no more than seven acres[2] seems to have been the median size (Hoskins, 1957, p. 148. Thirsk, 1957, pp. 42, 84, 96). Men with larger than average farms, or who were without sons or whose sons had left home to find work or land elsewhere, might have to make some use of hired hands, but it was more common for the peasant holding to be too small to provide a full time occupation for all those living upon it. This was particularly the case in pastoral districts because of the lighter labour requirements of animal husbandry, but even in the mixed farming districts there were slack seasons of the year when there was little to be done. There is no doubt, therefore, that there was much under-employment in the countryside at this period although the extent of this was mitigated by the practice of sending adolescent children of both sexes out to work on the larger farms in the neighbourhood as 'servants in husbandry', living-in with their employers. This simultaneously relieved their parents of the cost of supporting them, enabled them to learn a range of useful farming skills, and provided them with an opportunity to accumulate some savings with which to set up their own household in due course (Kussmaul, 1981, pp. 70–85).

Inevitably, however, the smallest holdings were, on their own, inadequate to provide the occupier with a living, particularly if he had many children, and for this reason peasant families often had some additional occupation which enabled them to earn a money income so that they could supplement the produce of their own holdings with purchased food. It was thus the poorer peasants who were more deeply involved in the exchange economy than those who occupied substantial holdings. In corn growing areas the most common source of supplementary income was work for wages on the land of a larger farmer, and there was a continuous spectrum from the petty farmer who worked for a neighbour on an occasional basis, through the cottagers with an acre or two of land, to those who had little more than a garden of their own to cultivate and depended almost entirely on wage labour for a living. In

---

[2] However, it should be noted that where, as in the Fens, extensive common grazing was available and the wealth of farmers consisted in their livestock rather than their sown acreage, the size of a holding does not tell much about the scale of farming carried on by its occupant, for the holding itself might be of less importance than the pasturage rights attached to it.

many pastoral districts this type of employment was scarce, but there were also local crafts which could be followed part time (*A.H.E.W.* IV, 1967, ch. VII). Of these the production of woollen cloth was probably the most widespread but there were many others, sometimes dependent on local sources of raw materials, such as wood-working, charcoal burning and small scale iron production in the vicinity of the royal forests. Where tin was to be found as in Cornwall, or lead as on the Mendips and in the Peak, or coal as in many places in the highland zone, peasants might also be miners. Where building stone was to be found, as in the Isle of Purbeck, many were part-time quarrymen. In coastal villages they often spent part of the year as fishermen. Everywhere some of them employed their spare time, and that of their draught animals, in carting, while almost every village had someone who brewed and sold ale. In 1500 the need for such additional means of livelihood was less widespread and pressing than it must have been two hundred years before, because farms were larger, rents lower and the number of peasants with virtually no land at all much smaller. It was also much less than it was again to become as the sixteenth and seventeenth centuries progressed, but even at the beginning of the period peasants were not necessarily farmers pure and simple. Indeed even if a peasant family did not pursue a secondary occupation to supplement its income, it did not devote the whole of its productive effort to farming, for as we have already noticed a good deal of time was devoted to tasks such as carpentry, building repairs, processing of food-stuffs, manufacture of clothing and household necessaries, and the collection of fuel, which in more recent times have been performed by specialists from outside the family in return for payment. The peasant family was thus able to make use of its own under-utilized labour resources to limit its need for a money income, and this was an important factor in its self-sufficiency.

The forms of agriculture and secondary employments which flourish best in any peasant society are those which require the least capital, for the latter is an asset with which peasant families are typically very ill provided. The poorer peasants of course had little opportunity to save anything at all, but even those who were somewhat better off were unlikely to accumulate much in the way of savings. This was largely because, if times improved, they were more likely to increase the proportion of their own produce which they consumed, or to work less hard or less continuously, perhaps abandoning or spending less time on a tedious and ill rewarded by-employment, rather than continue as before, or even to seek to expand their operations, in order to build up capital in the way that a commercial farmer would do.[3] This response meant that a

---

[3] It was a commonplace amongst entrepreneurs before the eighteenth century that their employees, urban as well as rural, were not interested in earning a money income beyond what they needed for

peasant's defence against hard times was not a financial reserve but an ability to reduce consumption and increase effort. It also meant that their farms were seriously under-capitalized compared to those of the commercial producers. They had less equipment, and indeed often seem to have managed with only a few crude implements; their buildings were less adequate; their farms were likely to be less conveniently laid out; they had less livestock and its quality was usually inferior, which meant less manure for their arable. Likewise they were able to do less to enhance the fertility of their soil by the application of other types of fertilizer, or to improve its quality by means of drainage. Their output per acre was thus certainly lower than that of commercial farmers, even before the difference was further widened by the greater rapidity with which the latter adopted the new techniques and new crops which were becoming available in the seventeenth century. (See also below Ch. 4 sec. iv.) This low productivity of peasant agriculture was a factor of considerable importance in the economic history of the sixteenth century, for it was in large part responsible for the extremely rapid rise in food prices in the early stages of the great inflation. As long as peasant farmers remained the dominant type of agricultural producer it was inevitable that increases in demand for agricultural goods would not be fully matched by corresponding increases in supply, even though they were less and less able to maintain their orientation towards subsistence production and were obliged to market an increasing proportion of their output. It was only as commercial farming gradually extended its activities at the expense of the peasantry that agriculture gradually became able to meet fully the demands made upon it, a stage which was not reached until the middle of the seventeenth century.

Another aspect of peasant society which requires comment was its conservatism. Its members were very much wedded to traditional ways of life and customary ways of doing things. Change was unfamiliar and unwelcome. If imposed from without it was likely to be greatly resented for its own sake, quite apart from any threat to the well-being of the community it involved. If ventured on by individuals in their midst it would, initially at any rate, be regarded with suspicion and hostility. A general reason for this conservatism was the nature of village life, which bred·a culture which was highly conformist. Another factor, which produced conservatism in respect of agricultural practices in particular, was the narrow margin by which the typical family was able to sustain itself, a margin which could all too easily be wiped out by misfortune such as crop failure, murrain amongst livestock, fire, flood or the premature death of the head of the household. The peasant could not afford to add

the support of their families, and once they had earned enough for that purpose they preferred leisure to a larger wage packet. See also below ii, pp. 32–3.

any avoidable risks to those which were inherent in his way of life, and whilst new methods or new crops might offer the possibility of greater returns, until their success had been demonstrated beyond all question, their adoption involved the possibility of failure. Security thus dictated adherence to the well tried methods inherited from earlier generations, and experimentation was a luxury he left to others. However once peasant farmers were satisfied that an innovation could be safely adopted it might spread amongst them with surprising speed, as the history of tobacco growing in the first half of the seventeenth century demonstrated (Thirsk, 1974).

The individualism of a peasant society, in which the nuclear family was the basis of economic organization, was tempered not only by the conformity of each family to the traditional ways, but also by the interdependence of the various families who lived in the same place. This was not simply a matter of neighbours occasionally helping each other, or pooling resources on a more permanent basis, for instance by sharing a plough and each providing part of the team needed to operate it. This of course occurred, and must have been widespread, for probate inventories show that throughout the period a high proportion of small farmers did not have enough draught animals to make up a full plough team on their own, and many villages provided a common plough, often kept in the church-yard when not in use, available to anyone who did not have his own. However, more important was the fact that they all belonged to a community which undertook at least some joint economic activity, and regulated the activities of individuals in the supposed interests of the group as a whole.

In pastoral areas the extent of communal activity and control was invariably much more limited than in arable ones, but even there the community derived importance from the fact that it managed the common grazing and waste land, which was often by far the most valuable resource available to the inhabitants, more important even than their own individual holdings. Nevertheless it was where open field husbandry prevailed that the rôle played by the community in economic life was most fully developed. Many practical problems inevitably arose from the fact that farms consisted of a number of long narrow unfenced strips scattered haphazardly around the huge fields and separated from each other by the strips of other owners. But it was above all the need to use the arable land for communal grazing purposes once the crop had been gathered in and during the time when it was left fallow, which made it necessary for the community to impose a comprehensive discipline on all cultivators.[4] All had to follow the same agricultural timetable. They

---

[4] Communal grazing rights over the arable were not found everywhere that open fields prevailed, and seem to have developed only where pasture was particularly scarce. In the Midland Plain, however,

had to plough when others ploughed, to sow crops which would fit in with the basic rotational pattern, and gather in their harvest when everyone else was doing so, for if they did not neighbours might suffer damage and the use of the fields as pasturage would be delayed. In open field villages the shortage of permanent pasture which made it necessary to use the arable land in this way often posed a problem even at the beginning of the sixteenth century, and it might therefore be necessary for the community to place limits or 'stints' on the number of livestock each villager could keep, as well as regulating in precise and minute detail where and when their owners could put them out to graze. The rights of the community, which were based on custom, thus superseded the rights of its individual members in a number of important respects.

These communal rights were exercised through some form of village assembly. This sometimes took the form of an assembly specially for the purpose of regulating communal affairs, particularly where a single village was divided into several manors, but more often appeared in the guise of the jury of the manor court, or the parish vestry. Whatever form it took, the villagers, or rather the leading landholders among them, for peasant society was never an egalitarian democracy, would enact by-laws to regulate the affairs of the village. They would also appoint officials to enforce them, and punish offenders by imposing fines; and they would ensure that members of the village fulfilled their elementary responsibilities to their neighbours, for instance by keeping their gates closed and in good repair, their fences mended, and their ditches scoured, so that one man's neglect did not mean loss or damage to another. In some places they also appointed common functionaries, for instance a shepherd or a cowherd who would be responsible for taking the village livestock out to the common pasture whilst the owners were in the fields. However the main function of communal control was that it provided a mechanism for making the fullest possible use of the land available, and for ensuring that everyone got a share in the relatively scarce resources upon which they all depended for their living. A large commercial farmer trying to maximize his profits would find the restrictions it imposed on him irksome, but for the average peasant it was an embodiment of the principle that the greedy and ambitious few should not pursue their ends at the expense of their poorer neighbours' well-being, and he placed a correspondingly high value on its survival. As for compliance with the restrictions and regulations, to him this meant no more than following the traditional methods of farming and we have seen that he had little or no wish to do otherwise (Blum, 1971. Ault, 1972).

such rights were general, and it was the open field enclaves in pastoral or semi-pastoral districts from which they were absent. For a recent work on English field systems, see Baker and Butlin, 1973.

The level of material well-being enjoyed by a peasant society depends essentially on the amount of land available to it compared to the size of its population. Where land is relatively abundant only the better and more productive soils need be tilled, the size of holdings can be large, and landlords are unable to demand high rents. The cultivators therefore flourish, not only because their farms yield them an ample subsistence but also because they are able to retain the bulk of what they produce for their own consumption. Few villagers will be unable to obtain sufficient land to support their families and for those few the scarcity of labour, which is the corollary of an abundance of land, will ensure that wage levels are high. On the other hand if the rural population begins to rise more rapidly than it is possible to expand the cultivated area, or if the amount of land available for peasant farming is constricted because of growing competition for it from other forms of economic activity, such as commercial farming, then very different conditions will begin to develop. Cultivation will spread onto infertile or difficult soils which yield a poor return for the labour spent on them. Holdings will become smaller as they are subdivided in order to provide a livelihood for larger numbers, and rents will be driven upwards by competition between potential tenants for scarce farms. An increasing proportion of the peasantry will find themselves unable to secure farms on any terms and will come to form a landless proletariat, wholly dependent on working for wages and various forms of non-agricultural employment, the rates of remuneration for which will be gradually forced downwards by the excess labour supply. Income is thus redistributed from peasant to landlords and employers, and living standards will be progressively reduced towards subsistence level.

Medieval England had experienced both these sets of circumstances. In the thirteenth and early fourteenth centuries, as we noticed at the beginning of Chapter 1, the population had grown very large and all the above consequences had ensued. Conditions for the rural masses, indeed, had apparently deteriorated to such a degree that some historians consider that the demographic catastrophe of the mid and later fourteenth century was in part a direct result of their desperate poverty. By the fifteenth century, however, the population was much smaller, and seems to have showed little or no tendency to increase for a period of several generations. Consequently a situation resembling that outlined at the beginning of the previous paragraph had come to prevail, and both the landholding peasantry, and those who relied mainly on wages, were enjoying a degree of prosperity that they had not known for centuries, and may never have experienced before. There were, of course, some of them who were very poor indeed, and harvest failures, such as those of 1482 and 1483, must still have brought destitution and even death to those with the smallest holdings, but the proportion of villagers seriously at risk in this way was much smaller than it had been two hundred years before. Nor is it true to say that there was no competition for land from commercial agriculture. Times when wool prices were high in relation to those for arable products, as they were between the early 1460s and mid 1480s, encouraged large scale sheep farming (*A.H.E.W.* IV, 1967, pp. 636–7). Manorial lords and their demesne lessees were anxious to extend their pastures and in some areas, notably in such eastern counties as Lincolnshire and the East Riding of Yorkshire, and in some parts of the Midlands, they did so by incorporating land which had formerly been cultivated as open field arable by small peasants. In the circumstances of the time, with demand for land slack and many villages having land untilled for want of tenants, this was often done without displacing anyone, although undoubtedly sometimes tenancies were brought to an end and the old occupiers evicted in order to create the sheep-runs. However it was probably rare for more than a handful of tenants to be involved, even when an entire village was converted to pasture and its very site destroyed. Modern research has shown that such 'lost' villages had usually been small and on unpromising sites from which people had drifted away, lured by the easy availability of better land elsewhere, so that they had already lost many of their inhabitants before the landlord completed the process by moving out the last few families (Beresford, 1954, chs. V–VII). In some limited localities this conversion of arable land for commercial farming was quite extensive: John Rous, who died in 1491, compiled from his own knowledge a long list of villages in Warwickshire, mostly from the southern part of the county, which had been destroyed. It caused some concern in government circles, where fears arose that stretches of empty and depopulated countryside would weaken the nation's defences against invasion, and legislation was passed in 1488 and 1489 in an attempt to check it. However taking the country as a whole, when the sixteenth century dawned peasant farming was not yet under serious pressure from the expansion of the commercial sector.

II THE EXPANSION OF THE COMMERCIAL SECTOR

iii Engrossing, enclosure and conversion to pasture

As the new century advanced conditions altered and there was set in motion a complex chain of developments which brought about great changes in the fortunes of the peasantry, and which by the end of the period with which we are concerned had resulted in the partial destruction of the class. The ultimate origin of most of these develop-

ments was the sustained increase in the population from the early
sixteenth to the mid seventeenth centuries although, as we shall see,
many of the effects of population growth were indirect. In historical
reality the direct and indirect consequences were inextricably linked,
often reinforcing each other, but in some circumstances tending in
different directions. However for the purposes of explanation it will be
easier to consider them separately.

We have seen that a rising population, accompanied as it was by an
increased degree of urbanization and a large growth of the number of
people in rural areas who were unable to produce all their own food,
meant a great increase in market demand for agricultural commodities
and continuous increases in their prices. The prospects for commercial
farming in the sixteenth and seventeenth centuries were thus very much
more encouraging than they had been in the later Middle Ages. Naturally
not all types of production were equally prosperous all the time for, as we
saw in Chapter 2, prices of different commodities did not rise at a uniform
pace. (See above esp. pp. 30–1, 37–9.) The price of wool was particularly
favourable to producers between about 1504 and 1518, as it had been at
one time in the later fifteenth century, and as it was to be again in the later
1530s and 1540s, and again at the beginning of the seventeenth century.
Expansion of cloth exports was one reason for these periods of high wool
prices, but another was the relatively low prices of grain which were then
prevailing and which gave domestic consumers increased purchasing
power, thereby boosting home demand for textiles. But at other times, for
instance in the second half of the sixteenth century, wool growing lost
some of its attractiveness and the constantly increasing demand for beef
and mutton from the wealthier groups in society made meat production a
more profitable use of pasture land. The periodic upsurges in the price of
cereals provided a golden windfall for farmers who were able to produce
large surpluses of grain for sale, but they fared less well during some of
the intervening periods when prices rose much less rapidly or even
dropped back.[5] Nevertheless before the last third of the seventeenth
century most, though not quite all, of these price movements were little
more than ripples on the swelling tide of prosperity enjoyed by
commercial producers, and the efficient farmer who had plenty to sell
rarely failed to make money for long whatever his speciality
(*A.H.E.W.* IV, 1967, ch. IX).

Slowly at first, but with increasing rapidity after about 1570, the scale
of the traffic in agricultural products increased: old markets found their

---

[5] Alternating periods when grain prices stood first high, then low, relative to agricultural prices in
general have been attributed by Dr. Bowden to natural cycles in weather conditions. *A.H.E.W.* IV,
1967, pp. 634–6; and V, Part ii, 1984, pp. 55–8.

business expanding, new ones became established, and there grew up a new system of private wholesale trading which by-passed the public markets altogether. By far the largest concentrated source of demand was the rapidly growing capital city which already by the later sixteenth century, and still more so in the seventeenth, was attracting food-stuffs and agricultural raw materials from so wide an area that there was probably no county in England where a minority of commercial farmers, usually the largest producers amongst them, were not supplying something towards it. In limited districts its influence was overwhelmingly powerful. Thus in Thanet which provided much of its barley, or the coastlands of the North East whence came much of its dairy produce, or by the later seventeenth century the pastures of the South Midlands where cattle and sheep were fattened for the butcher, the nature of the local agriculture was increasingly determined by London's requirements. The larger provincial towns, and the industrial workers of the main cloth manufacturing districts in East Anglia, the South West and the West Riding of Yorkshire, however, provided a market which in aggregate must have been nearly as big as London's. Finally there was the growing army of consumers in the small towns and villages up and down the country, not very numerous in any one place but found almost everywhere, who provided the bulk of the customers at innumerable local markets which the smaller producers chiefly relied on for the disposal of their crops and livestock, and which probably absorbed a larger volume of both than did all the main concentrations of population put together (Fisher, 1935. *A.H.E.W.* IV, 1967, ch. VIII).

In order to take advantage of the favourable market conditions of the sixteenth century commercial farmers naturally wanted to expand their operations, and their increasing profits gave them the capital to do so. Whether they were themselves owners or merely tenants they therefore wanted larger farms, and farms that could be run with the maximum of efficiency. There were two ways in which they could increase their acreage. One was, by purchase or by lease, to absorb the holdings of one or more other farmers, a practice which was known at the time as 'engrossing'. The other was to take in land which had not hitherto been cultivated at all but had remained as waste or common grazing ground, to plough it up, and turn it into arable or improved pasture for their own exclusive use. This the lord of a manor, and those licensed by him, had the right to do under the terms of the thirteenth century Statute of Merton (1235), provided that he left sufficient pasturage for the needs of the other commoners.

The search for efficiency, which meant lowered costs of production and perhaps increased output as well, and thus higher profits, involved the creation of compact farms, conveniently laid out in relation to the site of the buildings, and fields which were suitably sized for their purpose. Such reorganization was often desirable in areas where small enclosed fields were general, but it was in the open field districts that the commercial farmers found it most necessary. There large farms consisted of dozens or even scores of strips, some only a fraction of an acre in size, and widely dispersed so that some of them would inevitably be a long way from the farmstead in the village. No less of a nuisance was the control over husbandry practices maintained by the village community, and the right of commoners to use the arable fields as pasture after harvest time, which seriously restricted the large producers' flexibility and thus their ability to exploit to the full the commercial possibilities of the period. Thus the more enterprising and energetic open field farmers attempted to consolidate their strips as far as possible, by exchanges with others and by buying and selling, so that their farm could be operated without the waste of time and energy which the constant need to move men and equipment from one minute plot to another necessarily involved. No less important was the possibility that a consolidated block of strips could be separated off from the rest of the village land by fences and hedges, sub-divided in such a way as best suited the farmer's convenience, and freed from any form of communal control and from common rights. It could then be operated by him in the way which seemed to offer the most lucrative return.[6] Frequently the latter involved only a more intensive version of the same type of husbandry as the farmer had practised before, and as the remaining strip-holders continued to practise, but at certain times and in certain places more radical changes followed. In particular in many Midland districts where heavy soils were as well or better suited to pasture farming than to grain growing, and especially at periods when the prices of animal products were high compared with those of cereals, the enclosure of open field arable often resulted in its conversion to grass for the production of either wool or meat.[7] However even a man whose

---

[6] However it should be noted that enclosure did not of itself rid a man's land of common rights, and unless he were in a strong enough position to defy his neighbours he could only avoid them by paying some form of compensation. There was, therefore, much so-called 'Lammas land' in the sixteenth century, that is land that was enclosed but still liable to be used as common pasture after the harvest had been gathered in, although sooner or later its owner was likely to negotiate its complete freedom from all forms of communal control. Contrariwise an owner or owners might agree on the extinction of common rights even though their land continued to lie open and unenclosed (Kerridge, 1967, pp. 16–19). The historical reality was, in other words, more complicated than any attempt at simplification and generalization may seem to suggest.

[7] Another qualification must be added here. Farmers in these districts could increase their acreage under grass without enclosure by securing communal agreement to the laying down of some of their open field strips as grass leys, on which livestock could then be tethered or penned in. Indeed, the later Middle Ages seem to have seen a considerable extension of the acreage under grass by this means.

primary interest was in raising grain crops for the market would want to increase the amount of livestock he kept, since the dung of farm animals was a vital element in maintaining or improving arable yields, and the larger his flocks and herds the more bountiful his crops would be. The easiest way to do this without reducing his acreage under corn was to make greater use of the manorial common, putting out more beasts to graze on it than he had formerly done. Alternatively he could come to an agreement with someone who had the right to use the common of a neighbouring manor and pasture animals on it under another's name. Specialist livestock farmers, of course, could do the same in order to increase their pasture resources yet further.

None of the activities described in the preceding paragraph were new in the sixteenth century. Some men had long been engrossing farms, appropriating parts of the waste land within the boundaries of the manor where they lived, consolidating open field strips, enclosing them, converting arable to pasture and putting out larger numbers of animals on the common than their neighbours. But in the later Middle Ages, when land was abundant relative to the size of the population trying to make a living from it, they could usually do these things without seriously adverse consequences for their fellows. No one would be injured by encroachments on the manorial common when what remained provided more than adequate grazing for the animals of the other villagers; nor did anyone see harm in an ambitious yeoman taking two, three or even four farms when there were holdings which stood untilled for want of tenants; nor was conversion of arable to pasture a matter for adverse comment when grain prices were low and agricultural labourers to work corn farms difficult to find. However during the fifteenth century the incentives for commercial farmers to expand their operations had not been very powerful, except in limited localities and for limited periods. It was only in the sixteenth century that they began to affect all branches of agriculture and virtually all areas all the time, and as they did so the activities of these large scale producers began to appear in a rather different light. The rising prices which provided the incentive were caused largely by a rising population, and a rising population meant an increasing number of peasant families who wanted land in order to maintain themselves. As the numbers in the villages began to swell, so untenanted farms were taken up, land which had gone out of cultivation altogether since the fourteenth century was taken back into use, and eventually in one area after another a shortage of land for peasant farming began to develop. In districts where large areas of waste remained the shortage could be alleviated by winning more cultivable land from the wild, but in the more densely populated areas of mixed farming there was limited scope for this, and in many places, especially in the open field Midlands, none at all, even in the early sixteenth century. Indeed in some places the land shortage became very acute, especially in the later sixteenth and early seventeenth centuries, so that an intense land hunger developed.[8] This is illustrated by attempts to put exceedingly poor soils under the plough, for instance on the barren heathlands of Dorset, and hard fought legal disputes over grazing rights between neighbouring communities which had hitherto peacefully shared the use of a common for generations. It is also shown by the increasing need felt by village communities to impose 'stints' limiting the number of animals which individuals could keep on the common pastures: commons which had been large enough for all to use freely in the fifteenth century were often becoming seriously over-grazed when, by the second half of the sixteenth century, the number of households was perhaps half as large again (*A.H.E.W.* IV, 1967, pp. 200–12).

The problem was, therefore, that the needs of the two sectors of agricultural society were in direct conflict. The activities of the commercial farmers threatened to reduce the resources available to the peasant family farmers, whilst the system of communal rights and communal controls which provided the peasants' main defence against these activities, and to which they now clung with increased tenacity, interfered with the efforts of the farmer to take full advantage of market opportunities. From the peasant farmers' point of view engrossing meant that fewer families could get land to cultivate than if every tenant had only a single holding. If part of the common was appropriated by the lord of the manor or his demense lessee, so that what remained was inadequate for the needs of the other villagers, or if it was eaten bare by the flocks and herds of one or two large farmers, then it would be a serious matter for the small family farmers who depended on the common pasture to support the plough animals–horses on the light soils, oxen elsewhere–without which they could not carry on their arable farming. Loss of any part of the common land, let alone the loss of all of it, would be particularly serious for the poorest members of village society, the cottagers and landless labourers. They had no plough-teams but it provided them with the only available pasturage for a cow, a few sheep, pigs or geese, and a source of fuel and other trifles, which made the difference between some modest degree of comfort and independence and utter poverty (*A.H.E.W.* IV, 1967, pp. 403–9). Enclosure of part of the open fields, and the extinction of common rights this usually involved, would also mean some reduction in the amount of grazing

---

[8] See also below secs. vii and viii of this chapter where the direct consequences of population increase in rural society are discussed more fully.

available to the rest of the community. Conversion of a mixed farm to permanent grass, however, struck an even more fundamental blow at the village economy than was felt in the loss of common pasture, because it meant a reduction in the demand for labour. The disappearance of employment possibilities would not simply reduce the labourers' standard of living, it would make it impossible for them to survive at all.

How acute the conflict between the two sections of rural society became, and how serious were the consequences of engrossing, appropriation of common land by individuals, enclosure of open field and so on, depended very much on local circumstances. The main factors were the attractiveness of the area for commercial farming, which varied according to soil conditions and access to markets, and the balance between resources and the size of the peasant population which was trying to make a living from them. If the balance was a fine one, even a relatively slight disturbance of the *status quo* could be serious for all the family farmers and cottagers involved and disastrous for some, but if there was no great pressure on resources then considerable changes could occur without adverse consequences. In most of the North, the Welsh border counties, and the south western peninsula, and in some of the pastoral enclaves in the lowland zone, there were large areas of uncultivated mountain, moor, marsh or woodland, so that substantial inroads could be made on manorial commons without prejudice to anyone. Besides, the existence of such a reserve of cultivable land meant that engrossing was less necessary and less of a grievance where it did occur. Conditions, in other words, remained comparable to those which had prevailed over almost the entire country in the fifteenth century. Moreover in these areas of pastoral farming open arable fields were either absent altogether, or few and unimportant and without any elaborate framework of control, so that neither their enclosure nor their conversion to pasture was ever much of a problem. Most of those which existed in 1500 had already gone by 1600, and virtually all the remainder by 1700. County boundaries do not necessarily coincide very closely with natural regions but the point may be illustrated by the fact that in sixteen of the forty-two English counties less than 4 per cent of the surface area remained as open field late enough to be enclosed by act of parliament in the eighteenth century (Slater, 1907, ch. XIII).[9] Change in these districts usually proceeded by means of amicable agreement between the various parties to the manorial economy

[9] The counties were Northumbs., Durham, Cumbs., Westm. and Lancs. in the North; Chesh., Staffs., Shrops., Herefs. and Monm. on the Welsh border; Soms., Devon and Cornwall in the South West; Essex, Sussex and Kent in the South East. The amount of open field remaining to be enclosed by act of parliament varied from 3.6 per cent of the area in the case of Herefs. to none in those of Lancs., Devon, Cornwall and Kent.

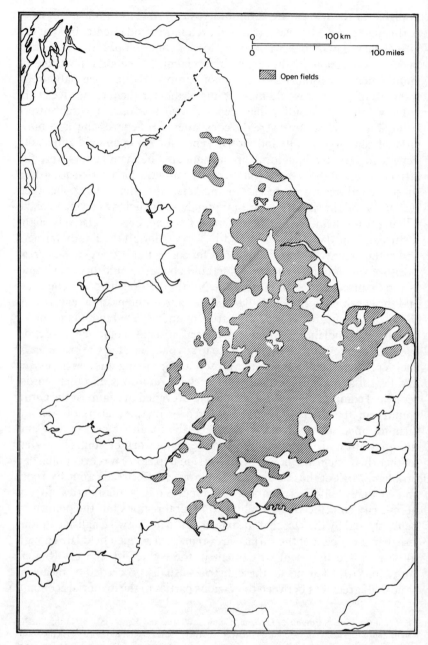

Map 2 Approximate extent of open fields, *c.* 1700. (After Slater, 1907, map
facing p. 73.)

and, although disputes sometimes occurred and the resentment of peasant farmers was sometimes aroused, neither happened with the frequency or the intensity found elsewhere.

It was in the mixed farming regions of the East, the Midlands, and the central South, where population densities were greater and the pull of market opportunities often stronger, that competition for land between commercial farming and peasant farming was most intense and the resultant conflict most bitter. In many places in these areas there was so small a margin between the resources available and what was needed to support the growing population that if any one farmer expanded the scale of his operations in a big way it was bound to injure others. Pasture land was generally limited, and often in acutely short supply, so that it was of the utmost importance to the villagers that manorial commons should be preserved intact. Peasants who lost their farms as a result of engrossing would have great difficulty in finding another tenancy, and were likely to be reduced to earning their living by working for wages, but if engrossing was accompanied by enclosure and conversion of open field arable to pasture then the likelihood was that there would be no work available. In that case they would have to leave the village, and perhaps the district, in search of land or employment.

This displacement of population as a result of the conversion of open field arable to pasture was an aspect of agrarian change which attracted a great deal of attention in the sixteenth century, from the government, from parliament, and from those moralists and others, such as Sir Thomas More and Bishop Latimer, who claimed to speak for the poorer members of rural society. For this reason it has also received much attention from historians. However conversion to pasture was widespread only during relatively limited periods when price trends made it particularly advantageous for farmers to increase their output of animal products, and even then it was largely confined to districts where a combination of soil conditions, and the difficulties of marketing a bulky product like grain, meant that pasture farming was a more suitable economic activity than the raising of cereals. Obviously areas already concentrating on pastoral farming were not affected, nor were those whose comparative advantage lay overwhelmingly on the side of growing corn. It was the Midland counties of Leicestershire, Lincolnshire, Warwickshire, Northamptonshire, Bedfordshire, Buckinghamshire, and to a lesser degree some of their neighbours, which were the principal victims of depopulating enclosure, or rather the parts of those counties, most of which contained enclaves in which pastoral farming had long been the rule, where open fields and mixed farming were still general at the end of the Middle Ages (Beresford 1954, ch. VII. *A.H.E.W.* IV, 1967, pp. 240–55). Neither the acreages nor the number of people affected can ever be known with any certainty, for although a series of government commissions of enquiry, in 1517, 1548, 1566, 1607 and 1630, assembled a large amount of information on the subject, their findings were certainly incomplete and often of doubtful accuracy (Kerridge, 1955). The evidence, however, confirms that the scale of conversion to pasture and the consequent depopulation has frequently been greatly exaggerated, and it is certain that only a small proportion of the total area, less than 10 per cent down to the early seventeenth century, even of the counties mentioned above, was involved. The total destruction of villages was uncommon in the sixteenth century, especially after about 1520, and most of the cases of enclosure discovered by the enquiries affected only a few dozen or a few score acres of land and two or three families in any one place. Thomas Haselrig of Noseley, Leics., who, as a result of the investigations of the Enquiry Commission of 1517–18, was found guilty of destroying five houses, reducing six others to the status of cottages and enclosing 480 acres (Scarisbrick, 1978), was thus a relatively large scale offender by the standards of the time.

Some historians believe that extensive depopulations may have been more common than the historical record suggests, arguing that those who perpetrated them would have been men too powerful to be brought to book. However it is improbable that there were many such cases, if only because it was rare at this period for a great landowner to exploit on his own account the demesnes of more than one or two of his manors. On the other hand it would be wrong to underestimate the local significance of this piecemeal change in the organization of the land and the use to which it was put, especially where it continued generation after generation. Thus in Leicestershire one village in six disappeared between 1450 and 1600 and more than one in three experienced some enclosure during the sixteenth century. And in Northamptonshire, the worst affected county according to the findings of both the 1517 and the 1607 commissions, over 14,000 acres were enclosed and 1405 persons displaced between 1488 and 1517, and another 27,335 acres were enclosed and 1444 more people displaced between 1578 and 1607 (Hoskins, 1957, p. 179; 1976, p. 70. *A.H.E.W.* IV, 1967, pp. 241–2). But it must always be remembered that enclosure of open field and conversion to pasture was only one of the forms taken by agrarian change, and that engrossing without enclosure, the appropriation of commons, or their over-stocking by rich yeomen and gentry, were equally important aspects of the extension of commercial farming at the expense of the peasant sector, and caused almost as much discontent and bitterness amongst the peasantry. Equally resented too, were the attempts of lords of manors to force up the rents and fines which their tenants paid for their holdings, and these occurred in every part of the country.[10]

iv Opposition to agrarian change

The opposition of the peasantry to changes which they felt to be threatening took two principal forms. Particularly if they had the support of some of the more substantial members of the community they resorted to the law. Where there had been breaches of manorial custom they combined to bring civil suits against their lord or his demesne lessee, and not infrequently won them. Where there had been breaches of the statutes directed against enclosures they laid information that led to criminal proceedings, or they took cases themselves to the Courts of Star Chamber or Requests, as did the tenants of Draycot and Stoke Gifford in Somerset when, sometime around 1540, Sir John Rodney deprived them of their common pasture on Stoke Moor by incorporating it into his park, and further enlarged it by demolishing two tenements and taking in part of their land (*T.E.D.* 1, 1924, pp. 29–30). Where they lacked the financial resources to engage in litigation or the confidence that they were likely to gain redress that way, their only alternative was violence. They organized riots during which fences and hedges were torn down, enclosures thrown open and the village livestock driven into land which had been appropriated. On a number of occasions local resentments grew so strong that disorders became widespread, there was open defiance of government authority and even armed rebellion. None of the major sixteenth century rebellions were purely agrarian in origin, although that of Ket in Norfolk in 1549 was overwhelmingly so, but in most of them agrarian discontents were prominent, even though religious motives and in some cases regional distrust of London policies, which also aroused the gentry and even some members of the aristocracy, were equally important elements. The Pilgrimage of Grace (1536) which affected large areas of the North as well as the lowlands of the East Riding of Yorkshire and Lincolnshire, and the rebellion in the South West in 1549 are the best examples of this (Fletcher, 1968. Beer, 1982, esp. chs. 3 and 4. Davies, 1973. Tawney, 1912, Part III, ch. I).

From the latter part of the century onwards peasant protests were less involved with those of their social superiors, since the latter were increasingly expressed through parliamentary opposition. They consequently appear in unadulterated form, although for the same reason they made a less dramatic impact. Thus there was a near rising in Oxfordshire

[10] The subject of rents and fines is dealt with below in sec. vi of this chapter.

in 1596, and again in 1607 in the three Midland counties of Northamptonshire, Leicestershire and Warwickshire which, as we have seen, had certainly been affected by depopulating enclosure. There was prolonged and well organized resistance, amounting almost to rebellion, in parts of Dorset, Wiltshire and Gloucestershire, between 1628 and 1631, when attempts were made to enclose the royal forests which had provided many small farmers with common pasture which was essential to their livelihood (Allan, 1952). Even more prolonged resistance occurred in the fenlands of Lincolnshire and Cambridgeshire, when the drainage schemes of the 1630s threatened to deprive the peasantry there of their rights of common in order to create large arable holdings, which the promoters could let at high rents to commercial farmers (Darby, 1940, pp. 49–64. Thirsk, 1957, pp. 120–7). Nevertheless neither the scale nor the frequency of these later disturbances in any way compared to the widespread and often ferocious peasant risings which occurred on the Continent in this period. One reason for the relative quiescence of the English peasantry after 1549 was undoubtedly that the most substantial among them, the yeomen, who would have been their natural leaders in resistance, became so deeply involved in commercial agriculture that their material interests, and indeed their whole outlook, came to have more in common with those of the gentry than with the family farmers and smallholders. Another was probably that, at least from the middle of the sixteenth century onwards, the majority of English landowners in practice behaved with greater restraint towards their tenantry than they have been given credit for. Ruthlessness there certainly was, but, as we shall see, it was probably the exception rather than the rule. (See also below sec. v of this chapter.) It was also important that the agrarian grievances of the cultivators were not compounded by heavy state taxation, such as was imposed on the French peasantry,[11] nor by the recurrent bouts of warfare which afflicted many other parts of Europe bringing devastation and ruin to the countryside and driving its inhabitants to desperation.[12]

However it was mainly because of the threat to public order which the continuance of the agrarian changes posed that the government became concerned and attempted to check them, although other motives were also involved. During periods of high grain prices fears that the conversion of arable to pasture threatened the nation's ability to feed

---

[11] Between the later 1520s and the beginning of the 1640s direct taxation did not much affect the small cultivator in England, and though it certainly did during the Civil War and its aftermath, it was not until the 1690s that heavy taxes were again levied for a prolonged period. See also below II, Ch. 11 secs. ii and iii.

[12] It is notable that the only significant campaigns fought on English soil in the period, those of 1642–6, did produce a movement of peasant resistance in the so-called 'Clubmen'.

itself were regularly revived, whilst a reduction in the number of family farmers was felt to be undesirable from a strategic point of view, since such men formed the back-bone of the armed forces in time of war. Besides, the prevailing view was that society ought to be an ordered hierarchy, in which everyone was content with the station into which they had been born. It was accepted that the rich should not seek to deprive the poor of their rights, any more than the poor should aspire to pull down the rich, and that if they did it was the government's duty to protect the weak against their powerful oppressors. The crown therefore threw its weight into the conflict on the side of the peasantry. Again and again, from the later fifteenth century until almost the middle of the seventeenth, it issued proclamations and secured the enactment of parliamentary statutes against engrossing, enclosure of open field land and the conversion of open field arable to pasture; it established commissions of enquiry in order to facilitate prosecutions in the common law courts; and it activated Star Chamber and the other prerogative courts against offenders.[13]

This prolonged campaign did not succeed in halting, though at some periods it probably did retard, the advance of commercial farming at the expense of the peasants and, in view of the strength of the economic forces behind what was occurring, it could not possibly have done so. Besides, the policy was opposed to the material interests of the landowning classes on whom the crown depended for the government of the localities, and its implementation by the J.P.s and other organs of local administration was at best half-hearted. Enforcement therefore had largely to be entrusted to informers and the prerogative courts and this made it doubly unpopular in the eyes of the gentry. By the seventeenth century, moreover, articulate public opinion was increasingly inclined to favour agrarian change, as the concern about its social consequences, which had preoccupied the writers of the early and mid sixteenth century, gave way to an appreciation of the economic advantage to the nation of a more efficient and productive agriculture. By the middle of the century, indeed, virtually every writer on such matters was as enthusiastically in support of enclosure, of making commons more productive and of using land for the purposes to which it was best suited, as their Tudor predecessors had been hostile. Finally long periods of good harvests and relatively low grain prices tended to allay the old fears about shortage of grain, and these provided the background to a repeal of some of the husbandry statutes in 1593 and, after their re-enactment in 1597

[13] However it should be noted that the crown never attempted to check the over-stocking of commons, which would have been quite beyond any possibilities of enforcement, and also largely ignored the problem of appropriation of common pasture by individuals.

following a run of disastrous harvests, to a second partial repeal in 1624. The 1630s was the last decade in which the crown made any effort to enforce the laws which remained, and by then its motive was less a determination to check the activities of enclosers and engrossers than a desire to raise revenue by imposing fines on them. This finally discredited its agrarian policy and played its its part in making those hostile to Charles I's personal government determined to be rid of the prerogative courts. Their abolition by the Long Parliament in 1641, and the eclipse of royal authority with the coming of the Civil War, thus marked the end of the government's attempts to protect the peasantry, and the changed climate of opinion ensured that the policy was not revived at the Restoration (Tawney, 1912, Part III, ch. I. *A.H.E.W.* IV, 1967, pp. 213–38).[14]

However the peasants themselves naturally remained hostile to any developments which threatened their way of life. For reasons we shall come to in the next chapter conversion of arable to permanent pasture was less common by the seventeenth century, whilst technical changes in agriculture and the growth of rural industries were increasing the demand for labour in the countryside, so that the consequences of engrossing were less catastrophic than once they had been.[15] But the appropriation of commons and the enclosure of open fields continued, remained a serious grievance with petty farmers and cottagers, and was almost invariably opposed by them. Even in cases where they were persuaded to agree to what was intended, subsequent disputes often revealed that they had been under heavy pressure from more powerful members of their communities, and had only consented with reluctance. Even if, as became increasingly usual in the seventeenth century, their vital interests were safeguarded by the preservation of a section of the common for their exclusive use, they rarely participated in schemes for enclosure or appropriation of common land, for they could ill afford the expense which would necessarily be involved. They would have to pay the costs of fencing, ditching and hedging the land allotted to them, and these costs would be much higher relative to the income produced by a small holding than to that yielded by a large one. Moreover, even if they could afford to pay for fencing, the fact that the great majority of small farmers, particularly in the principal open field areas, did not own the land they occupied, but held it from a landlord for some more or less limited tenure, meant they would be unwilling to invest money in making a long term improvement which might eventually be used as the justification for an increase in the rent. Their opposition to the attempts of landlords and the larger farmers to make changes thus continued to the

[14] See also below II, pp. 240–1.
[15] See below pp. 128–9; and for rural industries, II, Ch. 8 esp. secs. xi and xii.

end of the period, and indeed long into the eighteenth century, but deprived of the backing of the government and the support of respectable public opinion, it was increasingly forlorn and ineffective.

v The rôle of the landlords

One important factor behind the onward march of commercial farming at the expense of peasant agriculture, despite the forces hostile to it, was the desire of the landowners to increase the income from their estates, and indeed their need to do so during the inflationary period down to 1640. Many of the middling and lesser gentry were farming a large proportion of their estates themselves, and for them the obvious course was to get rid of some or all their tenants and take over their farms. If they were content to leave the actual exploitation of their land to others they would derive a larger, and certainly a more reliably paid, rent from one or two substantial tenants with capital of their own, working a large acreage, and producing for the market, than they would from a crowd of subsistence-oriented smallholders and poverty stricken cottagers. Landowners thus had every incentive to build up the more substantial farms on their estates, by permitting their occupants to take in part of the manorial common, or by adding smaller holdings to them when opportunity arose; and to create large farms from scratch by major appropriations of common land or by throwing together a number of small ones. In open field areas they had an equally compelling reason to promote enclosure, or at least to encourage their tenants to undertake it: the productivity of enclosed land was so much higher than that which remained open and subject to common rights that the rent it commanded per acre was 50–150 per cent higher, or even more.[16] If the desire of their larger tenants to enclose brought them into conflict with the smaller ones, then financial self-interest would normally ensure their support for the former. It was increasingly common, therefore, for large farms to be enclosed even in neighbourhoods where the smaller ones remained in the form of strips in the remnants of an open field system.

Nevertheless there were a number of reasons why the process of replacing small peasant family farms by larger and more efficient commercial farms was a slow one, and very far from complete by the end of the seventeenth century. One was that the number of potential tenants for large farms was strictly limited, for especially in the early part of the

[16] Generalizations about this matter are, however, beset with hazard. One problem is that, particularly in the inflationary period down to 1640, part of the increase in rent which occurred after enclosure was often due not to the enclosure itself but to the general increase in the value of all land in the neighbourhood.

period, there were relatively few men with sufficient capital to stock them and sufficient knowledge and experience to handle the managerial and marketing problems which running them involved.[17] Tenants of such farms were often landowners in their own right, minor gentry or yeomen; sometimes they were relatives or clients of their landlord; sometimes men who had made a success of a smaller tenancy and were climbing the socio-economic ladder. But even in the eighteenth century landowners often had trouble in finding suitable candidates for their largest holdings (Mingay, 1962), and in the sixteenth it must have been even more difficult.

Another reason for the relatively slow pace of change was that landlords themselves were often short of the capital which was required if an estate was to be comprehensively reorganized. It might be necessary to buy up the land of other owners, or to compensate sitting tenants, before open fields could be enclosed or farms enlarged. Larger farms would certainly necessitate larger farm buildings, whilst enclosure involved especially heavy expenses because not only were there fences to erect and hedges to plant, but there might be new access roads to make, and even completely new farmsteads to build. Established landowning families, especially amongst the lesser gentry, often had little liquid capital and could not undertake expenditure on the scale required. Nor, at least until the middle of the seventeenth century, was credit to be had on terms which would have enabled them to meet the cost by borrowing. (See also below pp. 150–1, 159.) Besides, many owners did not pay a great deal of attention to the management of their properties and allowed the existing state of affairs to continue unchanged for generations. Lack of interest in such matters was one explanation of this, but an inherited tradition of paternalism was another. Landlords whose families had an old established connection with a particular estate tended to allow their tenants to hold on easy terms, and to remain in undisturbed possession of their farms from father to son, partly as a matter of honour and partly because they valued good-will and loyalty more highly than an increased money income (Stone, 1965, pp. 214–17, 303–7). Nevertheless sooner or later,

[17] Use of the term 'large farms' clearly raises problems of definition. I am here meaning farms which were of a sufficient size to enable the occupier to operate them primarily as a money-making concern, rather than to supply his family with food, and the size required by this criterion clearly varied according to geographical conditions and the type of farming practised. In the open field Midlands, 50–70 acres was probably the minimum holding on which a man could operate in this way, and 100 acres would be required to place him securely in the category; elsewhere the appropriate dividing line might be different. I am not, however, intending 'large farms' to be interpreted in the way that Arthur Young and the other agricultural writers of the later eighteenth century used the phrase, that is to refer to holdings of 300 to 500 acres or more: in sixteenth century England such monster farms were very rare indeed.

in the inflationary times of the sixteenth and early seventeenth centuries, most landowners who neglected their estates were beset by financial difficulties which forced them, either to put aside indifference and old-fashioned notions about relationships with their tenantry, or if they could not afford to finance the necessary changes or did nothing until it was too late, to sell their land. If they sold, the estate would probably pass to someone who *could* afford to undertake the additional investment required to maximize the return on his purchase. Indeed it was typically after a property had changed hands and passed into the possession of a man who had accumulated a fortune in law, commerce, government office or some other business, that estate reorganization was undertaken. The activities of Sir Walter Raleigh on his newly acquired property at Sherborne (Dorset) between 1592 and 1602, and those of the second Earl of Castlehaven at nearby Stalbridge after 1618, provide cases in point (Bettery, 1977(2), pp. 94–5, 209). By the early seventeenth century it was therefore becoming unusual for estates to be left wholly undisturbed by their owners, but even so differences in personal inclinations, and in financial circumstances which affected both the need to undertake improvement and the ability to finance it, ensured that on some properties far more was done than on others. Nor were the financial circumstances necessarily the most important, for some, indeed perhaps most, landlords continued to feel a very real sense of responsibility for their tenants' welfare, even if it did not prevent them from making changes when circumstances dictated. Sentiments such as those contained in the advice of the Yorkshire squire Henry Tempest to his son in 1648, 'Oppress not thy tenants, but let them live comfortably of thy hands as thou desirest to live of their labours', were far from unusual amongst well established families and were not consciously hypocritical (Cliffe, 1969, p. 46).

However even if a landowner wished to reorganize his estate in order to increase the income it yielded there might be difficulties. There were, we have just seen, laws on the statute book which made illegal the destruction of small holdings to create large farms and the conversion of arable to pasture, although most of them only applied to those parts of the country where agrarian change caused the most serious dislocation. These were virtually a dead-letter for much of the time, but down to 1640 they were periodically enforced with considerable vigour, and seem to have had some deterrent effect. More important was the fact that an owner's freedom to do as he liked with his property was frequently limited by the rights of others, whether as members of a village community or as individuals, and their rights had as sound a legal basis as his own. If a man was rich and powerful, and those who stood in his way were few in number and weak, it might be possible for him to ride rough-shod over them, and particularly in the early sixteenth century this sometimes happened – how frequently is uncertain – although there is little or no evidence of it from the later part of the period. However, as we have seen, for a landlord to take high-handed action, even when technically within his rights, was to court violence, during the course of which serious damage might be done which would be expensive to repair, and it might precipitate a lengthy law-suit the costs of which would absorb all the profits accruing for years to come. Thus the mere threat of serious opposition sometimes deterred a landlord from proceeding with his intended improvements: at Orton and Great Haughton (Northants) at the beginning of the seventeenth century the determined hostility of the tenantry induced even the unscrupulous and financially desperate Sir Francis Tresham to leave them in peace (Finch, 1956, pp. 88–9). Generally, therefore, if a manorial lord did not own all the land that would be affected by any changes he was contemplating, he would attempt to secure the agreement of the other owners involved. This might involve lengthy and tortuous negotiations, but even in open field villages other large farmers were often as much interested as he was in appropriating a slice of the manorial common, or in doing away with communal control of husbandry and the strip system, and would not oppose him. Indeed the initiative for such changes often came from a group of prosperous yeomen rather than from the lord himself. Thus, explaining the situation on the formerly open field manor of Iwerne Courtenay in Dorset, a surveyor wrote in 1553 that after increases in rent had driven some of the tenants to give up their farms 'the residue made request unto the lord ... that they might use his land in such sort as he might be satisfied his rent, and they his tenants able thereby to amend their living and maintain hospitality', and with his consent their lands were accordingly reallocated and enclosed, 'and every tenant and farmer occupied his ground several to himself' (*T.E.D.* I, 1924, p. 57).

Even agreed enclosure might, however, be illegal in view of the various agrarian statutes in force at different times, but from the later sixteenth century onwards the parties to enclosure agreements often sought legal sanction for what they had done from the Court of Chancery. Agreement, therefore, sometimes ratified by a court decree, sometimes not, was certainly the most common method of enclosure in the seventeenth century, and almost equally certainly in the sixteenth too, although, as we have already noticed, not all agreements were as unanimous in reality as they purported to be (Leonard, 1905. Beresford, 1961. Kerridge, 1969, ch. IV. Butlin, 1979). But if the small proprietors were numerous and held a large proportion of the land in the village, then it would be difficult and probably impossible to get them to agree at all, and determined opposition on their part often succeeded in blocking the proposals put forward, so that the landowner's intention was either thwarted permanently, or at least until he or his successors could buy up so much property that no opposition remained. In villages where small owners were dominant, and there were many such in the Midlands although we shall see that their numbers were diminishing, the question of enclosing the open fields was unlikely to arise at all in the period with which we are concerned. Thus in the six counties of Northamptonshire, Huntingdonshire, Rutland, Bedfordshire, Oxfordshire and the East Riding of Yorkshire, over 40 per cent of the area remained open in the mid eighteenth century, and in five more counties over 30 per cent remained open (Slater, 1907, ch. XIII. See also Map 2). Yet even if one man owned all or most of the land in a place his own rent paying tenants might also be an obstacle to reorganization. This, however, depended very much on the nature of the tenancies involved and to these we must now turn.

vi *Tenancies and rents*

From the estate owner's point of view there were two main types of land, demesne and customary, the peculiar characteristics of which had evolved centuries before. Demesne land was his own to dispose of as he wished. He could either keep it in his own hands and farm it himself or through a bailiff, or he could let it out to tenants upon whatever terms were mutually agreeable. It could be let 'at will' or 'from year to year', forms of tenancy which enabled him to get rid of the tenants or increase the rent with the minimum of delay, but which equally enabled them to leave at short notice or threaten to do so if the rent were not reduced. The advantages of flexibility were thus partly off-set by a corresponding instability. Alternatively demesne land could be leased for a longer period, either a fixed number of years or for the life times of the tenant and his immediate dependants. Such tenancies made the lessee legally responsible for the payment of the rent for the whole duration of the lease, and so guaranteed the owner a steady income from his property, but they also gave him an unimpeachable title to remain in occupation, provided that he paid the rent and observed any other conditions which had been agreed, for the same period. The owner could not raise the rent or regain possession until the lease expired, and he therefore sacrificed some flexibility for the sake of stability. However, when the lease finally expired he regained complete freedom to do as he wished with the farm, and the former tenant had no further legal interest in it. It was also completely a matter for the owner in what form he took his rent. He could either follow the traditional practice, which had been general in the Middle Ages and remained common throughout the sixteenth and seventeenth centuries, of requiring a lump sum known as a fine[18] at the beginning of the lease term and a correspondingly lowered annual payment thereafter. Alternatively he could adopt the more modern practice of requiring an annual rent equivalent to the full value of the holding. Similarly it was up to him whether the rent was paid partly by deliveries in kind, as was common in the inflationary period down to the mid seventeenth century, or wholly in money as was normal after about 1650. In practice there were local and regional conventions about the nature of tenancies on demesne land and forms of payment. For instance leases for lives on which fines and very low annual rents were payable were, at any rate in the seventeenth century, general in the South West but hardly ever found in the eastern part of the country. However owners were not bound by these conventions and, if their inclinations or circumstances dictated it, there was nothing, apart from the local ill-feeling it would cause, to stop them introducing new tenurial forms to their demesnes.

Improvement and reorganization of demesne land could not be hindered by tenants who held 'at will' or on similar terms, but if it had been leased no change was possible which did not have the lessee's full co-operation until the lease had expired. On some estates this imposed very lengthy delays. During the period when there was no long term upward movement in prices, which had extended into the early sixteenth century, there had been a tendency for landlords to grant very long leases in an attempt to stabilize their rent incomes. Terms as long as thirty, forty, sixty or even eighty years were commonly granted at that time, and they continued in force well into the period of rapid inflation and expanding opportunities for commercial farming. After the early part of the sixteenth century the length of farm leases became much shorter, and twenty-one years became the maximum term which was normally granted to a tenant, although on many estates lettings were for even briefer periods such as seven or fourteen years. However, many landowners who acquired former monastic property after the Dissolution of the 1530s found it encumbered by very long leases which the abbots had granted in their last days often in order to make as much as possible out of fines before they were dispossessed by the king (Youings, 1971, pp. 56–61). Furthermore at all periods owners who needed cash were inclined to raise it by offering reversions to existing leases to sitting tenants, or by selling long leases of portions of their estates to investors seeking an outlet for their funds.

---

[18] In the sense here used the term has no judicial or punitive implications.

Such methods enabled them to raise capital without actually alienating any land outright, but they bequeathed to their heirs an estate whose annual income had been reduced, and on which any improvements might be impossible for generations to come. Even in the seventeenth century, therefore, owners were not infrequently prevented from making the most of their demesne lands by the survival of old lease terms.

The other type of land with which the estate owner was concerned was customary land, that is land occupied by tenants the terms of whose tenancies were regulated by the custom of the manor. There were local variants of customary tenure, some of which, such as the one known as 'tenant right' found on the Scottish border and involving an obligation to ride out in arms against invaders when called upon to do so, were highly distinctive. However the most widespread form of it was copyhold. Indeed, taking the country as a whole, in the first half of the sixteenth century the majority of the rural population, perhaps two thirds or even more, were copyholders. They therefore greatly outnumbered those who occupied demesne land and those who owned their own farms as freeholders, who may have numbered about one ninth and one fifth respectively. However there were regional variations to this pattern and whereas in much of the West and North up to 90 per cent were copyholders, in some parts of the eastern and south eastern counties the proportion was no more than half, and other forms of tenure were correspondingly more important. Freeholders, for instance, were especially numerous in Kent, in Suffolk and elsewhere in East Anglia (Tawney, 1912, pp. 21–7). Moreover since manorial customs differed greatly from one district to another, and even from one manor to the next within a very small area, the nature of copyhold was not identical everywhere.

Copyholders always paid fines at the commencement of their tenancies and low or even nominal annual rents, and most of them held for lives rather than for terms of years. The important differences lay in whether or not they had a right to a renewal when their terms expired, and how the fines then payable were arrived at (Kerridge, 1969 (1), pp. 35–45). On some manors there were copyholders of inheritance, whose right to renew their tenancies, to pass them on to heirs by hereditary succession, or to alienate, was specially recognized by the custom of their manors, and whose fines were either fixed or limited to what was 'reasonable'. This was the usual form of copyhold tenure in the eastern part of the country, and it has been estimated that about half of all copyholders held on such terms. There was nothing that a manorial lord could do to get rid of them if they stood in the way of estate reorganization, and there were strict limits to how much more income he could get out of them by increasing their fines. Any attempt to terminate their tenancies, to alter the terms on which they held, or charge fines higher than those sanctioned by custom, could be countered by legal action, for the law courts would uphold the custom of the manor whether it was breached by lord or by tenant (Kerridge, 1969(1), esp. ch. 3).[19] In practice, however, copyholders could not always afford to challenge their lords in this way, for doing so involved considerable expense, together with the inconvenience of absences from home and journeys to London, and doubtless lords did sometimes get away with wrongful evictions. However there is no reason to think that these were very common, even in the early sixteenth century, and they certainly became increasingly rare as time wore on. Most landlords were indeed reasonably law abiding and anxious to retain the good opinion of the neighbourhood, and were unlikely even to contemplate such action. There could, however, be a genuine dispute as to exactly what the custom of a particular manor was in respect of copyholds, and of course many of those whose tenancies had been ended quite legally naturally felt a burning sense of injustice. And inevitably there were unscrupulous landlords, particularly perhaps amongst those whom financial difficulties rendered desperate,[20] and amongst those money-minded businessmen who were buying their way into landed society from outside, and who neither shared the ethos of the old established gentry nor lived on the property they acquired, but they were probably a small minority. Usually the only way open to the lord of a manor to rid himself of copyholders of inheritance was to buy their farms if and when they were prepared to sell, and add them to his demesne. As we shall see shortly, throughout the sixteenth and seventeenth centuries small farmers frequently did have to sell up and, although the buyers were not always manorial lords by any means, these purchases did cause a gradual reduction in the amount of land held under this form of tenancy. The engrossing of farms, and the enclosure which often accompanied it, was thus more often the result of social change in the villages affected, rather than a cause of it as is so often assumed.

Most copyholders in the western part of the country, and some of those elsewhere, did not enjoy the right of inheritance and limited fines. They

[19] The obligations on manorial lords to limit fines to a 'reasonable' level meant that they could not set their demand so high that the copyholders' right of inheritance was thereby denied them.

[20] The crown, perhaps, can be included in this category, for it was urgent financial need which led James I's government to attempt to change the terms by which its tenants in the far North held their land, using the argument that since the union of the crowns had rendered obsolete their military obligations for the defence of the Scottish border, a revocation of their grants was justified. The resistance aroused by this attempt to abolish 'tenant right' largely frustrated the crown's intentions, and likewise defeated the efforts of some, though not all, of the private landlords who tried to follow its example. The whole episode, therefore, provides a striking example of how the threat of violence, combined with legal action, enabled peasants, at least sometimes, to defend their tenurial position despite the great difficulties they faced (Tupling, 1927, pp. 141–5).

held for lives and without any legally recognized right of renewal, although it was generally considered that they had a moral one, and in normal circumstances this would be respected by the lord of the manor. However, such people were clearly in a much weaker position than copyholders of inheritance, since if the lord wished to reorganize his estate he could refuse to renew.

Copyholders for lives were also vulnerable because, even if the lord did not bring their tenancies to an end, the absence of any custom limiting the amount of the renewal fine he could demand left them without any defence against intensified financial exploitation. In this they were in much the same position as tenants-at-will on demesne land or demesne leaseholders whose leases had expired, and like these other groups in the rural population, sooner or later during the course of the sixteenth century they were called upon to pay a great deal more for their land. Rents had been generally stable in the fifteenth century and had continued so into the early sixteenth, but the growing pressure of numbers in the countryside meant a greatly increased demand for land and this enabled landlords to raise their rents steeply from the 1520s until perhaps the 1630s, even in places where commercial farming was making little headway. The extent and timing of the increases varied considerably from one estate to another, sometimes being postponed until the last third of the sixteenth century, although in such cases they were usually the more drastic when eventually they did come. On the estates of the Petre family in Essex, for instance, rents were little altered between the 1540s and the mid 1590s, but they were then driven up six or seven fold within less than half a century. Taking the country as a whole increases of four or five fold between the mid sixteenth and mid seventeenth centuries were common place, whilst both on the Wiltshire estates of the Herbert Earls of Pembroke and on some Yorkshire properties there was at least an eight fold increase. The rents of the Acclom family's mannor of Bonwick, for instance, were only about £16 17s a year in Queen Elizabeth's reign but stood at £160 a year by 1637. Nor in all probability were such increases particularly unusual on well managed estates in other regions (Emerson, 1951. Kerridge, 1953. Cliffe, 1969, pp. 47–8).

On copyhold land everywhere, and on demesne leasehold in the western part of the country, the landlords normally left the annual payments unchanged and imposed heavier and heavier fines as the price of a new or renewed tenancy. On demesne land elsewhere their demands increasingly took the form of rack rents, that is yearly rents which represented the full annual value of the holding. Both methods of extracting more income from the actual cultivators were naturally very unpopular, especially so since unchanging rents and fines had come to be taken for granted in the later Middle Ages, and at certain times and places were more of an issue in the countryside than engrossing, enclosure or conversion to pasture. Nevertheless rack renting was probably the more disliked because in the sixteenth century it was something of an innovation, at least as far as peasant farmers were concerned, and because it was often introduced where a landlord had succeeded in converting copyhold land into demesne. Sometimes, indeed, the change to rack rents forced the poorer peasants to give up their farms altogether, whether or not this was the landlord's intention, for if their holdings were too small to pay the rent demanded and to feed their families, and no subsidiary sources of income were available to them, they could not carry on. For those who stayed, however, the economic consequences of the two practices were much the same. A man faced with the need to raise a large fine could either save up the necessary sum in advance, or he could borrow it and gradually discharge the debt over the years that followed, but either way he would have as great a need to increase his annual money income as did the man with a rack rent to pay. This he might be able to do partly by devoting more of his own or his family's time to subsidiary employments or to wage labour, but for most it was also likely to mean producing more for sale, and since the possibilities of increasing total output would probably be very limited on a small family farm, this meant marketing a larger proportion of what he produced at the expense of his own consumption. Higher rents and fines thus meant harder work, or a lower standard of living, or both. They also meant that the balance between farming for subsistence and farming for the market within the peasant sector as a whole was bound to tilt in favour of the latter. The implications for the individual were vividly described by Bishop Latimer in a sermon preached in 1549, when he told his hearers that his father had rented a farm in Leicestershire fifty or so years before for which he paid £3 or £4 a year:

and hereupon he tilled so much as kept half a dozen men. He had walk for a hundred sheep; and my mother milked thirty kine. He was able, and did find the king a harness, with himself and his horse. . . . I can remember that I buckled his harness when he went unto Blackheath field. He kept me to school, or else I had not been able to have preached before the king's majesty now. He married my sisters with five pound, or twenty nobles apiece. . . . He kept hospitality for his poor neighbours, and some alms he gave to the poor. And all this he did of the said farm, where he that now hath it payeth sixteen pound by the year, or more, and is not able to do anything for his prince, for himself, nor for his children, or give a cup of drink to the poor (Tate, 1967, pp. 156–7).

The upward movement of rent more or less came to an end even before the Civil War, and the virtual impossibility of maintaining the existing rent levels whilst war-time conditions prevailed in the early and mid 1640s clearly marked the end of an era for both landlords and tenants. In the second half of the seventeenth century it was rarely possible for landlords to make further substantial increases, except in cases where long leases negotiated when prices had been markedly lower had at last fallen in, or where major improvements such as enclosure had been undertaken. Indeed in many areas rents tended to fall back, particularly in the 1670s and 1680s, and on some estates the reductions were of the order of 20 per cent. However this return to lower levels of rent was mainly, if not wholly, a result of the lower product prices which affected arable and livestock farmers alike at that time, and so it did not represent any serious reduction in the burden which payments to the landlord involved. Indeed, it is clear from the numerous bankruptcies amongst tenant farmers in these years, that the earning capacity of many farms fell further than did rents. By the 1690s, moreover, as prices improved, rents again began to creep upwards, so that by the early eighteenth century most tenants were probably paying much the same as their predecessors had done fifty years before (*A.H.E.W.* v, Part ii, 1984, pp. 75–9). Besides, from the time of the Civil War onwards, taxation by the state became a more regular and more oppressive feature of national life than it ever had been before 1640. (See also below II, Ch. 11 sec. iii.) Tenants paying rack rents were not liable to the taxes on land which were repeatedly levied in the middle and later part of the century, particularly during the Civil War and its aftermath, in the mid 1660s, early 1670s and throughout the 1690s, since they were normally discharged by their landlord. But both copyholders and leaseholders for lives *were* liable, and particularly when the Land Tax was levied at four shillings in the pound, as in the 1690s, it represented a substantial increase in their outgoings, although one which was heavier in the South and East than in the North and West, because of regional differences in the accuracy of the assessments of land values upon which the tax was based. Besides, all occupiers of land normally had to pay their own Hearth Tax (levied from 1662 onwards) and any other parliamentary levies, such as the occasional poll taxes which were imposed on individuals or households rather than on land. Finally the weight of local taxation was also becoming greater by the later seventeenth century, as the growing numbers of indigent in the villages drove the poor rates steadily upwards. (See also below II, pp. 232–3.) If anything, therefore, the need of small farmers for a money income, and thus their need to produce for the market, was greater than ever, despite the fact that rents were no longer rising.

III SOCIAL CHANGE IN THE COUNTRYSIDE

vii The fate of the peasantry in the mixed farming zones

It was important for the economy as a whole that the peasants were forced to bring more produce to the market because it made a major contribution towards satisfying the growing demand for food-stuffs and agricultural raw materials, which commercial farming on its own could not have met despite the extent of its expansion. But for the peasantry their increased need for a money income made them less and less self-sufficient, and more and more dependent on their dealings with the market, so that they were much more exposed to the play of economic forces than they had formerly been. Some of the more fortunate and energetic of them were able to meet the challenge and became successful and prosperous commercial producers, but for the class as a whole existence became more precarious.

In mixed farming areas the poorer peasants had always been liable to suffer hardship, or worse, when poor harvests reduced the quantity of food grains that their farms yielded, so that after keeping back the necessary minimum for seed there was not enough left both to feed their families and to raise the money to meet inescapable financial commitments. The need to pay a large annual rent or to discharge a heavy fine made this problem worse. It also added another, since in years of bountiful harvest when grain prices dropped heavily they might get so little for what they had to sell that they were equally unable to pay their way. One year of scarcity or super-abundance would cause them difficulties, a succession of such years, which, as we have seen, commonly occurred in the sixteenth and seventeenth centuries, could ruin them. Certainly at Chippenham, Cambs., a village where family farming was largely eliminated during the course of the seventeenth century, its decline began with a crop of land sales by small copyholders in the immediate aftermath of the notoriously bad harvests of 1594–97 (*A.H.E.W.* IV, 1967, pp. 652–9. Spufford, 1974, pp. 75–83. Thirsk, 1957, pp. 192–6). And in many areas the agricultural depression of the later seventeenth century reduced the small farmer to a desperate plight, one lamented by Richard Baxter writing in 1691. He considered that they were worse off in material terms than the unmarried servants they employed, for unlike the husbandman the latter 'know their work and wages, and are troubled with no cares for paying rents, or making good markets, or for the loss of corn or cattle, the rotting of sheep, or the unfavourable weather, nor for providing for wife and children and paying labourers' and servants' wages'. The best the small farmer could hope for was to scrape by – 'its well if all their care and toil will serve to pay their rents' – but in the 1670s and 1680s, in their thousands they had been failing to do even this. They had been falling into arrears with payments to their landlords, being sold up and evicted, and in some cases simply abandoning their farms and fleeing to escape debts they knew they could never pay (Thirsk and Cooper, 1972, pp. 182–3). 'Ran away in debt to be a soldier', 'Dead insolvent', 'Went off in debt and left his corn', 'Carried off his goods by night and went off insolvent', 'There is nothing to be had: the man is dead and his wife and children are maintained by the parish', are examples of the comments which recur again and again in estate records from all over the country at this time.[21]

In the pastoral regions peasant farmers might be even more seriously straitened by harvest failures than those in the mixed farming zones, for they had to buy essential food-stuffs at greatly enhanced prices, but low grain prices would bring them nothing but benefit. Moreover the prices of their own livestock and animal products fluctuated less violently than those of grain, and although hard winters or outbreaks of disease which destroyed their flocks and herds could cause as much havoc as a really bad harvest in a district where grain was the main crop, such occurrences seem to have been much less common.

In addition there was another reason why the peasants of the pastoral farming areas had greater economic strength than those of the districts where cereal crops were the mainstay of the local husbandry. One of the most direct and immediate consequences of the growth of the rural population in the sixteenth and the early part of the seventeenth centuries, and the consequent need to provide a livelihood for larger numbers, was that peasant farms tended to get smaller. Peasant inheritance customs varied much from one district to another but primogeniture, the practice whereby a father left all his possessions to his eldest son, was never general in the way that it was amongst the wealthier classes, and some degree of partition between co-heirs seems to have been common. This did not normally amount to an equal distribution of property between all a man's sons, and usually involved either the breaking off of small pieces from family holdings, or the imposition on them of financial burdens in favour of younger children. However, even the latter, if practised by a high proportion of families over a period of several generations, would lead to a considerable reduction in the size of farms because the encumbrances often precipitated the sale of part of the property. Now in districts where the peasants had access to ample common pastures on which they could keep as much livestock as they

[21] Herts. R.O., Gorhambury Mss 1. A.67; XI, 25. Dorset R.O., D.124, box 173, bundle 3.

wanted, even tiny holdings were not incompatible with a reasonable degree of prosperity. But in the areas where commons were restricted, as they were in most parts of the country where mixed farming prevailed, peasants could not supplement the resources of a very small holding in this way, so that fragmentation of farms meant a progressively enfeebled community, a larger and larger proportion of whose members were trying to make a living from an inadequate amount of land and were thus particularly vulnerable to fluctuations in harvest yields and prices (Spufford, 1974, pp. 85–7, 104–11, 159–61). Fragmentation was particularly important in undermining the position of the landholding peasantry because, unlike rack renting and heavy fines, it also affected that section of the class whose tenures gave them protection against landlord exactions.[22] Indeed it could even be said that it particularly affected them. Demesne leaseholders could not divide their holdings, even if they wanted to, and although all types of copyholders normally could and freeholders always could, it tended to be those tenancies whose financial liabilities to their landlords were least burdensome, that is copyholds of inheritance and freeholds, which were furthest sub-divided. This was of course just because, despite minute division, they could still yield as good an income to their holders as larger farms which had to pay more to the landlord. But the extremely small size of the fragments into which they were often broken, especially by the seventeenth century, meant that their occupiers were just as liable to get into difficulties as were their fellows who held by less favourable forms of tenure.

The two factors which so seriously undermined the viability of the family farmers, increased rents and fines, and shrinking holdings, thus both had their greatest impact in the mixed farming areas, and it was in these that small scale peasant farming was most obviously in retreat in the sixteenth and seventeenth century. Small family farmers rarely had the opportunity to build up substantial savings to tide them over periods of difficulty.[23] Most of what little capital they had was represented by their farm stock and equipment, and if any part of that had to be sold their ability to carry on in future years would be yet further reduced. Failures amongst them were thus very frequent. Freeholders and copyholders of inheritance could get into debt as a result of some individual misfortune or the need to buy food in a time of scarcity, and be unable to pay off both

[22] It was mainly fragmentation, therefore, which explains the apparent paradox that family farmers declined most markedly in the mixed farming areas, which lay largely in the east and centre of the country, even though tenures were in general more secure there than in the more westerly districts: see also above pp. 87–9.

[23] This often forced them to borrow in order to survive a crisis, so that the terms upon which credit was available, in other words the issue of 'usury', had also become an important issue by the mid sixteenth century. See also below II, p. 232.

interest and principal until at last they were obliged to sell out. Tenants at rack rents could easily fall into arrears and gradually become more and more indebted to their landlord, until eventually he would seize their remaining stock to recover his money and force them to give up their tenancies. Those who had fines to pay might find that they could raise neither the cash nor the credit to renew a lease, and so have to quit of their own accord. When small freeholds or copyholds came onto the market the purchaser might be a yeoman seeking land on which to establish a younger son as an independent smallholder, but it was equally likely to be the lord of the manor wishing to expand his demesne farm, or some other prosperous member of the community building up a large property for himself. Similarly when petty tenant farmers failed, their land would often be added to one of the larger farms on the estate rather than let to another poor man. Thus, quite apart from any deliberate policy on the part of landlords, the economic weakness of small scale peasant farms in the grain growing areas ensured that there was a long-run tendency for their numbers and the proportion of the land in their occupation to decline.

The larger farmers who concentrated on production for the market were obviously not immune to the difficulties caused by fluctuating prices, but they were less seriously affected by them. Most important of all was the fact that their larger scale of production meant that in years of scarcity they stood to benefit from the resultant high prices in a way that small producers, who in such circumstances had virtually nothing to sell, did not. Long periods of low prices, such as afflicted grain growers in the 1560s and the first decade of the seventeenth century, and the producers of almost all agricultural commodities in the 1670s and 1680s, could reduce their profits very seriously and cause even worse difficulties for those with rents to pay, but even so they normally had greater financial reserves and could more easily borrow money to tide themselves over a crisis than peasant farmers. Some of them certainly came to grief, especially those who over-extended themselves by renting or buying more land than they could afford to stock, but for most of the period those who were reasonably efficient and reasonably lucky were able to prosper. Above all those who were freeholders, or were copyholders of inheritance and thus enjoyed security of tenure and whose rent and fines meant less and less in real terms as inflation continued, were able to do extremely well. Yet so too could tenants on demesne land paying a rack rent if they had a lease which gave them security for a number of years, and although twenty-one years was normally the maximum duration of this type of lease, a substantially shorter term could be sufficient. This would enable them to invest their own capital in their farms without fear of being deprived of the fruits of it, thereby raising productivity and increasing the volume of output, and since their rents could only be increased on the expiry of their leases, until that time all the advantage of the long term rise in product prices would accrue to them. Even if their rents were eventually increased by the same proportion as prices had risen, their other costs of production, such as the wages paid to hired labour, would not have increased to the same extent, so that they could pay a much higher rent and yet continue to flourish.

Many commercial farmers of the sixteenth and early seventeenth centuries invested the proceeds of their success in the purchase of more land if they were already owners, or in establishing themselves as independent proprietors if they had hitherto only been tenants. This was a process, which if continued in successive generations, could end in the acquisition of so much property that the whole economic and social standing of the family was transformed. A very few of the most successful farming gentry of the sixteenth century, such as the Spencers of Althorp in Northamptonshire, rose to become the county grandees of the seventeenth, largely on the basis of reinvested agricultural profits (Finch, 1956, ch. III). Likewise some of the most successful yeomen farmers of the early part of the period grew rich enough to buy whole manors, and like the Bales of Carlton Curlieu and the Hartopps of Burton Lazars, to take two Leicestershire examples, joined the county élite as knights or baronets during the course of the seventeenth century (Hoskins, 1950, pp. 154–8). Much more numerous, naturally, were those families who added field to field, and farm to farm, until they had become the principal landowners in the parish and were able to adopt the way of life of the gentleman. And far more numerous yet were those who prospered sufficiently to add something to their property without ever achieving a basic alteration of their position in society: gentry who gradually extended and consolidated the demesne lands of an inherited manor but whose estates never spread into another parish, and yeomen whose acquisitions amounted to a few dozen acres rather than several hundred. Some of these purchases were by sitting tenants from financially embarrassed landlords, and thus did not involve any change in the purpose for which the land was farmed, but many more were at the expense of small peasants, and as we have seen, were an important means whereby the area devoted to capitalist commercial farming was increased. Piecemeal purchases by those making money out of farming for the market were particularly numerous between about 1570 and about 1640, a period which other evidence confirms to have seen the most rapid expansion of farming for the market (Campbell, 1942, pp. 70–9. *A.H.E.W.* IV, 1967, pp. 301–6). In the mid and later seventeenth century, first war-time conditions in the 1640s and then long periods of low prices combined with heavier taxation made it more difficult for the farming gentry and yeomanry to continue their expansion. Land available for sale thus more often went to large owners, and although such people preferred to have their estates tenanted by substantial farmers rather than peasants, their purchases were probably less often followed by a change in the way the land was exploited than were those made by men who were actually farming for profit themselves.

In the mixed farming regions, therefore, there was a slow but continuous process in operation throughout the sixteenth and seventeenth centuries whereby both the ownership and, what was perhaps more important, the occupancy of land came to be concentrated in fewer hands. Peasant farmers who were obliged to give up their holdings, for whatever reason, became submerged into the growing class of cottagers and landless labourers, and were one of two sources from which these two groups were being increased. The other source, which until the early seventeenth century was numerically more important, was the natural increase of the rural population, since in districts where there was little or no new land available for cultivation growing numbers inevitably meant that many were unable to acquire holdings. The trend was thus towards a society in which there was a widening gulf between rich and poor, between a small but increasing number of prosperous large scale farmers on the one hand, and a large and increasing number of almost or completely landless people on the other, and in which the middle group of small family farmers was gradually being squeezed out. The culmination of these developments lies well after the end of the period with which we are concerned, in the era of parliamentary enclosure in the later eighteenth and the first half of the nineteenth centuries, but already by the beginning of the eighteenth century they were far advanced in some places, and there were signs of them almost everywhere where grain farming prevailed. Thus at Chippenham on the Cambridgeshire chalkland between 1544 and 1712 the number of farmers with over ninety acres had risen from two to seven, the number of all other landholders had fallen from forty-three to eleven, and landless householders had risen from twenty-one to thirty-one (Spufford, 1974, p. 73). Even in a village like Wigston Magna in Leicestershire where, largely because there was no manorial lord intent on expanding his demesne, peasant farms of ten to twenty acres remained numerous in the late seventeenth century, there was nevertheless a large number of cottagers with little land or none at all, and at the top of the tree a small group of rich farmers and absentee owners with 100 acres or more (Hoskins, 1957, pp. 194–204).

Opportunities for landless labourers to make a living, however, were not equally good everywhere, and this class was unevenly distributed around the countryside. In places where manorial control was strong, and all or most of the land belonged to just one or two proprietors who were concerned about the administration of their estates, erection of new cottages to house a swelling population of the landless would not be permitted. Indeed old cottages were likely to be demolished when they fell vacant, and only as many labourers as were required by the larger tenant farmers to work their land would be permitted to live in the village. The need to spend money repairing the buildings was thereby avoided, and the poor rates and other inconveniences which arose from the presence of poor and under-employed people were kept to a minimum. Younger sons of peasant farmers, and those who lost their farms, would therefore generally have to leave and look for employment elsewhere. These were what came to be known later as 'closed' villages, and if there had been any conversion of arable to pasture they might provide a livelihood for very few labourers indeed, the most extreme form of the closed village being, of course, the 'deserted' one where all the land was in the hands of a single farmer who had put it down to grass and was almost the only remaining inhabitant. However, in places where manorial control was weak or non-existent, which might be the result of a manor being dismembered and sold off piecemeal, or of ownership by an uninterested absentee, a very different social pattern emerged. Those without land would not be obliged to leave, and, especially if there were ample space for cottage building and plentiful employment opportunities, there was likely to be immigration from outside so that large populations of poor cottagers built up. As we shall see such a development was more common in pastoral districts, but even in open field areas there was a minority of 'open' villages of this type. A well documented example is Sherington in Buckinghamshire where there was a substantial inflow of population from neighbouring townships which had been enclosed and converted to pasture. As a result the number of cottagers rose from eighteen in 1580 to sixty-three in 1708, and in the 1660s half the households in the village had to be exempted from the Hearth Tax on grounds of poverty (Chibnall, 1965, pp. 195–204).

In most open field mixed farming districts the growth of such pauperized village populations was limited by the employment available, especially before the seventeenth century, since casual and seasonal work on the larger farms in the neighbourhood was often all that was offered. In a few places there were rural handicraft industries, such as cloth making in the environs of Norwich or in the Wyle and Nadder valleys near Salisbury, but these were more characteristic of the pastoral areas (*A.H.E.W.* IV, 1967, pp. 12–14). In the second half of our period employment for the rural poor became more widely available. This was partly because the more progressive farmers were beginning to adopt labour intensive crops, notably the turnip, but also fruit and vegetables, tobacco and dyes such as woad, madder and saffron. (See below Ch. 4 sec. v.) It was also because new handicraft industries were developing, for instance lace-making in Buckinghamshire from the end of the sixteenth century, and the knitting of stockings in Leicestershire, Nottinghamshire and elsewhere in the North Midlands from about 1670 onwards. (See below II, Ch. 8 sec. v.) In one 'open' village in Leicestershire, Wigston Magna, about one sixth of the population were wholly dependent on knitting for their livelihood by the end of the seventeenth century, and the opportunities for work which knitting offered were attracting a steady flow of immigrants who had been displaced by enclosure for pasture elsewhere in the county (Hoskins, 1957, pp. 211–12). Nevertheless the open villages of the mixed farming regions could never absorb all those for whom there was no longer room in the countryside around them, and throughout the sixteenth and seventeenth centuries there was a drift of population from those regions, both to the towns and to the more sparsely settled pastoral areas where there was still room for newcomers.

viii Social developments in the pastoral districts

If we turn now to the pastoral districts we find that in general small scale peasant farming fared considerably better and was still very strong in 1700. Certainly there was some tendency towards larger farms, and for yeomen and farming gentry to acquire land at the expense of small farmers, but it was less marked. To the end of the seventeenth century and beyond, therefore, society remained more egalitarian, characterized by a more even distribution of wealth and less glaring contrasts between rich and poor. This was partly because, especially in the remoter parts of the highland zone, the rich did not have the opportunity to grow so rich, but it was mainly because everywhere the poor were less poor and there was no growth of a completely landless rural proletariat. Less volatile prices for the products of animal husbandry were clearly one important reason why the peasantry in these areas successfully withstood the changes and pressures of the period. Another was the greater availability of commons, for provided that a peasant had unstinted grazing for his beasts he could make a good living off a holding which on its own could not have supported him at all. In such circumstances, moreover, sub-division of holdings as a result of partible inheritance customs did not weaken peasant farming and thereby open the way to engrossing and the destruction of the peasant community, at any rate not to the extent that it did in the corn growing regions. Instead it led to a permanent increase in the number of peasant farms, in that large populations of petty livestock farmers grew up during the sixteenth century and continued to flourish throughout the period, as is illustrated by the populous fenland communities of Cambridgeshire, Lincolnshire and neighbouring counties, whose main occupations were the raising and fattening of cattle and dairying. Thus at Willingham, Cambridgeshire, between 1575 and the 1720s there was no growth of large farms but a very great increase in small holdings of sixteen acres or less, and the proportion of entirely landless people in the village actually fell from 38 to 32 per cent, despite a large increase in numbers (Thirsk, 1957, chs. 1 and 5. Spufford, 1974, ch. 5).

Moreover population growth contributed to an extension of peasant farming in another way, which did not and could not happen in the more densely settled mixed farming areas: that is through extensions to the cultivated area. Such extensions were made in one of two ways. Either land was reclaimed from forest, fen or moor and allocated to tenants in an orderly fashion organized by the lord of the manor or his representative, or encroachments were made piecemeal, sometimes with the lord's permission but more often without it, by squatters who erected a cottage for themselves and fenced in a small area around it. Manorial control was often very weak in areas of sparse population so that unauthorized settlement frequently proceeded virtually unchecked, and, provided the new arrivals agreed to pay a rent when their presence was eventually discovered by the lord, they would normally be left undisturbed. In these ways very large areas of land come into agricultural use in the North, down the Welsh border, in the south western peninsula, and in those forest areas of the lowland zone where comparable conditions prevailed. Existing farms were often enlarged and substantial new ones sometimes created, but the most striking result of it all was an enormous growth in the number of very small holdings extending to only an acre or two, or even less, many of whose occupants were people who had been forced to move out of nearby mixed farming districts for reasons discussed above. Most of these small holdings were, in themselves, far too small to provide a livelihood, but they gave access to the common or waste land from which they had been won, so that the occupants had ample pasturage for livestock and were able to supply themselves with fuel and other things (*A.H.E.W.* IV, 1967, ch VII). A classic instance of the phenomenon in question is the rapid growth of the villages in the royal forests of Northamptonshire, whose average size more than doubled between 1524 and 1670, whereas that of the non-forest villages in the county increased by only 40 per cent (Pettit, 1968, chs. VII and VIII). Another area, different in many respects but similar in that there were large areas of waste and plenty of room for new families, were the valleys running up into the Pennines. Here too an increasing local population, swelled by immigrants from outside, produced a society characterized by very large numbers of very small holders. In the Rossendale area of Lancashire, for instance, the number of separate holdings rose from seventy-two in 1507, to treble that figure by 1608, and to 315 by 1662. By the latter date nearly two thirds of the households occupied holdings worth less than £5 per annum in rent (Tupling, 1927, pp. 76, 163).

A further reason why small scale peasant farmers continued to flourish in the pastoral zones was the greater opportunities open to them of supplementing their income from non-agricultural sources. In some parts such as central Suffolk, the western Cotswolds, on both sides of the Wiltshire–Somerset border, and East Devon, population densities had been sufficiently great, even in the fourteenth and fifteenth centuries, to promote the growth of rural cloth manufacturing industries organized on the domestic system, which provided small farmers with part-time or seasonal employment. In many other districts, however, their emergence was delayed until the sixteenth or early seventeenth centuries. Not all pastoral communities came to derive a significant part of their livelihood from industrial wage earning, but in most cases the need of the people for an additional source of income encouraged the exploitation of local mineral deposits, which were more widespread in the largely pastoral highland zone than elsewhere, or of other raw materials. Alternatively, if there were none, it often attracted entrepreneurs searching for plentiful supplies of cheap labour. Examples of the first are provided by the early growth of iron production and the metal working trades around Sheffield in South Yorkshire and in parts of the West Midlands. Examples of the second are the development of textile manufacture on both sides of the Pennines, in the West Riding of Yorkshire, notably in the huge parish of Halifax, and in eastern Lancashire including Rossendale. The growth of such forms of employment proceeded in step with the growth of the peasant population, so that they became an essential part of the local economic structure. (See also below II, Ch. 8 secs. xi and xii.) To those involved they were no mere by-employments, as is sometimes implied, but a crucial element in an integrated way of life which depended on both agriculture and wage earning for its viability. They were also an additional reason why so many pastoral areas attracted immigrants. It was not only somewhere to live, but also work, which such districts were able to offer. Their incipient industrialism, proto-industrialization as it has been called, was thus as much a cause as a result of the type of society which developed there (Thirsk, 1961. Mendels, 1972).

4

THE PROGRESS OF AGRICULTURE

i The achievement of English agriculture

Throughout the sixteenth and seventeenth centuries native agriculture not only provided the population of the country with almost all its food and drink, but also furnished manufacturers with many of their raw materials. Fish was the only important item in the diets of large numbers of people which was not the product of English farms, for the only other food-stuffs brought in from outside were exotic luxuries whose production required a different climate: wines, spices and sugar, for instance, and beverages like tea and coffee which were becoming fashionable by the end of the period. English grain farmers not only provided the nation with its daily bread, they also supplied the brewing, distilling and starch-making industries, whilst the hops which brewers were making increasing use of as time wore on were also home grown, mostly in Kent, at least by the seventeenth century. Livestock farmers provided meat and dairy produce, but they also produced hides and skins to be turned into leather and parchment, tallow to be used in the making of candles and soap, and above all wool to keep busy the many tens of thousands of spinning wheels and looms, whose output clothed both rich and poor, and provided the country's main export commodity. Some of the dyes the textile industry required, notably woad (blue) and weld (yellow), were also grown inside the country, though, as with hops, more widely from the later sixteenth century onwards than in the early part of the period. Similarly an unknown, but certainly significant, proportion of the increasing quantities of linen, canvas, rope and netting manufactured in England was made from native grown flax and hemp. Finally, the dependence of the transport industry on agriculture must not be forgotten. The horses which were essential for the conveyance of both people and goods, whether by road or by inland waterway, were almost all reared inside the country, and, what was an even greater call on its productive capacity, were kept fit for work on a diet of native grown hay and oats.

The dependence on agriculture – of the people for food, industry for raw materials, and transport for motive power – was such that the increase in the population during the period with which we are concerned necessarily meant great increases in demand for its products. We saw in Chapter 1 that the population of England rose from somewhere around 2.3 million in the 1520s to about 5 million by the 1630s, a figure regained before the end of the period despite a slight drop in the interim. (See also above Table 1 and Fig. 1 in Ch. 1 sec. i.) There was thus an increase of perhaps 2.7 million, or approximately 130 per cent, and it is an historical fact of great significance that virtually all the increased supplies of agricultural commodities required to feed, clothe and employ these extra people were forthcoming from internal sources. It is true that down to the middle of the seventeenth century output did not rise rapidly enough to prevent a long term rise in prices, especially grain prices, so that the living standards of the poorer members of the community dropped heavily. (See above Ch. 2 sec. i.) It is also true that in year of serious harvest failure there was not always enough grain available, even with the help of imports, to prevent prices rising so far that some of the poorest members of the community were unable to buy sufficient food and therefore died of starvation or disease. Nevertheless such subsistence crises occurred very infrequently, even in the later sixteenth century seem mainly to have affected the highland zone, and by the early seventeenth to have been confined to it. (See above Ch. 1 sec. iv.) In most years of the sixteenth century there was in fact a small and, down to the 1590s, an increasing export of grain. In the first half of the seventeenth century this export trade dwindled away, and the country appears to have become a net importer for a time, although again not on a very large scale: the record 160,545 quarters of grain imported to London in 1638 represented the annual output of perhaps 1 per cent of the country's arable acreage (*A.H.E.W.* IV, 1967, pp. 524–7, 617–18).

The change in England's status from that of net exporter to net importer of cereals coincided with the culmination of the long period of population increase, but was probably more a reflection of commercial developments than a sign that the country had ceased to be able to feed itself. On the one hand merchants were better able, thanks to greater capital resources, commercial experience and a widening range of overseas contacts, to bring in grain from overseas, mainly from the countries along the southern shore of the Baltic, which was the chief food surplus region of Europe at this time. On the other hand the growth of a more efficient system of internal marketing and distribution led to the absorption by consumers at home of the small 'surplus' which had previously been sent abroad. That this is the correct interpretation is confirmed by what would otherwise be a strange paradox: that the period when England apparently ceased to be able to spare any basic food-stuffs for export was also the period which witnessed the final disappearance of subsistence crises, even in the mainly pastoral North and West, where little land was devoted to growing grain. After the terrible years 1596 and 1597 the only other such crisis which affected a large geographical area was the one which struck the North in 1623, and that seems to have been as much the result of industrial unemployment during a trade depression, which deprived many poor people of purchasing power, as it was of any absolute scarcity of food.[1] A further contributory factor in the disappearance of occasional famines may also have been the provision of poor relief for the most desperately needy: intermittent and inadequate though the distributions may have been, especially early on, they were probably sufficient to prevent people starving who would otherwise have done so. (See also below Ch. 7 sec. ii.)

However by the second half of the seventeenth century the absence of subsistence crises was clearly also, and mainly, due to the fact that agricultural output was at last rising more rapidly than the population.[2] This in turn was partly because the rate of growth of the latter had slowed down drastically, and indeed turned into a slight decline for a time, but it was also because improved farming techniques superimposed on a continuing expansion of the cultivated area had produced an acceleration in the rate at which production was being increased. As we have seen in Chapter 2 the long upward movement in grain prices came to an end around the middle of the seventeenth century, and thereafter the relative over-supply of the home market with grain products is suggested by the downward drift in their prices until the atrocious harvests of the 1690s temporarily reversed the trend. (See above Ch. 2 sec. ii.) Imports had ceased to be necessary by the 1660s (Hinton, 1959, pp. 37–42, 105), and England again became an exporter of grain, but on a larger scale than before. The concern of landlords at the effect that low grain prices were having on farm profits, and therefore rents, found expression in acts of parliament which first lowered the maximum price below which grain could be freely exported, then permitted the export of corn whatever the price on the home market (1670), and finally introduced bounty payments (1672) in order to provide positive encouragement to exports. (See also below II, pp. 242–3.) By the first decade of the eighteenth

[1] See above pp. 8–9, 16–19 for a discussion of subsistence crises.
[2] It also owed something to the fact that the output was becoming more varied. Increased availability of dairy products and bacon provided some buffer against a shortage of food grains, but most important was probably the increase in the amount of spring sown grain which made harvests less vulnerable to adverse weather conditions than when most people depended on autumn sown creals. See also below p. 139.

century these averaged 283,000 quarters a year, which was food for 140,000 people or about 2.5 per cent of the then population. By that time England was well on the way to becoming for a while, one of the major granaries of Europe, on which less fortunate countries were coming to depend for their regular supplies (John, 1976).

Imports of livestock had also become of some importance by the early seventeenth century. Hitherto the emptier areas of the North, Wales and the South West had raised a sufficient number to satisfy the requirements of the graziers in the more favoured parts of the country who fattened them for the market, but increasingly the latter were coming to draw on Irish, and to a much lesser extent Scottish, sources of supply. Imports from Ireland reached their peak in the early 1660s: in 1665 57,545 cattle and 99,564 sheep came thence, together with the equivalent of another 14,632 cattle in the form of barrelled beef. Scotland provided few sheep and a smaller number of cattle, perhaps 30,000 in 1662 (Cullen, 1968, pp. 29–31. Chartres, 1977 (1), pp. 20–3), but although these combined totals are considerable they represent no more than at most 15 per cent of the cattle and 4 per cent of the sheep slaughtered annually at that time.[3] Moreover in 1666 the Irish trade was prohibited by parliament in the interests of the English stock raising districts, and the total volume of imports promptly shrank, for the Scottish livestock trade did not increase sufficiently to fill the gap until the early eighteenth century (Campbell, 1964). Some dairy products, mainly butter, were also imported from Ireland in the seventeenth century until they too were banned in 1666, but England was on balance an exporter of butter and cheese for most of the period covered in this book.

The only other important agricultural commodity in which the country failed to remain self-sufficient was wool. In the sixteenth century there had still been a surplus of wool above internal requirements which was exported, and though the wool trade was only a shadow of its medieval glory even at the beginning of the period, the quantities remained significant until the 1550s: in the year 1538–43, for instance exports averaged more than $1\frac{1}{2}$ million lbs per annum (Carus-Wilson, 1954, p. xx).[4] However after 1558 there was a rapid decline, and by the 1580s exports had become negligible. After 1614, indeed, the export of wool was actually made illegal in order to help the native cloth manufacturing industry against its foreign rivals, whom, it was felt,

---

[3] In 1695 Gregory King estimated the number of beef cattle slaughtered annually to be 800,000, and the number of sheep at 3,600,000 (Thirsk and Cooper, 1972, p. 797). Allowance has been made for a likely increase in slaughterings between the 1660s and 1690s to arrive at the percentages suggested in the text.

[4] 4,500 sacks of 364 lbs each.

should not be allowed to benefit, even in a very slight degree, from English raw materials. Moreover soon afterwards English clothiers began to make use of foreign wools, and small but increasing quantities were imported from Spain. At first this was mainly because changing fashions meant a growing demand for fabrics which required an especially fine wool, which sheep fed on English pastures could not produce. However, well before the end of the century the continued expansion of the cloth industry, and the high price of English wool, meant that a substantial fraction of the industry's requirements of even those grades which England could produce were being partly satisfied from abroad, particularly Ireland (Bowden, 1962, pp. 46–8, 155–62, 184–217). As early as 1671, and again in 1698, imports of Irish wool well exceeded 300,000 'great stone', perhaps 5 million lbs or more, and the value of imports of wool from all sources averaged nearly £200,000 a year in the first five years of the eighteenth century (Cullen, 1968, pp. 35, 42. Schumpeter, 1960, Tables XV and XVI). At the latter rate they were equivalent to about one tenth of domestic production.[5]

England may not have remained completely self supporting in agricultural products throughout the two centuries of this study, but she never fell far short of it, even during the culmination of a long period of growing population in the early seventeenth century. By the last third of the century, moreover, a sizeable import of wool and a lesser one of livestock was balanced by exports of grain, dairy products and also leather. Nor is there any doubt that England's record of near self-sufficiency was a great deal better than that of many other European countries. Scotland, Scandinavia and large areas of France not only remained subject to subsistence crises throughout the seventeenth century, but in the two latter cases well into the eighteenth; the densely populated Dutch Republic was heavily dependent on both imported food-stuffs and imported agricultural raw materials throughout the period; and much of the Mediterranean region failed to match increases in population by increases in the output of food so that by the end of the sixteenth century it too had become dependent on outside sources of supply even in years of normal harvest. No doubt the countries of both the extreme North of Europe, and the extreme South, suffered from climatic disadvantages from which England was largely exempt, but a fortunate geographical position is certainly not a sufficient explanation for her agricultural success which, as we shall see, also owed much to the changes in rural society and the institutional structure of farming which we discussed in the last chapter.

[5] In 1695 Gregory King estimated the annual value of the wool produced inside the country to be £2 million (Thirsk and Cooper, 1972, p. 782).

ii Expansion of the cultivated area

It was as a result of three principal developments that English agriculture was able to meet the greatly enhanced demand for its products in the sixteenth and seventeenth centuries. An increased proportion of total output was diverted from peasant consumption to the market; secondly there were large additions to the cultivated area; and thirdly there were improvements in productivity. Not a great deal need be said about the first of these. The extension of commercial farming at the expense of peasant farming clearly had this effect: dispossessed peasants and their families still consumed agricultural products of course, but as labourers they will have consumed less because of a lower living standard, and the difference was thus available to contribute towards satisfying general market demand. The difference between the consumption of the small family farmer and the labourer may have been considerable, for Dr Bowden has estimated that the latter earned only about £9 a year in the early seventeenth century whilst the net profit from a 30 acre arable farm, including what the farmer retained for himself in kind, was £14–£15 or more in an average year (*A.H.E.W.* IV, 1967, p. 657). Besides, the consumption of many of those who remained as farmers must have been progressively squeezed by the increasing weight of rents and fines which obliged them to find a larger cash income and thus to sell a growing proportion of what they produced. However the declining proportion of agricultural output which was absorbed by the producers themselves was less important in increasing the supply of commodities to the market than were increases in total production.

These increases are likely at first to have come very largely from an extension of the area under cultivation, and a more intensive utilization of land which was not actually cultivated on a permanent basis or at all. Unfortunately there is no way of measuring either of these developments, but as we have seen in Chapter 3 both the appropriation of common land by commercial farmers, and piecemeal encroachment by small peasants and squatters were proceeding throughout the period, and were accompanied by an increased exploitation of the areas of waste which remained as pasturage for farm stock. In much of the lowland zone there was little scope for either, even in 1500, let alone in 1600: for instance it has been estimated of Leicestershire that by the latter date 95 per cent of the county was under cultivation and no more than 1 per cent remained as woodland (Hoskins, 1950; 1963). This forms a marked contrast with the situation in highland zone counties such as Devonshire, where even if the uncultivable wastes of Dartmoor and Exmoor are excluded, at least 20 per cent of the area was still under its natural vegetation cover even at the end of the sixteenth century, a proportion which rose as high as 50–60 per cent in some districts (Hoskins, 1943). Taking the south western peninsula as a whole several hundred thousand acres must have been brought into cultivation in the sixteenth and seventeenth centuries. Along the Welsh border, too, there was a great deal of under-utilized land, and in the single Shropshire parish of Myddle, which does not seem to have been exceptional, at least 1000 acres, over one fifth of the total area of the township, was added to the cultivated area between the later fifteenth and the mid seventeenth century by the cutting down of woods and the draining of meres (Hey, 1974, p. 39). In the northern counties, again, similar conditions prevailed and on an even larger scale, though there a greater proportion of the mountain, moor and forest continued to be used only as rough grazing until after 1700.[6] We have seen that there were enclaves of thinly populated country in the lowland zone, but the only respect in which eastern England unquestionably offered greater opportunities for the extension of cultivation than the North and West was in the reclamation of marsh and fen. Along many parts of the coast, from Sussex to the East Riding of Yorkshire, the action of the sea in depositing silt caused the shore line to recede year by year, so that at intervals the inhabitants were able to take in a new piece of saltmarsh by building a protective bank, so that it became dry pasture secure from inundation and could eventually be planted as arable. There were scores of parishes, particularly around the Wash and on the Thames estuary, whose area was increased by several hundred acres during the period, and in some places the rate of reclamation was much faster than this: at Tetney on the Lindsey coast over 1000 acres were recovered from the sea in the two generations before 1608. It is true that in other places the sea made inroads into the land, but in the sixteenth and seventeenth centuries the gains far outweighed the losses (Thirsk, 1957, pp. 15–21, 62–9, 129–34. Kerridge, 1967, pp. 223–5). Much more dramatic than the piecemeal recovery of coastal marshland were the large scale drainage projects whereby the inland fens were laid dry. This, however, is discussed below on p. 110.

The motive force behind this movement to extend the cultivated area was, of course, the demand for more land both for commercial farming and for peasant occupation. Indeed the high rents which could thus be obtained not only induced landowners to sanction the breaking up of land which had been left untilled because no one had previously wanted it, but

---

[6] In the South West, and probably elsewhere in the highland zone, considerable areas over and above those taken into cultivation on a permanent basis were brought under the plough temporarily, and then abandoned again, especially in periods of particularly high grain prices or intense local population pressure (Fox, 1973).

also to turn over to farming parts of their estates which had been kept inviolate for sporting purposes. Deer parks, often well wooded, were numerous at the end of the Middle Ages. They were usually many hundreds, sometimes several thousands of acres in extent, and even in some parts of the South and Midlands occupied a not inconsiderable fraction of the available land. In Nottinghamshire, for instance, as late as 1700, there were 22,000 acres of parkland, which was 4 per cent of the county. However, between the mid sixteenth and the mid seventeenth century these game reserves were being disparked and turned over to agriculture in their dozens. There were still more than 800 parks at the end of the sixteenth century, but many had already disappeared: a Kentish list of 1596 mentions that twenty-three out of the fifty-four which had formerly existed in the county had been disparked within living memory (Prince, 1967. Fowkes, 1967. Chalklin, 1965, p. 12). More extensive even than private deer parks were the royal forests. These were areas which, though not exclusively devoted to game or by any means devoid of human habitations, had since the early Middle Ages been subject to special laws intended to preserve the wildlife and restrict the extent of settlement within their bounds. Some of them covered huge tracts of countryside. Rockingham Forest in Northamptonshire, for instance, occupied most of an area eighteen miles long and eight miles across (Pettit, 1968, p. 12), and in many otherwise thickly populated counties they were the only really sizeable areas of under-utilized land remaining. In the 1620s and 1630s many were wholly or partly disafforested, which meant that they were freed from forest law and sold, after which the new owners could do as they wished with what they had bought. This did not necessarily mean a change in land use, and stands of timber were usually replanted if felled, but much of the former forest had not been thickly wooded but more or less open and used by local villages as common pasturage. The government had envisaged that such land should be made subject to permanent cultivation after disafforestation and much of it clearly was, although in a number of places, such as Gillingham Forest in Dorset and Braydon Forest in Wiltshire, there was considerable opposition from the dispossessed commoners, which forced the crown to modify its original intentions (Pettit, 1968, pp. 65–70. Allan, 1952).

Much of the land brought into cultivation in the sixteenth and seventeenth centuries, especially the former parks and forests, was of very low fertility and required considerable improvement, for instance by the application of marl, to make it really productive. The cost of doing this was always considerable, and coming on top of the costs of clearance, fencing and sometimes the construction of new farmsteads, meant that the creation of large areas of new farmland involved a substantial investment of capital by those undertaking it. The recovery of marshland from the sea similarly called for the expenditure of large sums, sometimes several pounds per acre: Sir Thomas Culpepper, for instance, spent £1000 on the 'inning' of 200 acres of Dengemarsh in Kent in the later 1640s (Chalklin, 1965, pp. 13–15). However the capital required for even the largest marshland reclamation paled into insignificance beside the sums absorbed by the drainage of the Fens in the second quarter of the seventeenth century.

The technical and managerial expertise for the implementation of a series of very ambitious drainage schemes was provided by the Dutch engineer Vermuyden, but the financial resources came mostly from local landowners, acting as individuals or in consortia, of which that headed by the Earl of Bedford was the most notable, with some contribution from the crown. Between them they raised what were, for the period, truly huge amounts of money: it was said that the works in Hatfield Chase alone cost £200,000, and that Bedford and his associates had spent £300,000 between 1630 and 1653. Great new drainage channels had to be dug, up to forty, fifty or, in the case of the twenty-one mile long so-called Bedford River, no less than seventy feet in width; embankments had to be thrown up; and elaborate sluices constructed to regulate the flow of water. However, as a result, 70,000 acres in the East Riding of Yorkshire, many tens of thousands in Lincolnshire, and no less than 400,000 acres in the southern Fens, mostly in Cambridgeshire and Huntingdonshire, known collectively as the Bedford Level, were made fit for arable cultivation. The Lincolnshire drainage works did not survive the 1640s when the local people, who had been deprived by them of common rights vital to their livelihood, took advantage of the prevailing disorder to destroy them so that the land returned to its previous condition as rather watery common pasture subject to more or less regular inundation in winter. Further south, however, damage done during the 1640s was repaired, again under Vermuyden's supervision, in the early 1650s, and despite the increasing difficulties which were encountered in containing floods in the later seventeenth century, the Bedford Level represented a permanent addition to the country's productive capacity. The Fens had been by no means unproductive before, but crops of grain and cole-seed could now be grown for the first time, and larger numbers of sheep and cattle than ever could be kept, so much so that an observer in 1655 remarked that 'the country thereabouts is now subject to a new drowning, even to a deluge and inundation of plenty' (Darby, 1940, chs. I–II. Harris, 1953. Thirsk, 1957, ch. 5. Gough, 1969, ch. 12).

Finally the latter part of the seventeenth century saw the beginnings of a movement to extend continuous arable cultivation to yet another type of land which had hitherto been under-utilized. The chalk downs of the South, the limestone wolds of the East and North East, and the sandy soils in many areas had been too poor and thin to bear crops under the farming techniques available in the sixteenth and early seventeenth centuries, and were therefore for the most part used as rough sheep pasture. However, the coming of new types of fodder crops, which is discussed in more detail later in the chapter, transformed the prospects of farmers on these lands. They were able to support far more livestock than before. This meant a greater quantity of manure was available as fertilizer, and this in turn made it possible to convert a larger and larger proportion of the former sheep-walk to crop-land, on which not only the fodder crops, but also grain, could be grown. This was a process which continued into the eighteenth century, and reached its culmination well after the end of our period, but it was already in full swing by 1700. John Aubrey, the antiquarian, estimated that between 1660 and 1685 about a quarter of the vast expanse of Salisbury Plain was converted to arable, and within a generation or two the ploughing up of downland and heath was attracting frequent comment from contemporaries (Jones, 1965. Kerridge, 1967, p. 26). Daniel Defoe, for instance, who was writing early in the eighteenth century, was much struck by the advance of arable cultivation on the downs of Hampshire and Wiltshire, and commented that thanks to new methods of husbandry they now bore 'excellent wheat, and great crops too, tho' otherwise poor barren land, and never known to our ancestors to be capable of any such thing; nay, they would perhaps have laugh'd at any one that would have gone about to plough up the wild downs and hills, where the sheep were wont to go' (Defoe, 1928, 1, p. 187).

The net effect of two hundred years during which farmers constantly extended their fields at the expense of moorland, forest, coastal marshes, deer parks, royal hunting grounds, fenland, down and sandy heath, was to add several million acres to the continuously cultivated acreage of the country. In 1695 Gregory King estimated that the latter was about 21 million acres (Thirsk and Cooper, 1972, p. 779), a figure which is probably a little too high, but which is likely to be of the right order of magnitude. It is a reasonably conservative guess that one fifth of that had been taken into use since the early sixteenth century, which would imply an increase in the cultivated area of about 25 per cent during the period. Particularly during the early part of the period, when increases in the productivity of existing farm land were clearly slow, the extension of cultivation must have been a major source of increased output. Yet since the population seems to have risen by more than four fifths between 1500 and 1600, unless it occurred on a very much larger scale than seems probable, it cannot have accounted for more than a limited fraction of the total increase. Changes in the way in which the land was cultivated, and the intensity with which it was cropped, must, in the long run, have been more important.

iii Constraints on productivity

Productivity levels in English agriculture at the end of the Middle Ages were extremely low by modern standards, both in crop production and livestock husbandry. Figures are hard to obtain, and for peasant farms impossible. Some calculations have been made from surviving sets of fifteenth century farm accounts relating to demesne lands, but it is difficult to assess how representative they are since yields must have varied very widely from district to district, and from year to year in the same district.[7] However an average wheat crop in the southern half of the country was probably eight or nine bushels per acre, which would have represented a return on the seed sown of not more than four or five fold at the very most. This is much the same as the yields obtained in North Africa in the 1920s and compares very poorly with the 70–80 bushels per acre obtained by English arable farmers at the present day (Bennett, 1935. Slicher Van Bath, 1963 (1), pp. 39–41. Farmer, 1977). The carrying capacity of pasture land is even more difficult to ascertain, but it is clear that not only could the livestock farmer of 1500 have kept fewer beasts than his modern counterpart, but that they would have been smaller creatures capable of producing much less milk, or meat, or wool per head.

The low returns which farmers got from their fields reflected three inter-related factors: the limitations of the agricultural technology available to them; their own poverty; and the forms of organization within which most of them were working. Farming tools and equipment were clumsy and inefficient. There had been no systematic improvement of crop strains or animal breeds, and pasturage consisted of whatever vegetation grew of its own accord on land left undisturbed by the plough. As for the range of crops in use in mixed farming districts, it was very restricted, and food grains, beans, peas and vetches would virtually exhaust the list in most of them. This was partly through lack of knowledge, but partly also because the pressing need of each peasant to grow enough food to support his family obliged him to concentrate

---

[7] A further difficulty facing the historian attempting to enquire into crop yields in this period is that neither measurements of area, nor those of quantity, were standardized throughout the whole country.

heavily on cereals. Neither root vegetables, nor clover, nor any of the other 'artificial' grasses, such as sainfoin, which later provided rich feed for animals and greatly extended the scope and value of arable rotations, were yet grown.[8] There were, of course, none of the chemical fertilizers on which modern farmers rely so heavily, and only very limited use was made of the many natural aids to soil fertility, such as marl and chalk, which were widely available in the countryside, because of the great expense involved in collecting or extracting them and applying them to the land. Animal dung was the form of fertilizer most generally relied upon. As Bishop Latimer, himself the son of a yeoman, put it in a sermon preached in the mid sixteenth century: 'a ploughland must have sheep; yea, they must have sheep to help fat the ground; for if they have no sheep to help fat the ground, they shall have but bare corn and thin'. However the poverty of most rural communities in mixed farming areas meant that the average farmer had relatively little livestock of any sort. Thus in open field Leicestershire in the early sixteenth century even the well-off peasant with 40–50 acres of land would have few more than one sheep per acre and half a dozen cows (Hoskins, 1950). They were thus unable to produce a sufficiently large quantity of dung to ensure good crop yields. Since neither varied rotations nor intensive manuring were possible, farmers were obliged to rest their land periodically in order to allow it to recover heart by natural processes. This is not a very efficient method, and it has the further disadvantage of being a very wasteful one, for the obvious reason that it involves leaving a proportion of the farm land untilled each year: half of it if fields were fallowed every other year, or one third if they were fallowed one year in three. There was thus a considerable difference between a farm's cultivated acreage and the acreage actually under crops at any one time.

The poverty of the mass of peasant farmers, which deprived them of the capital to build up their flocks and herds, or to improve their land, was itself largely a result of the low productivity of their land and their inability to crop all of it simultaneously. For the principal consequence of the miserable returns they obtained was that a holding, which in more recent times could provide a man and his family with a good living, was barely able to sustain them at all, the more so since the produce from a very high proportion of the land actually bearing crops, as much as a quarter if the ratio of yield to seed was no more than 4:1, had to be reserved to provide seed for the following year. Besides, a disproportionately large fraction of what capital farmers did have available had to go in the acquisition of draught animals to plough the necessarily large acreages of low yielding corn land, whilst in areas where pasturage was

[8] At least in England, although by the late Middle Ages they were in use in parts of the Netherlands.

scarce it was a serious matter that so much of it had to be devoted to their support. Thus both capital and pasturage resources which might otherwise have been available for other forms of livestock, capable of producing meat, milk or wool, which would have increased and diversified the farmers' output, were absorbed by the need to keep horses or oxen. Nor, in the conditions of the sixteenth century, was there any prospect of the iron link between the peasant farmers' poverty and low productivity being broken, and indeed it became even more strongly forged as the effects of increasing population began to tell. Sub-divided holdings and higher rents and fines meant greater poverty, and a further reduction in their ability to invest in their farms. Growing scarcity of pasture in many parts of the lowland zone, which led to the over-grazing of manorial commons and the introduction of stints, often made it increasingly difficult for villages to keep even the livestock they could afford to acquire, whilst the acreage of ploughland which required manuring was greater than ever.[9] In areas where woodland was scarce, such as the chalk and limestone uplands and some parts of the Midland Plain, the exhaustion of local supplies of fuel as the numbers of people grew made it necessary for the poorer members of the community to burn dried animal dung in their homes, as is the practice in many of the more arid areas of Asia at the present day. The fuel shortage was thereby alleviated, but the land was deprived of a proportion of the fertilizer it so urgently needed.

The form of organization which imposed a drag on productivity was, of course, the open field system and the unimproved common pastures associated with it, and their prevalence over large areas of the country meant that neither the land, nor the labour bestowed on it, were even as productive as the best of contemporary farming methods might have permitted. It is true that the open fields were not nearly as inflexible, nor possessed as many disadvantages, as was believed by a former generation of historians who followed the lead of agricultural propagandists of the late eighteenth century like Arthur Young. A farmer did not have to grow precisely the same crops on his strips as did all the others who held land in the same field: provided he kept to approximately the same timetable of ploughing, sowing and harvesting, he could grow whatever suited his convenience. Indeed with the agreement of his neighbours he could even put some of his strips down to grass, and nothing illustrates the flexibility of the open fields so well as the increasing number of these leys,

[9] Scarcity of pasturage was, in its turn, largely the result of low arable yields which made in necessary for communities to plough up so large a proportion of the land available to them in order to raise sufficient creals upon which to live.

surrounded by temporary or even by semi-permanent enclosures, which appeared in some parts of the Midlands during the later Middle Ages (Hoskins, 1950). Nevertheless the fact that hard–headed tenants would pay so much higher a rent for fully enclosed land demonstrates that open field farms yielded less to those who worked them than did enclosed areas of comparable acreage. (See above p. 81.) It may be that the need to be constantly on the move from one part of the fields to another did not waste as much time and energy as is often asserted. Nor that the presence of unploughed baulks and headlands, separating both the furlongs into which the fields were divided and often the indivudual strips as well, wasted land to any serious degree, for they provided necessary access ways and were an important source of pasturage. But friction between neighbours arising from the close proximity of their intermingled strips, over matters ranging from outright theft of standing crops to the spread of weeds from ill tended land, seems to have been frequent and to have been a disincentive to the more energetic to invest maximum effort in their husbandry (McCloskey, 1975). Inadequate drainage was also frequently a problem in the open fields where the confused pattern of the ownership of the innumerable long strips made it difficult to remedy, but even in enclosed areas the inability of small farmers to afford the expense, and sometimes their ignorance of the appropriate techniques, meant that much land which could have benefited from drainage regularly became water-logged, ruining crops and causing rot and liver-fluke amongst the sheep. Besides, rough common pastures often provided a poor sub-sistence for the livestock which, in consequence, were of deplorably low quality, and their use by all and sundry meant that a single diseased creature could infect all the others in the village. Moreover, one of the most important advantages which was potentially available to a farmer who had more animals than his neighbours was the greater quantity of dung with which he could enrich his arable. But this could only be realized if his lands lay separately from those of the rest of the community and his sheep and cattle were kept apart from the common flock or herd and folded exclusively on his own fields.

Finally, although the need to secure communal agreement did not prevent change occurring at all, there can be little doubt that it often retarded innovation and limited its scope, and that to an extent which differed much from place to place, the whole system of communal control tended to inhibit the activities of the vigorous, enterprising and efficient, and to protect the smaller and less efficient producers. As we saw in the previous chapter maximization of economic efficiency was not the purpose of open field village organization, whose ends were, in a sense, social rather than economic.[10] Indeed the system of communal regulation was, like the under-investment characteristic of peasant society, both cause and result of poverty. It existed because of the need to share out resources in such a way as to enable as many people as possible to make some sort of a living from them. But the consequence was necessarily that total output was lower than it might have been had such considerations been disregarded.

iv Regional specialization and the flow of capital into agriculture

During the course of the sixteenth and seventeenth centuries these inter-connected constraints on agricultural productivity began to break down, and the main solvent was the rise of commercial farming. Higher productivity, in other words, did not come as a result of peasant society as a whole pulling itself up by its boot-straps and breaking out of the vicious circle of poverty, under-investment and low yields, for only a minority of its most successful members could in practice ever achieve that. It came very largely through the partial elimination of the petty peasantry and the gradual transfer of land from its members to farmers of substance, in ways, and for reasons, which were discussed in the last chapter.

One long term consequence of the advance of commercial farming, which certainly had implications for productivity, was increasing local specialization, in certain regions, on those types of production which best suited the natural endowments of the area. This did not occur to the same degree everywhere and it was certainly more apparent in the South East and East Anglia, with their ready access by road, river or coastal shipping, to the London market, than it was in the more distant parts of the kingdom. Nevertheless the growing concentration on beef and mutton production, and on dairying, in the coastal lowlands of Northumberland and Durham, which was evident by the end of the sixteenth century, illustrates the fact that the tendency was not confined to any particular part of the country (*A.H.E.W.* IV, 1967, pp. 25–8). In some cases local specializations were essentially new and their development brought about striking transformations. For instance, Leicestershire and much of neighbouring counties such as Northamptonshire, Bedfordshire and

---

[10] A number of historians have recently turned their attention to the question of the origins of the open fields, and to their persistence in some parts of the country for many centuries. Some of them have argued that, contrary to appearances, there were distinct economic advantages in the system, whether in terms of insurance against the risks inherent in a relatively primitive agriculture, or of making the best use of the available labour both within and outside the peasant family. These and other arguments have, however, been presented with more theoretical ingenuity than empirical evidence. See particularly McCloskey, 1975; 1976. Fenoaltea, 1976. Wilson, 1979. Also Dahlman, 1980.

Buckinghamshire, were mainly devoted to arable farming at the beginning of the sixteenth century, but two hundred years later their heavy soils were largely under grass, which was a much more suitable use for them. By the early part of the eighteenth century the first of these counties in particular was famous for its pastures, and for the sheep, cattle and horses reared there, which supplied the textile industry with raw material and London with both meat and motive power for its many drays and coaches. It had become, as Defoe expressed it, 'a vast magazine of wool for the rest of the nation', whilst its livestock were brought up to the capital in such numbers 'that one would think so little a spot as this of Leicestershire could not be able to supply them' (*V.C.H. Leics.* IV, 1954, pp. 211–13, 220–2. Hoskins, 1963. Defoe, 1928, II, p. 89). The spread of fruit and hop growing in Kent provides another example of a new local specialism in this period, but it was more common for increased specialization in an area to take the form of greater emphasis on one or more aspects of an established system of husbandry, or one or more products from amongst those which it had long been producing. Thus during the sixteenth century there was greatly increased production of wheat, at the expense of a once equally important barley crop, in much of North and East Kent, and the opposite development in which barley in large part replaced wheat in the furthest extremity of the county beyond Canterbury and in the Isle of Thanet (Chalklin, 1965, pp. 73–82, 90–5).

It would be wrong, however, to give the impression that under the influence of a widening market for agricultural produce, farmers in all districts were coming to concentrate upon an increasingly narrow range of products, for in some areas change took the form of diversification rather than specialization. Thus in some extensively wooded areas such as the Forest of Arden, still sparsely settled in 1500 and where the principal economic activity during most of the sixteenth century was the raising of beef cattle, continued local population growth associated with immigration and the development of rural industry created a local market for a wide range of food-stuffs. Thus by the mid seventeenth century there had evolved a more varied agriculture which placed much greater emphasis on both dairying and the raising of grain (Skipp, 1978, esp. chs. 4–7. Yelling, 1977, pp. 184–7). Nevertheless taking English agriculture as a whole there is no doubt that there was a much greater degree of regional specialization in 1700 than there had been in 1500.

In districts such as the East Midlands, which had been open field in 1500, progress towards greater specialization depended largely on the progress of enclosure. However, irrespective of changes in land use, which did not necessarily follow, enclosure and the gradual erosion of the area in open fields itself contributed to higher output per acre to an important degree. Even if enclosed land was managed on the same plan as when it had lain open it would almost certainly produce more. But more important was the fact that many of the improvements open to a man with some capital were either completely dependent on enclosure, as in the case of better drainage, or as in the case of marling and, in the seventeenth century, the growing of new crops, were very much easier, certain to yield a better return, and therefore more likely to be undertaken. The importance of enclosure in this respect is suggested by the general agreement of agricultural writers from the mid sixteenth century onwards that it was in the counties such as Suffolk, Essex, Kent and Devon, where virtually all the land was laid out in enclosed fields, the farming methods were most progressive and most worthy of imitation. Enclosure, however, was only one aspect of the increase in agricultural investment which came about as a result of the expansion of commercial farming at the expense of the peasantry, and it is this increase as a whole which should be seen as the first of the two key elements in the process whereby the productive capacity of English agriculture was eventually transformed. The second, which was partly dependent on it, but which will be discussed separately, was the introduction of improved techniques.

Successful commercial farming generated a high rate of profit during most of the sixteenth and early seventeenth centuries, thereby providing its practitioners with funds which they could reinvest in their enterprises. If they were tenants, as most were, they would concentrate on building up the circulating capital with which they operated. First and foremost this meant that they would build up larger flocks and herds than small peasants could ever hope to acquire, which meant more dung for their arable and thus higher yields. If shortage of pasture made it difficult to support more livestock they could afford to rent additional grazing land, if necessary at a considerable distance, as commercial farmers from the chalk and limestone uplands of Lincolnshire increasingly did in the coastal marshland of that county, and those of the interior districts of Kent did in Romney Marsh. Thus in the mid sixteenth century, when the typical Leicestershire family farmer tilled 30–35 acres of open field arable and had a similar number of sheep and a small handful of cattle, Thomas Bradgate of Peatling Parva, a wealthy yeoman, had at his death in 1539 six horses, 400 sheep and 74 steers, milch kine and calves. Later in the century, fully one third of the farms in the county had fewer than twenty sheep, whereas one in ten had over a hundred (Thirsk, 1957, pp. 148–9. Chalklin, 1965, p. 13. Hoskins, 1950; 1963).

Besides getting more livestock the farmer of means would be able to obtain better quality beasts than the ordinary peasant because he could afford to pay a higher price for them. He was also more likely to be able to meet the expense of providing himself with the full range of equipment which his operations rendered desirable, and of obtaining the best strains of seed available, whereas the peasant would have to manage with the bare minimum of implements and the cheapest and most readily available seed. To cite the case of Leicestershire again, in the sixteenth century the paucity of the equipment owned by the poorer peasant farmers is indicated by the fact that they often had neither a cart nor a plough of their own (Hoskins, 1950), and there is no doubt that such people elsewhere were equally ill equipped. The large scale farmer would also be better able to buy in fertilizers from off the farm, and to pay for costly but beneficial improvements such as marling, chalking or drainage. Thus even before any marked technical improvements to farming methods there can be no doubt that the larger and more commercially orientated farmers normally secured a higher output per acre than did most peasants, but their advantage in this respect must certainly have increased as better methods began to spread in the seventeenth century.

One reason for this was that by that time their holdings were likely to be enclosed, even if situated in a district where those of smaller farmers were not (Kerridge, 1967, p. 18), and this made it easier for them to experiment with unfamiliar practices. Besides it was the larger producers, the farming gentry and the yeomanry, who could afford to take the risks in adopting new forms of husbandry, could afford to incur the initial expense or temporary loss of income which such changes often involved, and could deal with the problems of marketing which might arise when a farm changed the structure of its output. It was thus amongst them that technical advances spread first, and most innovations only percolated down to the peasantry much later, if they ever reached them at all. As we shall see there was at least one important exception to this generalization in that some labour intensive industrial crops, which required little or no capital, were readily taken up by small holders, and indeed in the case of tobacco after 1619 spread amongst them very quickly indeed (Thirsk, 1974). Nor would it be true to say that, down to 1700, peasant agriculture remained untouched in other respects by the changes in farming practices which were going on around it, but undoubtedly it was touched very much less profoundly than was that of the larger scale, more commercially orientated producers. The continued aggrandizement of large farmers at the expense of small must, therefore, have played an increasingly important part in the long term rise in agricultural productivity of the second half of the period.

Those who owned their own land had themselves to finance all

additions and improvements to fixed, as well as to circulating, capital, as
did those who held on tenancies, such as copyhold of inheritance, which
effectively debarred the nominal owner from any share in the future
increases in the value of their holdings. However the landlord–tenant
system, as it had evolved on demesne land and non-inheritable copyhold
in the last century or so of the Middle Ages, ensured that most other
occupiers did not have to. The relationship between the two parties,
indeed, was such that both had an interest in enhancing the value of the
property. Large farms were rarely let at will or on very short leases.
Lettings, at any rate from the mid sixteenth century onwards, were
typically for between seven and twenty-one years, so that the tenant had
sufficient security of tenure for him to be able to invest his own money in
short and medium term improvements, such as liming or marling,
without fear that he might be cheated of their fruits by eviction or an
immediate increase in rent. On the other hand the owner knew that at the
eventual expiry of the lease he would regain possession, or be able to
secure a higher rent or a larger fine, and he was therefore ready to
undertake those long term improvements, such as enclosure, drainage
works of an elaborate nature and the erection of new farm buildings,
whose expense and permanency was such that an occupier with a limited
tenancy would not be prepared to pay for them. There was thus a division
of financial functions. On one side the farmer provided his own working
capital, that is farm stock, seed and equipment, and undertook routine
repairs and such improvements to the fixed capital, that is the land and
the buildings, as would yield most of its advantages within the span of a
single lease term. And on the other side the landlord financed those which
would continue to yield a return into the indefinite future. To take a
specific example from an estate in Hertfordshire belonging to Sir Samuel
Grimston, when in 1686 Thomas Aylward the tenant of the large Hedges
Farm in Sopwell wanted a new barn, Grimston undertook to build it, for it
was to be a large five-bay structure with a solid tiled roof. Its subsequent
maintenance, however, was to be entirely Aylward's responsibility.[11]
However the relationship between landlord and tenant was flexible, and
just as a landlord might pay for short term improvements in return for an
immediate increase in rent if the tenant could not afford them, or even
contribute to working capital by allowing him a rebate on his rent in
difficult times, so an affluent tenant might make long term improvements
in return for an extra long lease.

In practice it seems to have been relatively rare, particularly down to
the middle of the seventeenth century, for established proprietors to

[11] Herts. R.O., Gorhambury Mass IV. F. 243, 36b.

spend accumulated savings on estate improvements, perhaps because
they did not often have any, although the many newcomers to landed
society who were building up estates out of profits made in other spheres
more often did so. Established landowners usually financed improvements out of current income, or failing this by getting tenants to
undertake the necessary work in return for a reduced fine, or a lower rent
during all or part of their tenancy. When in 1688 another of Sir Samuel
Grimston's tenants required additional barn accommodation he agreed
with the baronet to erect a 'Dutch Hovell with four posts and a cap of deal
to hold 30 loads of hay', and his rent was accordingly lowered from £30 a
year to £12 for the duration of a seven year lease.[12] However, there is no
reason to regard such an arrangement as being any less reinvestment of
estate income than if the estate owner had laid out ready cash saved from
fines and rents received in earlier years. The landlord–tenant system
thus had the potentiality to call forth a much higher level of agricultural
investment than would have been possible if virtually all the capital had
to come from either owners or occupiers. However for this potentiality to
be realized it was not only necessary that there should be tenants making
substantial profits which they *could* plough back into their farms, but also
that landlords should have a sufficiently powerful incentive to plough
back part of *their* receipts. The expansion of commercial farming meant a
great increase in the number of the former able to play their part, and it
also encouraged the latter to play theirs. Unless they knew that they
would secure a good return on their money landlords would not invest in
their estates; and as long as these were largely tenanted by peasants whose
poverty and subsistence orientated approach to farming prevented them
from paying a higher rent for improved land or new buildings, they
would not do so. But the high rents that commercial farmers would pay
for improved farms provided the required incentive, and there is no
doubt that the growth of commercial farming in this period was
accompanied by an increase in landlord investment from the relatively
low level to which it had fallen since estate owners had withdrawn from
the direct exploitation of their own demesnes in the late fourteenth and
early fifteenth centuries. The more rapid rate at which open fields were
enclosed, the many large scale projects for the reclamation of land from
the waste, and the growing number of new farm buildings erected
between about 1560 and 1640, all provide proof of this increase.

Nevertheless the flow of capital into agriculture, though undoubtedly
greater than in the later Middle Ages, and increasing, remained small by
later standards, especially in the sixteenth and the early part of the

[12] Herts. R.O., Gorhambury Mss IV. H. 43, 44.

seventeenth centuries. This is illustrated by the fact that despite the acceleration in the rate of enclosure and in the taking in of new land since the fifteenth century, both were proceeding much less rapidly than they were to do between 1760 and 1830. Neither all large farmers, nor all landlords were necessarily able to afford to invest much, and indeed we have seen that relative scarcity of capital was one factor which limited the rate of agrarian change. Nor would they necessarily choose to invest even if they could afford it, for there were many other possible uses for savings, such as house building, advancing the career of a younger son, or paying the marriage portion of a daughter. Alternatively they might prefer to use potential saving to finance a more lavish lifestyle: the yeomanry are believed to have had a high propensity both to save and invest, but the aristocracy and large sections of the gentry seem rather to have had one for conspicuous expenditure. Moreover even if a farmer or landlord did save and invest, for much of the period improvement of those parts of his estate already tenanted and yielding a rent was not the most likely form for his investment to take. He was more likely to extend the proportion of the estate actually under cultivation by financing the taking in of new land, and if he had large sums at his disposal he would almost certainly use it to buy more property, for, given the code of values prevailing in early modern England, this would bring the buyer not only an income yielding asset but also a social return in the form of increased status which no amount of improvements to his existing possessions could secure. Some improvements, particularly enclosure and other forms of farm reorganiz- ation, might indeed depend on one man buying up the possessions of others so that he became the dominant owner in a parish, but the patient assembly of a consolidated 'ring-fence' estate, bit by bit over a long period, was often a less attractive proposition than the purchase of whatever parcels of land happened to be on the market at the moment when the would-be buyer happened to have money to lay out. As for smaller sums, they were likely to be lent at interest to or through the medium of neighbours and acquaintances. Rates of interest were so high, 10 per cent being usually obtainable until 1625 and 8 per cent between 1625 and 1651,[13] that he could obtain a greater, and certainly an easier, return from lending money to others than from employing it himself. The probate inventories, not only of the gentry, merchants and shop- keepers, but of working farmers too, show that a significant proportion of them had money out on loan, especially by the early seventeenth century. Indeed well before the end of the period lending and borrowing money,

---

[13] These were the maximum rates of interest permitted by law from the time when usury was made legal in 1571: in practice for most of the period market rates coincided with 'legal' rates, although for short periods they did dip below them. See also below II, pp. 232–3.

without doubt more often to finance consumption than for productive investment, was commonplace in rural society. In the East Midlands and Norfolk as much as 13 per cent of the inventoried value of personal estates left at the time of death in the period 1650–1720 was in the form of credits owing, and in some parts of the country up to a quarter, or even a third, of all those leaving inventories were either owed money at the time of their death or else were themselves in debt to others (Skipp, 1970. Hey, 1974, pp. 55–7. Holderness, 1976 (2)).[14]

Besides the positive attractions of these alternative uses for money there was another reason why, for a long time, capital which was potentially available for agricultural improvement was not used for that purpose. This was that for most of the period down to the middle of the seventeenth century price conditions were such that most farmers could garner substantial profits, and most landlords could secure substantial increases in rent, without undertaking improvements. From the time of the Civil War onwards, however, easy profits were no longer to be had in any branch of farming, and for nearly a generation between the later 1660s and the early 1690s many producers, particularly producers of grain crops and wool but to some extent those who relied on other animal products also, found their profits diminished or even disappearing completely (John, 1960. Thirsk, 1970. *A.H.E.W.* v, Part ii, 1984, pp. 1–15). Large numbers of small farmers went out of business altogether at this time, and although the larger ones seem to have had a much better survival rate, the low prices prevailing gave them an incentive to raise output per acre and reduce their unit costs of production which had previously been lacking. As for the landlords, many of them had been forced to invest money in their estates to rehabilitate them after the neglect, or worse, they had suffered in the Civil War. And others, like Sir Ralph Verney who laid out £1000 or more on the enclosure of Middle Claydon (Bucks.) in the mid 1650s, did so to try to restore family finances shattered by the loss of income which sequestration of estates at the hands of political enemies involved (*A.H.E.W.* v, Part ii, 1984, p. 145. Broad, 1973, ch. 7). Then in the 1670s and 1680s, faced with falling rents, mounting arrears, tenants near bankruptcy and empty farms for which no tenants could be found, owners again had the strongest possible reasons to make improvements: to enable existing occupiers to carry on, and to render vacant holdings more attractive to potential takers. Some may have been deterred, by the evident unprofitability of their tenants' operations, from throwing good money after bad, but on balance it is likely that more landlord capital was

---

[14] Not all credits and debits recorded in inventories necessarily related to formal lending and borrowing, but it seems that a large proportion did.

sunk in enclosures, new buildings and the like in the last third of the seventeenth century than in any other period of equal duration between 1500 and 1700. Certainly the rate at which enclosure was proceeding in Leicestershire seems to have increased at this time, and Mr Machin's study of the chronology of farm-house building shows a much higher level of constructional activity in the countryside than in the pre Civil War decades, or than in the mid eighteenth century for that matter. Indeed, according to a recent comparison of the agricultural evolution of England and France, the greater willingness of English landlords in the agricultural depression of the later seventeenth century to provide financial support for tenants in difficulty, and to improve their farms, was one of the principal reasons for the divergence in the agricultural evolution of the two countries and for the notoriously greater efficiency and productivity of English farming by the eighteenth century (Hoskins, 1963. Machin, 1977. Cooper, 1978).

Besides the factors just discussed the seventeenth century saw a long term drop in the rate of interest obtainable from money lending which cannot have been without some effect on the volume of productive investment in agriculture. The maximum legal rate was reduced from 10 per cent to 8 per cent in 1625, and again to 6 per cent in 1651, in each case following a drop in the market rate. By the later seventeenth century 5 per cent was often the most that lenders could obtain, although this did not become the legal maximum until 1714, and in consequence the relative attractiveness of improvement against usury was greatly increased. Many potential improvements which a farmer or landlord could not be sure would yield as much as 10 per cent on the capital invested in them would certainly appear in a different light when the alternative was lending at only 5 per cent. That working farmers made conscious and explicit calculations of the rate of return they were likely to derive from capital ploughed back into their farms is improbable, although they must have had some basis for their investment decisions, but the more sophisticated of the gentry and the large estate owners, or their land stewards, certainly did do their sums, at least by the latter part of the period. Thus when Sir Samuel Grimston undertook to lay out £50 on new building and repairs on a farm called 'the Robin Hood' in Kingsbury (Herts.) in 1685, he increased the rent by a sum equivalent to exactly 5 per cent of his expenditure.[15]

The fall in the rate of interest was significant also because it made it easier to finance improvements by borrowing money on which interest had to be paid, but equally important in this respect were the

[15] Herts. R.O., Gorhambury III B. 99, 100a.

developments which made long term borrowing possible. Prior to about 1620 the types of security in normal use enabled lenders to insist on repayment of their loans at very short notice, and gave them the right of foreclosure on the security if it was not forthcoming on the appointed day. This made it impossibly risky for anyone to sink borrowed money into anything as inconvertible as an enclosure scheme, drainage works or a new set of farm buildings, and in practice additions to fixed capital were hardly ever financed by means of loans in the sixteenth or early seventeenth centuries. However in the early seventeenth century there evolved the concept of the equity of redemption, which made it possible for mortgages to remain outstanding indefinitely, whilst lenders who wanted their principal back could assign their security to another who would assume the rôle of creditor in their stead. Provided that a borrower continued to pay the interest on his debt he no longer needed to fear foreclosure, and thus a new means of mobilizing funds for investment in agriculture, or indeed any other sphere, was opened up for those who were owners of land. This was to be very important indeed in the future, although it seems to have been only towards or even after the end of the seventeenth century that it became at all common for landowners to take advantage of long term mortgages to improve their estates, and even then they were far more commonly used for less productive purposes. Nevertheless as early as the 1620s a few landowners, of whom Lord Brudenell was one, were borrowing in order to finance enclosure, and in the 1630s a number of those involved in the drainage of the Fens, including the Earls of Bedford and Portland, mobilized the capital they required by mortgaging part of their property (Finch, 1956, chs. VI and VII. Stone, 1965, pp. 355–7).

There are thus a number of reasons for thinking that there was a long term increase in the rate of agricultural investment, although even in 1700 it was still low by the standards of the later eighteenth century. A larger and larger number of commercial farms were coming into being and they were increasingly well provided, in terms of both quantity and quality, with land, buildings, stock and equipment. This development provided the setting for the introduction of new techniques because there is little doubt that these tended to be introduced on farms whose lands had already been improved in other ways. Moreover, although only one of the innovations to be discussed in the next section, that is the construction of water-meadows, involved substantial additions to fixed capital, all of them required some additional investment from the farmer. This was, as we shall see, because they involved him in keeping a much larger quantity of livestock than before.

v Advances in agricultural technique
and the introduction of new crops

In the sixteenth and the early part of the seventeenth century, the rate of increase in the productivity of English agriculture was certainly slow. It is also clear that it derived mainly from the gradual extension of the area farmed in large, commercially orientated and relatively well capitalized units, at the expense of peasant holdings, and from organizational changes, especially the enclosure of open field arable, which were closely associated with this. Commercial farming, however, was much influenced by market forces and responsive to the pressures they exerted, and these induced changes in farming methods which eventually led to important technical breakthroughs. It was only when, in the mid and later seventeenth century, the effects of these advanced agricultural techniques were superimposed on top of continuing, and perhaps accelerating changes in structure and organization, that productivity began to increase more rapidly.[16]

For at least the first two thirds of the sixteenth century there are few signs of technical progress in agriculture. In some places the increasing pressure of numbers on the land led village communities in open field areas, or individual farmers in enclosed ones, to adopt more intensive cropping systems which reduced the proportion of the cultivated area lying fallow each year. The conversion of a two field system to a three field one, such as occurred at Sherington in Buckinghamshire sometime between 1514 and 1561 (Chibnall, 1965, pp. 221-2), increased the acreage under crops by one sixth and the conversion of a three field to a four field one increased it by one twelfth. Where the land was of good quality this might raise output significantly, but where it was poor and little animal manure was available the larger sown acreage might be largely or even wholly off-set by a fall in yields from land which was now being over-exploited by its cultivators. It is not at all clear how widely such changes were introduced for they rarely left any mark in the records unless they subsequently gave rise to some kind of dispute, and anyway before the new crops of the seventeenth century made possible more intensive manuring and restorative crop rotation they cannot necessarily be accounted progress.

The origin of most of the technical advances which were made by English farmers within our period seems to have lain in attempts to ease

---

[16] Accelerating because there is reason to think that the growth of relatively large commercial farms at the expense of small family farms was proceeding more rapidly in the difficult conditions which faced producers during much of the later seventeenth century.

the constraints imposed on producers in the mixed farming areas by shortage of pasture. This shortage limited the amount of livestock they were able to maintain, and thus their ability to take advantage of market demand for animal products, but it also limited the supplies of manure available for their ploughland thereby holding down their crop yields, and this was a problem that more intensive rotations may often have exacerbated. To some extent shortage of animal manure could be compensated for by the use of other substances which were either complementary or alternatives, and from the second half of the sixteenth century onwards it is clear that those farmers who could afford to do so were devoting much greater attention than before to obtaining them. They were paying considerable sums for the extraction, carting and application of whatever natural substances happened to be locally available, particularly marl, chalk or calcareous sand, all of which neutralize soil acidity and therefore made whatever manure had been applied more effective. If none of these were to be had, or if they were thought to be insufficient or inappropriate, farmers were buying processed substances, either ones specifically intended for agricultural purposes such as lime, the production of which was greatly increased after about 1560, or organic waste products from towns, agricultural processing industries or manufacturing, such as stable manure, street refuse, malt dust, soap ashes and pulverized iron slag (Kerridge, 1967, ch. v. Havinden, 1974). These practices probably had their greatest effects upon productivity in districts of naturally low fertility, especially where old common pasture, park and woodland were being ploughed up for arable, but everywhere they raised crop yields, and before the end of the seventeenth century even permanent pasture was receiving similar treatment, at least in the South Midlands (Yelling, 1977, p. 187. Broad, 1980).

During most of the period down to the mid seventeenth century relative prices tended to encourage farmers to increase their grain production rather than their output of livestock products. However there were periodic interludes when the prices of animal products were relatively more favourable, for instance from the mid 1560s to the early 1580s, and again for most of the first two decades of the seventeenth century, and these gave farmers, particularly those for whom the costs of growing cereals or of transporting them to market were relatively high, a considerable incentive to expand the livestock side of their enterprise at the expense of grain production (*A.H.E.W.* IV, 1967, pp. 634–41). It is unlikely to be coincidence, therefore, that of the first two technical advances which began to make this possible, convertible husbandry and floated water-meadows, the one seems to have begun to gain ground in the first of these two periods and the other in the second of them.

Convertible husbandry, ley farming or up-and-down husbandry, as the practice was variously known, was a plan of farm management whereby, instead of land being kept either in tillage with periodic fallows or as permanent pasture, it was kept under crops for a few years, then laid down to grass for a few years, then ploughed up again for crops, and so on. The alternation itself improved the quality and thus the productivity of both ploughland and grassland, but more than this it remedied the arable farmer's pasture shortage and enabled him to keep more livestock. As a result he had a more ample supply of manure for that part of his holding which was to bear crops, so that an increase in yields would in considerable part counter-balance the reduction in sown acreage which resulted from turning the other part into temporary pasture. He thus achieved a larger total output and one more evenly balanced between grain and animal products. He also had a much more flexible undertaking, for he was able to shift the emphasis of his production from one to the other as price conditions might dictate. Convertible husbandry was thus not only important for the contribution it made towards increasing the productivity of English agriculture, but also because it was a major step in the process whereby the latter made itself more responsive to the demands of the market.

In the early sixteenth century the practice seems to have been a local peculiarity of the farming system of limited parts of the Midlands, the south western peninsula and the North, but after about 1560 it apparently began to spread outside its original homelands. It was first introduced on holdings already enclosed, and newly enclosed land which in the earlier part of the century might have been converted to permanent pasture was instead increasingly being farmed in this way. This provided considerable encouragement for enclosure, but it also took much of the heat out of the enclosure issue, since almost as many labourers as before were required and the process ceased to be synonymous with depopulation. In unenclosed villages the adoption of convertible husbandry posed greater difficulties. It is true that, provided the necessary communal agreement was forthcoming, it was perfectly feasible to place temporary fences around certain groups of strips, or even complete furlongs, and lay them down to grass, and in some districts this had long been the practice. In Leicestershire, for instance, it has been estimated that by 1600 one fifth to one sixth of an open field farmer's acreage was likely to be under grass in this way, and the proportion increased with the passage of time. In practice, however, it seems to have been unusual for arable and grass to have been systematically alternated in the open fields (Hoskins, 1963. Kerridge, 1967, pp. 107–8). Moreover, the evidence for the extent of the spread of convertible husbandry, even in enclosed districts, is ambiguous. Mr Kerridge believes that it spread very widely indeed, that by 1660 it had been adopted on half the farmland in the Midlands and on a good proportion of the remainder by 1700, and that in many other areas its advance was scarcely less rapid or its victory less complete. On the other hand some others have been sceptical about these claims and consider that Mr Kerridge has probably exaggerated the speed and completeness with which the practice was adopted, especially outside the Midlands, and certainly it seems to have been still unknown in many areas where it would have been suitable, even in the later eighteenth century (Kerridge, 1967, pp. 194, 212–21. Mingay, 1969 (1 and 2)).

There is less disagreement concerning floated water-meadows which were certainly more or less confined to those areas where physical conditions favoured their construction, and which were never of importance elsewhere. The process of 'floating' involved the construction of an elaborate irrigation system of channels, drains and sluices, which made it possible to divert the flow of a stream onto the meadow and to cover the whole surface with a thin sheet of flowing water. They were expensive to construct, but enormously beneficial to the farmer for the land was protected from winter frost, fertilized by deposited silt and adequately watered in summer. The grass started to grow much sooner than under natural conditions, thus providing animal feed very early in the year, and gave much heavier, as well as more numerous, hay crops during the summer. Water-meadows, therefore, like convertible husbandry, greatly increased a farm's capacity to support livestock, which in turn meant higher yields on arable land. Some forms of controlled flooding of riverside meadows had been practised at least since the fourteenth century, but fully fledged 'floating' appeared first in Herefordshire just before the end of the sixteenth century. It then spread to the valleys of the chalk downlands of southern England in the early part of the seventeenth, or possibly was developed there independently. By the 1620s water-meadows were well established, though not yet numerous, and thereafter spread more rapidly so that well before the end of the period they had become a familiar and essential feature of husbandry along the southern half of the Welsh border, and throughout much of Dorset, Wiltshire and Hampshire. And as they spread, so the size of the local sheep flocks increased, to such a degree indeed that early eighteenth century observers like Defoe were openly astonished. Most of the water-meadows were financed by landlords for the tenant of a large farm or a group of such tenants, or by gentry farming their own land, but in some cases common meadows were floated through the initiative of leading villagers, and the money for construction and subsequent maintenance came mainly from a group of prosperous yeomen through the levying of a rate on the lands of all those who stood to benefit. In view of the fact that they involved even greater capital outlays than enclosure, often costing several pounds per acre so that any given scheme could run to some hundreds of pounds, the relative speed of their adoption, especially in the middle decades of the seventeenth century, is impressive testimony of the ability of commercialized agriculture by that stage to raise the capital needed for even the most expensive improvements (Kerridge, 1967, ch. VI. Bettey, 1973; 1977 (1)).

Both convertible husbandry and water-meadows were apparently indigenous innovations which owed nothing to foreign practices, even though the former had long been known in parts of the Low Countries. It is not so clear, however, whether the same can be said for the range of new fodder crops which began to gain ground soon after the middle of the seventeenth century. All the plants involved were native to England or already naturalized, but there is a strong likelihood that the example of Flemish protestant refugees settled in eastern England, and the lessons learnt abroad, especially in the Netherlands, by royalist emigrés such as Sir Richard Weston in the 1640s and 1650s, provided the initial inspiration for their adoption as field crops. Certainly there was a considerable import of seeds from Holland in the early days of their use. However the economic stimulus for their subsequent spread was the same as that which lay behind the earlier set of technical advances: that is the need for farmers pursuing a mixed husbandry to increase their capacity to carry livestock at a time when grain prices were unfavourable to them as producers.

After the middle of the century, indeed, there was a period of agricultural depression much longer, much more severe and widely felt, than anything which had been experienced over the previous 150 years. Prices moved in such a way that the profits to be made from grain farming were almost continuously under pressure for the rest of the period, and over several decades the economic climate imparted a persistent bias towards livestock husbandry, even though for part of the time, in the later 1670s and 1680s, the prices of animal products too, or at any rate the profits to be made from them, were depressed. The impetus given to improved methods was correspondingly powerful, and there is no doubt that there was a distinct acceleration of the rate at which technical progress was occurring as this second wave of innovation began to spread across the countryside, well before the first had spent its impetus. But quite independently of the economic context, and reflecting the general increase in scientific curiosity, innovation was clearly in the air by the middle decades of the century. Growing numbers of both estate owners and large scale farmers were taking an informed and intelligent interest in new agricultural methods, sometimes seemingly as much for their own sake as for their immediate financial possibilities. News of experiments, successful and unsuccessful, circulated by means of private correspondence, especially among the extensive contacts of the lively minded publicist Samuel Hartlib, and the decision of the newly founded Royal Society to commission reports on English farming on a county by county basis indicates the very genuine interest in agricultural practice exhibited by the country's intelligentsia. An indication that this interest extended more widely throughout society was the greatly increased volume of agricultural literature which was published in the mid and later seventeenth century, for it would not have been produced had there not been a ready market for it. Works by writers like Blith, Yarranton, Worlidge and Hartlib himself, provided theoretical instruction in the new methods, and certainly contributed to their dissemination, although it is difficult to say how much (*A.H.E.W.* v, Part ii, 1984, pp. 542–66).

Shortage of winter feed for sheep and cattle was an inevitable concomitant of a shortage of pasture, and post-medieval farmers had for some time felt the need for additions to the very limited range of fodder crops available to them.[17] Thus some carrots had been grown for this purpose in the sandy parts of East Anglia since the latter part of the sixteenth century, but they needed soil conditions not widely met with elsewhere and their use never became common in other parts of the country. Not until turnips, hitherto grown commercially only by market gardeners, were introduced as a field crop in Norfolk and Suffolk in the 1650s, did farmers discover a root suitable for cultivation under a wider variety of conditions. From the mid 1660s onwards turnips quickly spread throughout East Anglia, and then to many other areas, so that by the end of the century they had appeared almost everywhere that the light well drained soils they required were to be found. Meanwhile other new forms of animal feed were also making headway. Sixteenth century pasturage, whether permanent or temporary, seems to have been simply a natural growth of grass and weeds, of relatively low nutritional value to livestock. Systematic attempts to improve its quality apparently began around the turn of the sixteenth and seventeenth centuries, especially by seeding the land with hay dust instead of allowing nature to take its course. The resultant sward was an improvement on what had gone before, but it still consisted of a very wide variety of plant species, some of

[17] Oats, peas, beans and vetches were the principal fodder crops of the later Middle Ages and the sixteenth century. In some places other types of grain, particularly barley, were grown partly for human consumption and partly to feed to stock.

a much higher nutritional value than others. However the particular usefulness of the various forms of clover, sainfoin, trefoil and rye-grass, which grew spontaneously over much of the country, had long been recognized, and at much the same time as turnips were introduced to the fields, the practice grew up, perhaps independently in a number of districts widely scattered throughout the southern and eastern third of the country, of cultivating them selectively or in proportioned mixtures. Sainfoin appeared first in the Cotswolds, clover first in the Weald, and by 1700 one or other of the 'artificial' grasses, as they are commonly called, was established in almost all districts of light soil save those of the far North (Kerridge, 1967, ch. VII. Overton, 1977; 1979. Lane, 1980).

The greatest advantage of turnips was that they provided a nutritious feed for animals during the winter months when grass stopped growing, and thereby freed farmers from the limit which the size of their hay crop had placed on the scale of their livestock husbandry. They were most appropriately grown as a hitch crop on land that would formerly have been left fallow so that their cultivation did not have to be at the expense of anything else, and the increased quantity of manure available from the additional livestock that could now be kept compensated the ground for the loss of its rest. The hoeing which turnips required was also beneficial since it cleared the land of weeds for the following year's crop of grain. As for the 'artificial' grasses, not only were they more nutritious than the natural mixtures they replaced, but it was quickly observed that they actually enhanced the fertility of the land on which they were grown because, as nineteenth century scientists were to discover, their roots had the property of fixing nitrogen in the soil. Of course the precise way in which these new crops were used depended on the farming system of the locality, but a whole series of new arable rotations were developed in order to incorporate them, as a result of which the frequency of fallowing was considerably reduced, although the practice could not yet be altogether dispensed with.[18] Nevertheless this partial elimination of bare fallows was in itself an important step towards a more intensive use of land. Meanwhile, where convertible husbandry was practised leys of natural grass came to be replaced by leys of clover, sainfoin or whatever was locally appropriate, and in some places it seems that the availability of the new grasses provided the stimulus for convertible husbandry to be adopted for the first time (Kerridge, 1967, chs. VII–VIII). Everywhere the new fodder crops were adopted farmers were able to keep much larger inventories of livestock, and as a secondary result secured higher yields from their arable. Thus it was said of farmers in Monmouthshire in the

---

[18] In many areas a fallow year continued to be the essential preparation for the principal grain crop of wheat or barley.

1690s that those who had 'fallen into the vein of clover, and . . . which kept no kine before now keep some 12, some 20 . . .' Similarly on the rich loams of North Kent, a region of large farms much of whose produce went to supply the London market, a combination of convertible husbandry and artificial grasses permitted an increase in the size of the typical farmer's herd of cattle from six in the period 1600–20 to over thirteen by the end of the century (John, 1965. Chalklin, 1965, pp. 96–7).

There is no doubt about the importance of the new crops, and it is no exaggeration to say that they represented the greatest single source of increased productivity that English agriculture experienced before modern times. Nevertheless the extent to which the benefits arising from them had been realized before the eighteenth century is a matter of some controversy. Again it is Mr Kerridge who has argued the case for their widespread adoption within a relatively short period after they first appeared, asserting that their diffusion was largely complete no later than about 1750. Other historians, however, do not believe that the facts will bear this interpretation (Kerridge, 1967, pp. 339–42; 1969 (2). Mingay, 1969 (1) and (2)). It appears to be certain that a minority of the more progressive farmers in most parts of the country where their cultivation was practicable had adopted turnips, clover and the other artificial grasses by 1700, although the latest research suggests that the acreages sown remained very small on most farms. But equally it seems that their use was not common amongst small producers until very much later; and certainly there is abundant evidence for the backward nature of the farming methods of the peasantry, especially in open field districts, as late as the third quarter of the eighteenth century (Overton, 1977. Morgan, 1978, ch. III). One way and another it seems probable that, outside East Anglia, the innovations we have just discussed had had only a limited impact by 1700.

This was not, however, as was once believed, because the open fields as such were an obstacle to the adoption of the new methods of husbandry. It was certainly easier for farmers whose fields were enclosed, and whose freedom of action was not limited by communal regulations, to make changes in their methods, for they had no one to consult but themselves, and all the advances seem to have been made first in areas where enclosure was already largely complete by the seventeenth century. Suffolk and Norfolk, the site of the first experiments with root crops, provide the most obvious illustration of this. However, open field communities could and did make such alterations to their field course, and even to the physical lay-out of their fields, for instance by subdividing them to create a larger number so that a more elaborate field course could be introduced, as was necessary for the incorporation of the new crops into their farming systems. In some places indeed, especially where some sub-division of the open fields, rather than the fields themselves, were the cropping units, arrangements were already sufficiently flexible, without the need for reorganization. It has been shown, for instance, that as early as the 1670s sainfoin was being grown in open fields in Oxfordshire (Havinden, 1961). Yet there is no doubt that where open fields prevailed the need for communal agreements did retard the pace of change. It is probable that agreements were most easily obtained in villages dominated by relatively few big farmers, and that where the land was held by a larger number of petty peasants the old ways continued unmodified until long after 1700. The small man could not afford to buy the extra stock which fodder crops would make it possible for his land to carry, and so, whether he farmed open strips or enclosed fields, the new systems could not be for him.

Finally it must be remembered that the new crops were much more appropriate to some types of soil than to others. It was farmers on the light and medium soils who could take advantage of them most successfully, and the greatest benefits accrued to those on the chalk and limestone uplands which it had previously been impossible to use for crops, and which had hitherto remained as grazing for sheep. The much larger sheep flocks which the fodder crops made it possible to support meant that sufficient manure became available to maintain the fertility of a much larger acreage of arable than before, and in consequence huge expanses of sheep-walk were put under the plough for the first time. (See above pp. 110–11.) On the other hand there were districts, especially in the Midlands and low-lying parts elsewhere, where heavy ill drained clays made the cultivation of turnips quite impossible and greatly restricted the use that could be made of artificial grasses. Indeed not until the introduction of cheap and effective techniques of under-drainage in the mid nineteenth century could the new crops be successfully introduced to these parts of the country. The reaction of farmers in the clay vales to unfavourable grain prices in the later seventeenth century was thus inevitably different. Where they had the necessary freedom of action they enclosed and converted their land to pasture: according to one estimate one quarter of the area of Leicestershire was enclosed during the seventeenth century, or according to another more than half between 1607 and 1730. Generally it would seem this was conversion to permanent pasture rather than to the temporary grass of convertible husbandry, for even with the help of the latter they could not produce grain cheaply enough to compete with the producers on the light soils.[19]

---

[19] Consequently there was even a movement away from convertible husbandry to permanent pasture in parts of the Midlands after *c.* 1650 (Broad, 1980).

They therefore came to concentrate almost exclusively on either the fattening of livestock or upon dairying. Where enclosure was not possible heavy soil farmers did the next best thing and increased the proportion of grass leys in the open fields. To quote the case of Leicestershire once again, by the end of the seventeenth century such leys frequently covered up to a quarter or even a third of the acreage of unenclosed villages. Meanwhile similar developments took place in other Midland counties, notably in large parts of Northamptonshire, Bedfordshire and Buckinghamshire (*V.C.H. Leics* II, 1954, pp. 204, 223. Thirsk, 1970. Hoskins, 1963. Broad, 1980).

The most far-reaching technical innovations in agriculture in the period before 1700 were primarily concerned with strengthening the livestock side of the mixed farming systems of the lowland zone, although they had a secondary impact on the productivity of arable land as well. There were, however, others which affected the latter directly. Perhaps the most important was the introduction of improved crop strains, which were either more resistant to disease, or ripened earlier, or gave a higher return on the amount of seed sown. The timing and extent of such introductions is unfortunately obscure, for by their nature they tend to leave little trace in the records, but the seventeenth century certainly saw superior types of wheat, barley and peas making headway in several distinct areas. There were also gradual improvements to routine husbandry practices, better preparation of the seed-bed, better methods of seeding, and the like, whose cumulative importance may have been great (*A.H.E.W.* IV, 1967, pp. 168–73. Yelling, 1977, pp. 172–3).

More fully documented is the steadily widening range of new crops, over and above those used as animal fodder, which entered the farmers' repertoire, again mainly in the seventeenth century. Even before the end of the sixteenth some of those with ready access to urban markets, especially in the environs of London and along the Thames valley, were coming to specialize in the commercial production of fruit and vegetables, and a hundred years later their numbers and the areas where they were found had greatly increased: in Kent, for instance, by 1700 fruit growing had spread into virtually all parts of the county where it was later to be found. Hops too had been grown before 1600, having been first introduced from the Continent in the fifteenth century, but they did not make much progress until after that date when their cultivation became increasingly widespread in Kent, elsewhere in the South East and in Herefordshire. Tobacco was, of course, American in origin, but was probably introduced by way of Holland. It proved well suited to English conditions and spread rapidly after about 1620, especially in Gloucestershire and Worcestershire, and there is little doubt that the kingdom would have become a major producer had not successive governments persisted in a determination to suppress it in the interests of trade with the colonies, and eventually succeeded in doing so, although not until the last quarter of the century. There was also considerable expansion in the cultivation of a series of other industrial crops, some quite new, others old established but hitherto grown only in very restricted localities and in small quantities. Cole-seed, which produced an oil used for illumination and in the manufacture of soap, was gaining ground in the Fens and elsewhere in eastern England from the 1590s onwards. Flax and hemp provided the fibres from which linen and canvas, rope and netting were manufactured. Woad and weld were both dyes used in the cloth industry, so was madder which was introduced from the Netherlands in about 1630. Teasels were also used in cloth making, for raising the nap of the finished product, whilst liquorice and saffron were chiefly in demand for medicinal purposes (*A.H.E.W.* IV, 1967, pp. 173–7, 195–7. Thirsk, 1970; 1974. Chalklin, 1965, pp. 88–95). Even by the end of the seventeenth century none of these crops were being grown on a really large scale, and most of them remained more or less local in their distribution, but taken together they had come to form a significant part of agricultural output, for in 1695 Gregory King reckoned that one million acres were devoted to them out of the 11 million acres which he estimated were used as arable (Thirsk and Cooper, 1972, p. 782).

Clearly the spread of the many new crops discussed in the previous paragraph was another aspect of the reaction of farmers to the relatively unfavourable grain prices which prevailed during much of the seventeenth century, for all of them, except flax and hemp, tended to be found in the corn growing areas. However, price incentives do not seem to have been the only factor involved. The other was apparently under-employment in the countryside, for without exception the methods of cultivation required by the crops under discussion were highly labour intensive. Plentiful supplies of labour were in fact important to most of the agricultural innovations of the period, especially when the partial elimination of bare fallows increased the acreage in productive use and thus the number of permanent workers a farm required, whilst higher harvest yields meant that more hands were needed to gather in, and turnip culture in particular created a new peak period of demand for labour in March. But not even the turnip was as demanding of labour as market gardening or the various industrial crops, and these tended to be grown either by big farmers in places where there were large populations of cottagers who could be employed by them, or where peasant smallholders remained numerous. Some of the industrial crops, notably hops and the various dyes, required considerable capital outlay and so were always a monopoly of the more substantial farmers, but others did not and were very much poor men's crops, particularly vegetables, tobacco, flax and hemp. The absorption of hitherto unemployed labour of course implies an increase in productivity per head of the agricultural population, and the increase in productivity per acre is indicated by the rates of profit which all these crops were capable of yielding (Thirsk, 1970). These were much higher than were obtainable from conventional husbandry and seem often to have reached £20–£30 an acre, and in ideal conditions some growers made even more from vegetables, hops and tobacco. By comparison mixed farming on average soils was unlikely to return a profit in excess of £1 per acre.

vi Agriculture and the evolution of the English economy

The extent of the improvements in agricultural productivity which had come about by the end of our period cannot be precisely measured, but were undoubtedly substantial. Mr Kerridge believes that by the seventeenth century even relatively unenlightened farmers were able to get yields twice as good as those which had been obtainable in the later Middle Ages, and that the most progressive got four times the medieval yields from both their corn land and their grass land, whilst the total improvement on the best managed lands was greater still, five times or more, because of the introduction of crops in place of bare fallows in many arable rotations (Kerridge, 1967, pp. 330–1). The significance of these assumptions depends very much on how widely disseminated the technical improvements had become by 1700, i.e. how large a proportion of farm land was being managed in such a way as to secure a four or five fold increase over the yields of *c.* 1500, and we have seen that this is uncertain and controversial. It is also thought by many that the assumptions themselves are unduly optimistic. There were still farmers in early seventeenth century Gloucestershire, and no doubt in many other places, whose yield : seed ratios were so low (4 : 1) that they can have improved little in the preceding 100 or 150 years (Slicher Van Bath, 1963 (1), p. 47), and on the other hand there seems to be a lack of documentary evidence of the very high ratios which Mr Kerridge believes farmers using the most advanced methods ought to have been able to obtain. In view of the likelihood that only a very small proportion of farmers had fully absorbed the new methods by 1700 it seems safer to assume that, taking the country as a whole, arable yields had not much more than doubled since the end of the Middle Ages. As far as wheat is concerned evidence from Norfolk and Suffolk suggests average yields of 14–16 bushels per acre in the later seventeenth century, and although methods may have been untypically advanced in East Anglia there was a preponderance of naturally low yielding light soils in the region.[20] We are hardly in a position to speak of national averages, but it may be that wheat yields of this order were as common as those of 8–9 bushels had been in the fifteenth century. This would suggest an improvement of roughly 75 per cent, but it is likely that the yields of barley and oats, whose combined acreage certainly greatly exceeded that of wheat, increased by a larger proportion (Overton, 1979. Yelling, 1977, p. 204).

If productivity per acre of sown arable roughly doubled between 1500 and 1700, and the cultivated acreage increased by about a quarter, then assuming, without much evidence either way, that the pastoral side of farming experienced comparable improvement, one might suppose the increase in agricultural output to have been approximately 150 per cent. However one would have to take account of the fact that the fertility of land which was not taken into continuous cultivation until as late as the sixteenth or seventeenth centuries was often of below average quality, although this was not true of drained fenland, and that it had not been entirely unproductive hitherto. On the other hand an allowance would have to be made for the more intensive use of land: for instance the change from two field to three field systems, the introduction of fallow crops, and the more complete stocking of what had formerly been under-utilized pasturage in the remoter regions of the highland zone. Taking these other considerations into account it would be a reasonable guess that total agricultural production had risen by something more than two and a half times,[21] which seems to be consistent with the growth of population, the import and export trade in agricultural produce, and what is believed to have happened to industrial output and living standards. The chronology of this increase must inevitably remain a matter of speculation, but since it is now apparent that at around $5\frac{1}{4}$ million the population was as high or higher in the 1650s than it was to be in 1700, and since with the disappearance of subsistence crises in the first half of the seventeenth century the country was nevertheless able to feed all these people, it seems that a large part of it must have already taken place by about 1660.

The assumption that the output of grain and livestock products increased in roughly the same proportions over the period as a whole is not an unreasonable one, although it is perhaps more likely that in fact that of

---

[20] The application of new methods on light soils produced the greatest increases in yields, but these often remained absolutely higher on heavier, richer soils even though the techniques applied to them remained fundamentally unchanged (Yelling, 1977, p. 172).

[21] A much lower figure for the increase in agricultural output has been put forward by E.L. Jones, but this is based on the extent of population growth alone and must be a serious underestimate since he assumes the unrealistically *high* population figure of 3 million for the year 1500 (Floud and McCloskey, 1981, 1, p. 68).

the former increased by rather more than the latter. Certainly the production of the two groups of commodities did not grow at the same rate in all parts of the period. Between 1550 and 1620 or even 1650, for instance, the grain crop must have expanded faster than did the output of the pastoral side of farming. Moreover the composition of that grain crop was altering. Rye was gradually losing its place on English farms in favour of wheat, but also in some parts of the country, the West Midlands for instance, there seems to have been a reduced emphasis upon the autumn sown grains in general,[22] matched by a corresponding increase in the acreage of spring sown oats and barley. This was a change that rendered cereal production less vulnerable to severe winter weather, and must therefore have helped to make year to year fluctuations in the total quantity of food grains available less violent than before, with important implications for the ability of the poorest to feed themselves in bad years (Appleby, 1979). During the mid and later seventeenth century the spread of innovations which strengthened the livestock side of mixed husbandry must have meant that the output of fodder crops and animal products had risen proportionately more than that of grains for human consumption. Certainly in 1695 Gregory King reckoned that the annual value of animal products, and the hay consumed in their production, was £12 million, which was clearly greater than the £10 million at which he valued grains of all sorts. Moreover, as we have already seen, there was also by this time a considerable output of industrial crops, few of which had been grown on any scale before 1600, let alone 1500, and some of which had not been grown at all. The value of these King put at £1 million a year, whilst fruit and vegetables were worth a further £1,200,000, so that between them they accounted for 9 per cent of total agricultural output (Thirsk and Cooper, 1972, pp. 782–3. Thirsk, 1978, p. 177). The increased variety of agricultural production in this period was thus almost as striking as the increase in volume, and scarcely less important to the economy.

In an economy so heavily dependent on agriculture as that of England in the sixteenth and seventeenth centuries the performance of the farming sector was bound to be of crucial importance to the well-being of society as a whole. In the short run this is seen most dramatically in the influence of the harvests, whilst in the long the ability or inability of the economy to generate growth was largely determined by the success or failure of agriculture. England never ceased to be able to feed her own people in normal years at any time during these two centuries, but it is nevertheless clear that between the 1520s and the middle of the seventeenth century the production of agricultural goods in general, and

[22] That is wheat and rye.

in particular that of essential food-stuffs, did not quite keep up with the growth in demand caused by a rising population, so that their prices rose very steeply, outstripping those of non-agricultural items. The results of this were a redistribution of real income in favour of producers and at the expense of consumers, and a change in the terms of trade between agriculture and industry in favour of the former. The first of these developments is seen in its most extreme form in the fall in the purchasing power of the wages of urban labourers, which by the early seventeenth century was down to only two fifths of its late fifteenth century level. (See below pp. 217–8.) The living standards of other social groups, such as rural labourers who did not need to purchase all their own food, but were able to produce part of it for themselves, or those who were better off and therefore did not spend so large a proportion of their income on those basic essentials which had risen furthest in price, were certainly affected much less seriously.[23] The industrial sector of the economy not only suffered from the increased price of many of its raw materials, but also from the fact that the growth of its markets was limited by the falling living standards of large sections of the population.[24] The consequences of the failure of agriculture to expand sufficiently to meet demand in full were thus prosperity for landowners and commercial farmers, irrespective of their efficiency, mainly at the expense of the landless poor of town and country, and to some extent also at the expense of the better off members of urban society as well. Secondly the development of industry was held back, thereby limiting the growth of non-agricultural employment which might otherwise have absorbed more than it did of the surplus labour which the growth of population was creating: the continuance of a labour surplus in turn accentuated the poverty of the non-landholding poor. Down to the early part of the seventeenth century, therefore, it could be said that the English economy was characterized by windfall profits for commercial farming, restricted development in other branches of the economy, and the impoverishment of the masses.

During the course of the seventeenth century these conditions gradually changed. Two distinct though probably related occurrences, the ending of the long upsurge in the population, and substantial improvements in agricultural productivity as a result of technical advances,[25] meant that after the middle decades agricultural production

---

[23] Indeed if they had sufficiently buoyant incomes these groups did not necessarily experience any drop in their standard of living at all, but all the same rapidly rising farm prices diverted part of the real value of their increased incomes to agricultural producers.

[24] For a fuller discussion of this issue, see below II, pp. 28–9.

[25] They were related because, as we have seen, the pressure on farm profits, which was so largely responsible for the willingness of farmers to innovate, was a result of the unfavourable price trends

was growing more rapidly than demand. The consequences of this new situation were to be immensely important for the future, and although they were only just beginning to work out by 1700, they were already becoming apparent. Prices, especially grain prices, began to fall. The easy, almost unearned prosperity of commercial farming passed away: good profits were now only to be had by the improving and the efficient. This led to yet further advanced in productivity as the progressive methods were adopted more and more widely, and so the downward trend of prices was reinforced. The terms of trade between the agricultural and non-agricultural sectors of the economy began to move in favour of the latter. Cheaper raw materials enabled industrialists to keep their costs down, but even more important was the fact that some of the real income which the poorer groups in the community had lost was being restored to them as cheaper food-stuffs ensured that money wages went further, and that any increase meant a real addition to their purchasing power. Effective demand for things other than basic food-stuffs was thus increased. Partly this benefited animal farming, since consumption of meat and dairy products per head clearly rose, and that branch of agriculture retained a greater degree of prosperity than did grain growing. But it also benefited rural and urban manufacturers, and the seventeenth century, especially the latter part of it, and even more the early eighteenth century, witnessed a continuous, if unspectacular, growth of industrial production and a diversification of its forms. In consequence there was an increase in industrial employment which provided work and incomes for many who would otherwise have been idle and poor, and a growing demand for labour at a time of little population growth led to some increases in wages. The agricultural factor was, as we shall see, not the only one in the expansion of the domestic market, nor was it only the domestic market which accounted for the growth of manufacturing since the expansion of the export trade also played its part. There is no doubt, however, that the growth of internal purchasing power, by the mechanism just discussed, was a principal factor in the industrial expansion of the second half of the period. (See also below II, p. 31.) Certainly by the end of our period prosperity was much more widely diffused than it had been before 1650, and it is possible for the historian to see in retrospect that a process had begun which, continued into the eighteenth century, was to carry the country to the threshold of an Industrial Revolution (John 1961; 1965).[26]

of most agricultural commodities, and this in turn was in large measure a reflection of demographic movements.

[26] Professor John's arguments refer to the first half of the eighteenth century, but the trends he is concerned to establish had their origins in the later decades of the seventeenth.

5

THE LANDLORDS

i Introduction

One of the most important characteristics of English rural society at the end of the Middle Ages was that the great majority of peasant cultivators did not own the land they occupied, but held it as tenants of a landlord. Their economic experience has now been fully discussed, and the present chapter will be devoted to that of the owners of the soil. If we begin by considering the social distribution of landed property at the beginning of the period, the first point to make is that a large part of it, at least a quarter and possibly approaching one third, was in institutional ownership in the hands of the Church and the crown. The estates of the latter had been greatly increased by Henry VII's seizure of the properties of many of his political opponents, but even so those of the Church, that is of numerous monasteries, bishoprics, cathedrals and collegiate churches, as well as minor institutions like hospitals and chantries, were very much the larger of the two.[1] Small owners below the standing of gentry probably owned no more than one fifth, whilst the remainder, some 40–45 per cent, was seemingly in the hands of the gentry and aristocracy (Table v).

The composition of the last of these three groups was continuously changing, as it always had been, mainly because in an age of relatively high death rates and low expectation of life, families were constantly dying out in the male line so that their property passed by means of marriage and inheritance to others. By a continuous process estates were being amalgamated with each other, or split up into smaller units, and in each generation new landed dynasties were constantly coming into being, at all levels of wealth, to replace the old. Buying and selling of land in the later Middle Ages there certainly was, but there seems to have been more of it at the level of the smallholders and working farmers than of the estate owners, and there appears to have been insufficient land on the market

[1] The landed income of the crown in the years 1502–5 has been estimated at c. £40,000 a year; that of the Church in 1535, when values had not yet risen sufficiently to make a comparison invalid, was something over £320,000 a year (Wolffe, 1971, pp. 219–20. Hoskins, 1976, p. 121).

Table v *Distribution of landownership in England: percentages of cultivated land owned*

		Mid 15th century (1436)	Late 17th century (1688)
Aristocracy and gentry {	Great magnates	15–20	15–20
	Middling and lesser gentry	25	45–50
Yeomen, family farmers and other small owners		20	25–33
Church } Crown }		25–35	5–10

Sources: Mingay, 1976, p. 59. Cooper, 1967.

either for established proprietors greatly to enlarge their estates by means of purchase, or for more than a trickle of outsiders to buy their way into the gentry.

As a result of the way in which they came into existence there was no uniformity to the size and shape of estates. Small ones often consisted of one or two substantial farms lying adjacent to one another and a few cottage properties where the necessary labourers lived, but they might equally well take the form of a cluster or a scattering of small and medium sized holdings. At a somewhat higher level, that of the middling gentry, they might consist of a couple of manors in the same or neighbouring villages, or at the other extreme, like that of the Furse family of Morshead (Devon) in 1627, of one central block of lands with numerous outlying parcels, some very small, in no less than nineteen different parishes up to thirty miles distant (Hoskins, 1952). As for the estates of the larger owners, they were rarely compact or even confined to a single geographical area, and those of the very largest were always exceedingly heterogeneous in composition since they invariably represented a combination of the properties of several families brought together by the accidents of inheritance. Thus the Stanley Earls of Derby and the Manners Earls of Rutland, two of the greatest territorial magnates of the sixteenth century, had acquired their huge possessions mainly in this way, whilst in the middle part of the period two separate branches of the Cavendish family rose to the Earldoms of Devonshire and Newcastle respectively almost entirely by the same route (Stone, 1965, pp. 192–4).

The lesser and even the middling gentry usually cultivated much, sometimes almost the whole, of their estates themselves, and so derived their income primarily or entirely from the sale of agricultural products. The larger estates, however, were essentially units of ownership and not of economic activity. A home farm was normally kept in hand to supply the owner's household with food-stuffs, and sometimes, especially in the sixteenth century, the lands of a few other manors were reserved for keeping sheep, for rearing or fattening cattle or breeding horses, according to district. In Norfolk, for instance, Sir Nicholas Bacon had perhaps 4000 sheep in six distinct flocks in the 1550s, whilst other magnates such as the Fermours and Townshends seemingly had as many as 10,000–20,000. There is, however, no parallel in this period to the large scale commercial arable farming enterprises carried on by many of the landed magnates, especially the ecclesiastical ones, of the thirteenth and fourteenth centuries, who often retained most of their manorial demesnes in hand and exploited them in this way. By far the largest part of the area of most great estates, even in the sixteenth century, was let out to tenants, and the estate owners derived the bulk of their income from the rents and fines paid by the latter. By the early seventeenth century even the pastoral farming activities of the great landowners were being curtailed, presumably because the intense demand for land and rapidly rising rents made it more profitable to let, and well before 1700 almost all of them were rentiers pure and simple (Simpson, 1961, pp. 64–5. Stone, 1965, pp. 296–303). A minority, however, always derived part of their income from sources other than agricultural land, a very few from the possession of court office or the exploitation of economic concessions, such as monopolies, obtained from the government; more, especially by the latter half of the period, from mining or industrial ventures. (See below II, pp. 70–4.)

ii *The multiplication of the gentry, 1500–1640*

The pattern of landownership outlined at the beginning of the previous section was to undergo a profound change as the period wore on. The single most important factor in bringing this about was the partial dismantling of the enormous estates of the Church and the crown from the 1530s onwards, thus transferring several million acres from institutional to private proprietorship. The Dissolution of the Monasteries, as part of the English break with Rome, involved the acquisition by Henry VIII's government of all the possessions of the 650 or so former religious houses, whilst both Henry himself and his successors also deprived the bishops of an unknown but certainly large proportion of their estates. By the time the plunder of the Church at last ceased in the latter part of

Elizabeth's reign[2] at least two thirds of what it had owned before the Reformation had been seized by the crown. The original intention, back in the 1530s, may well have been for the crown to retain the bulk of what it thus acquired, thereby ensuring a revenue that would have been more than sufficient for all normal purposes, and had such an intention been adhered to the political history of the country might have been very different. In the event, however, the urgency of the royal need for money to finance the war effort of the 1540s led to the adoption of a policy of sales, and already by 1547 two thirds of the monastic estates had been disposed of. In the following reign, that of the boy king Edward VI, not only most of the remaining monastic lands, but also the properties of the chantries and other lesser ecclesiastical institutions, were put onto the market bringing the total amount raised by selling to some £1,260,000 by 1554, whilst yet more, including much episcopal land, was granted away by the great lords who dominated the government, either to reward themselves or to win political support (Youings, 1971, ch. 5. Hoskins, 1976, ch. 6. Jordan, 1968, pp. 103–24).

By this stage few of the windfall gains the Reformation had brought to the royal patrimony remained unalienated, and when financial crises, again brought about by involvement in war, obliged Elizabeth to sell yet more property, first in the early 1560s and then again on several occasions after 1589, it was not only confiscated land but also the hereditary estates of the crown which had to go. Her Stuart successors continued the selling, and on a much larger scale, as their ministers wrestled with the financial problems caused by the impact of inflation upon inelastic sources of revenue, compounded by James I's extravagance, an expensive foreign policy in the 1620s, and the eventual breakdown in the relations between crown and parliament. By 1640, therefore, the landed property of the crown had been largely whittled away. Most of the ancient royal forests remained, though some even of these had been disafforested and sold off, and the sovereign still had a wide selection of palaces and parks to choose from, but of the many hundreds of rent yielding manors and farms which had still belonged to Queen Elizabeth at her accession only a scattered remnant survived. The crown may still have had a considerably larger estate than any single private proprietor, but in the seven counties studied by Professor Tawney, whereas in 1558 it had owned 9.5 per cent of all manors, by 1640 it held only 2 per cent (Stone, 1965, p. 166. Tawney, 1954). The likelihood is, therefore, that not less than one fifth and possibly nearer to one quarter of all English

---

[2] The spoliation of the church estates was halted, but not to any great extent reversed, during the reign of Queen Mary (1553–8).

land passed into private hands in this way. What remained to the Church and crown was finally appropriated and sold by the victorious parliamentarians after the Civil War, but these sales were revoked in 1660 and therefore left no permanent mark on the structure of landed society.

In the mid sixteenth century, when the monastic lands were being dispersed, some very large agglomerations of property were created mainly from this source by government officials and courtiers, certain of whom obtained much of it on very advantageous terms. Thus the great assemblage of manors acquired by Sir John Russell in Devonshire, Sir William Herbert in South Wales and Wiltshire, and Sir William Paulet in Hampshire and elsewhere, raised these individuals and their successors, respectively Earls of Bedford and Pembroke and Marquesses of Winchester, to the status of territorial magnates in a single generation. Even at this period, however, the bulk of the land was sold in relatively small lots at relatively high prices, and the same was certainly true of the sales of the late sixteenth and early seventeenth centuries. In both periods the main buyers were local gentry seizing the opportunity to round out or extend their inherited estates. In no sense did the crown sales call into existence a new class of landowner, and their main importance was thus periodically to increase the supply of land on the market, thereby making it easier for those who wished to buy to find what they wanted. But at no stage, except perhaps briefly in the 1540s, did they dominate the market, and far more property changed hands between private owners than passed from the crown to the latter. There are reasons for thinking that the volume of buying and selling had been growing even before the Dissolution of the Monasteries, and there is ample evidence that it continued to grow through the mid sixteenth century and beyond. It must have received considerable stimulus from the Dissolution, both directly through the need of some existing proprietors to finance their purchases of crown lands by the sale of outlying parts of their estates, and from resales by those who had acquired more than they could afford to hold, and indirectly from the effects such sales had in breaking down traditional prejudices against the sale of land at all unless there was literally no choice (Habakkuk, 1958. Kew, 1970. Outhwaite, 1971. Hoskins, 1976, pp. 136–8, 146–7). Nevertheless the increasingly active estate market of the later sixteenth and early seventeenth centuries was not merely a chain reaction set going by the land sales of the crown. Rather it was an independent development brought about, on the one hand by the increasing tendency of landowners to become enmeshed in financial difficulties which forced them to sell, and on the other by the continuous accumulation of capital, on a much larger scale than ever before, in the hands of those who wished to invest it in land.

It has often been argued, notably by R.H. Tawney who thought that the great magnates were most acutely affected, that the financial problems of the private landowners were mainly caused by the impact of inflation upon insufficiently elastic sources of income. It is said that many of them, their estates encumbered by long leases and customary tenants who could neither be evicted nor obliged to pay a realistic rent, and lacking both businesslike attitudes to estate management and the capital to reorganize and improve, found that they were unable to increase their receipts sufficiently to maintain the real value of their incomes (Tawney, 1941). And indeed for those for whom the maintenance of levels of expenditure appropriate to their inherited position was both a social and a psychological necessity, the result of declining real incomes would inevitably have been eventual ruin. Yet it seems most improbable that a long term decline in their purchasing power can have been the lot of a very large section of the landlord class, for economic forces were working so strongly in favour of those who controlled the supply of land, at least until about 1640, that only the particularly unfortunate or the very incompetent can have found themselves in this position. Many may have experienced limited periods when the real value of their landed incomes was falling, especially in the early stages of the price rise when leases granted before the upward movement in prices was really under way had still to expire, but most of them will have made up or more than made up, for this before it had caused irreparable damage (*A.H.E.W.* IV, 1967, pp. 690–5. Dewar, 1969, pp. 21–2). It was not inflation as such that was the real trouble, but the social pressures which combined to force up the conventional standards of expenditure required at any particular level of landed society well above any increases arising from the higher cost of goods and services.

One of the most serious aspects of this, because it affected a capital liability and one which was potentially liable to recur in each generation, was the rising cost of providing for daughters. Marriage at this level of society was essentially an arrangement to ensure the succession to property, and in return for the settlement of the husband's family estate upon the children which it was hoped would be born, and for a guaranteed financial provision for the wife if she were to be left a widow, the latter's father paid over to the husband, or if he were still alive to his father, a substantial cash portion. Without a portion a girl would not be able to marry at all, which would be a disgrace to the family, and without a portion commensurate with her social standing she would be obliged to marry beneath her, which was also a disgrace, and in so status conscious a society a recipe for marital discord. Younger sons could make their own way in the world, and although few fathers would gratuitously cast them off unprovided for, if the state of the family finances demanded economies these were more likely to be at their expense than at that of their sisters. One reason why marriage portions were becoming a heavier financial burden was that landowners had *more* daughters to marry off than formerly: the demographic trends ensured that more were being born and surviving to marriageable age, whilst after the Reformation the socially acceptable but cheaper alternative to marriage, entrance to a nunnery, was no longer available. Besides, the amount of portion required was rising steeply and, at least after 1600, more steeply than landed incomes.[3] The average offered by landowners in the upper ranks of the peerage, that is earls, marquesses and dukes, rose nearly five fold between the late fifteenth and early seventeenth century, from an average of £750 to £3550, by which time few fathers were getting away with less than one year's income per daughter. By the period 1675–1729 portions at this level in society had more than doubled again to an average of £9350 per daughter! Less grand individuals paid smaller sums, but ones that were probably just as large in relation to their resources. The proportion of a landowner's wealth which had to be devoted to the marriage of daughters was thus increasing, which made it more difficult than ever to meet the liability out of savings, and in practice if it could not be discharged out of the incoming portions obtained by sons when *they* got married,[4] then it often necessitated sale of an outlying portion of the estate. Some families, whose heirs married particularly rich brides, or whose daughters did not survive to marriageable age, undoubtedly did very well out of the portion system, but others who had to find husbands for several daughters in successive generations, and who were unwilling to sacrifice their marriage prospects by economizing on their portions, shouldered a financial liability which was likely to lead to extensive sales and could end in total ruin (Stone, 1965, pp. 637–49, 790. Cooper, 1976, pp. 221–4, 306–12).

Standards were also altering in matters of housing. As internal peace came to be taken for granted under the Tudors, and armed feuding

---

[3] Portions were being forced upwards in real terms, in part because of the large sums offered by lawyers, merchants and other moneyed men who wanted their daughters to marry into the families of the established gentry and were prepared to pay over the odds for the privilege. In part also it was because in time of demographic growth there was a greater rise in the number of girls amongst the landed classes than in the number of heirs to estates, who, because of the custom of primogeniture, were far more desirable husbands than younger sons: this upset the balance of supply and demand in the marriage market (Stone, 1965, pp. 645–9).

[4] Younger sons did not normally inherit any part of their fathers' estate, or if they did it was only a small portion: they were most commonly provided for by being given a lease of some land for their lifetime only, or perhaps a life annuity. This meant that normally they could not expect to marry nearly such wealthy brides as eldest sons, and in practice it was only the latter who could make a really substantial contribution towards meeting the cost of providing for daughters.

between members of landed society ceased to be a feature of English life, it was no longer necessary for the country residences of the rich and powerful to be designed as fortresses capable of resisting attack. This made it possible for their lay-out to be modified with more of an eye for domestic convenience, whilst changes in the way of life of the élite brought with them an increasing concern for personal privacy and material comfort. And so, greatly encouraged by the splendid mansions erected by wealthy new-comers to landed society, of which Sir Thomas Kytson's Hengrave Hall (begun 1530) and Sir John Thynne's Longleat (begun 1546) are famous examples, there was a great wave of country house building. Especially in the later sixteenth and early seventeenth centuries an increasing number of landed families, feeling that their old manor houses and castles were no longer an adequate symbol of their status, either entirely rebuilt or enlarged and remodelled them. And in doing so, and in trying to emulate those with more liquid resources than themselves, some certainly spent more than they could afford. Nevertheless the costs of a new house were not in themselves necessarily, or even very often, inordinate: the enormous sums lavished on a handful of prodigy houses by leading courtiers, such as the £39,000 spent by the Earl of Salisbury on Hatfield between 1607 and 1612, or the even larger sums laid out by the Earl of Suffolk at Audley End, were in no way typical, and most gentlemen were probably successful in financing their building projects out of income (Airs, 1975, chs. 1 and 8. Stone, 1965, pp. 549–55. Stone and Stone, 1972).

What was perhaps more serious than building costs as such was the increasing elaboration with which contemporary taste demanded that houses, whether new or old, be fitted up – with glazed windows, elaborate chimney pieces, plaster-work, wall-hangings, carpets, furniture and the like. The house of a minor country squire like John Langholme of Conisholme in Lincolnshire who died in 1528, might be almost devoid of contents, save for the bare essentials for living, a little plate and some arms and armour (Cornwall, 1974), but a hundred years later things were very different. Life in the English country house was becoming more gracious, but in the process it was becoming more expensive. Nor was it only in the furnishing of their houses that the gentry betrayed their growing appetite for the good things of life. As early as the 1540s there is evidence of upper class demand for luxuries sucking in expensive import goods on a scale which worried those concerned with the economic health of the nation, whilst in the late sixteenth and early seventeenth centuries soaring imports of sweet wines, dried fruits, sugar, spices, fine linens and velvets, together with the buoyant market for new native luxury industries such as crystal glass and silks, must have been in considerable part due to the purchases of the landowners.[5] New patterns of consumption inevitably established themselves first among the wealthiest of the élite, but by process of imitation they rapidly spread down through the upper reaches of the social pyramid, setting standards which it was difficult to ignore since at this time maintenance of a suitable level of display was an essential mark of both nobility and gentility. They may have had their most spectacular manifestations amongst those in court circles, a minority of whom, such as the seventeenth Earl of Oxford and the ninth Earl of Northumberland in the 1580s, spent so recklessly on clothes, entertaining and gambling, that they seriously undermined their whole economic position and were forced into massive sales of property (Stone, 1965, ch. x). However, there is every reason to think that throughout landed society they caused economic stress, making it very much more difficult for gentry families to live within their means than once it had been. Even a sober and frugal country gentleman like the early seventeenth century Sir John Oglander of Nunwell in the Isle of Wight constantly found that his expenditure was threatening to out-run his income (Bamford, 1936, pp. 229–41). And for those who by inclination were less careful than he, it was easy, in this climate of increasingly lavish levels of conspicuous consumption superimposed upon a general inflation, to run by degrees into serious debt.

Landowners, indeed, were incurring debt with increasing frequency as the period wore on, not only for the reasons just indicated but because it was becoming easier to borrow money with the emergence of an embryo capital market, at first in London but by the seventeenth century in many other districts also. It was perfectly possible to obtain credit and to raise loans at interest before the legalization of usury, and indeed the latter was as much a consequence as a cause of the increasing use of credit at all levels of society. However the Act of 1571 undoubtedly contributed to the rapid expansion in the volume of funds available for landowners to borrow which clearly occurred in the later sixteenth century, and this permitted over-spending on a much larger scale than had previously been possible. Those who incurred substantial debts at this period, however, almost invariably had sooner or later to sell land to liquidate them. On the one hand interest rates were high, usually the full amount allowed by law, that is 10 per cent until 1624, then 8 per cent between 1624 and 1651. On the other, at least until the 1620s, there was no possibility of a creditor allowing a debt to remain outstanding indefinitely, until a period of retrenchment, increased rent income or the materialization of an expected inheritance made it possible for the debtor to discharge it

[5] See below II, Ch. 8 secs. iii and v; and *ibid.* pp. 123–6, 209–10.

without realizing assets. Whether the security was a personal bond or the mortgage of land, loans were made only for short periods, rarely exceeding six to twelve months, after which they had to be repaid or a new advance negotiated, if necessary from another lender. If the latter could not be done, or done in time, which was all too likely whenever a period of financial stringency occurred, whether the result of trade depression or heavy borrowing by the crown at even higher rates of interest as in 1624–28 and 1638–42, then the borrower had either to sell, or to risk foreclosure (Stone, 1965, ch. IX. Habakkuk, 1981, pp. 205–6).

One way and another, therefore, numerous estate owners great and small were finding it necessary to put part, or sometimes all, of their lands onto the market. Large scale proprietors could, of course, sustain extensive sales and yet retain a sufficient estate to keep their position in landed society, although sometimes even major gentry families like the Treshams of Rushton (Northants.), the Horseys of Clifton Maybank (Dorset) and the Cooks of Gidea Hall (Essex) came to complete ruin (Finch, 1956, pp. 76–99. Ferris, 1965. McIntosh, 1978). But for the smaller squires, with just a single manor, being obliged to part with it meant their disappearance from the ranks of the gentry, and disappear they did in this period in their hundreds. Their places, however, were taken by others, for the increasing number of those selling land was matched by an increasing number of buyers.

Probably the largest single source of demand for property was from those who were already members of landed society. Such people usually acquired the wherewithal to buy in one of two ways. Either by good luck or good management they were farming the right sort of land in the right place, and were thus able to take full advantage of the favourable conditions for commercial agriculture which prevailed during most of the period down to 1640. Alternatively they had married rich brides and were investing their marriage portions in addition to their inherited estates. In some counties, such as Devonshire, Leicestershire and Lancashire, most of the new recruits to the gentry were successful yeomen farmers, whilst even in Yorkshire where, owing to the presence of York itself and the port of Hull, the rôle of non-agricultural capital was greater, a full half of new gentry families acquired their estates by this route. A great many of the purchases by the yeomen and farming gentry were inevitably small parcels of land or single farms, acquired in order to facilitate enclosure or some other form of estate reorganization, and mainly at the expense of the small family farmer, but even the yeomen are sometimes found buying hundreds of acres or complete manors (Hoskins, 1950; 1952. Blackwood, 1976. Cliffe, 1969, pp. 16–19. *A.H.E.W.* IV, 1967, pp. 301–6).

However when it was a matter of buying ready made estates

established owners were everywhere joined by those who had become wealthy through the pursuit of professional or business careers, as lawyers, government officials, merchants or cloth manufacturers, and in some districts such purchasers were so numerous as to become a dominating influence in local society.[6] North West Kent, most of Essex and the whole of Hertfordshire and Surrey were such areas because of their propinquity to London; so was Northamptonshire because of the large amounts of crown land for sale and the good prospects of improvement by enclosure for pasture; and no doubt there were others (Everitt, 1966 (1), p. 37; 1969 (2), pp. 19–22. Hull, 1950, ch. VI. Holmes, 1974, pp. 12–14 and Appendix 3). For land was the universal outlet for the savings of all who prospered to any considerable degree in the sixteenth and early seventeenth centuries. One reason why this was so was the social status which attached to its possession. Acquisition of an estate did not of itself endow a man with gentility, but it opened the way for a man to merge into the gentry by enabling him to live like a gentleman, that is without needing to labour himself, to play his part in local affairs, and to marry his children into neighbouring gentry families. And for his heir who inherited the estate, gentry status and a place amongst the ruling élite was, in practice, assured. The other reason why moneyed men had so voracious an appetite for land at this time was the difficulty of finding alternative investments. Other and more remunerative forms of investment certainly existed, for instance urban housing property, rent charges and annuities, lending money at interest, participation in shipping and commercial partnerships, and the various joint stock ventures floated for purposes ranging from mining to colonial settlement. But the first two of these, whilst sound securities, were not available in sufficient quantity, whilst the others were either too troublesome, too risky, or in the last case too speculative, to be a way of providing a reliable income for the indefinite future.

Land on the other hand was readily available in units of almost any size, furnished the best security the age could offer, and provided that it was well chosen in the first place and competently managed thereafter, would yield an income whose real value would be maintained irrespective of any increase in prices. Whether very rich, or only modestly affluent like Thomas Mawson, the tanner of Leicester, who is found buying several farms in the nearby village of Wigston Magna in the mid seventeenth century, those with money thus tended to sink most of their capital into

---

[6] Few of these new arrivals in landed society were truly parvenu in the sense that they sprang from a genuinely humble background. A high proportion, indeed, were themselves of gentry origins, typically being the younger sons of established landed families, who, having no expectation of inheriting the paternal property, had had to make their own way in the world.

land (Hoskins, 1957, pp. 196–7). In the case of the wealthy, indeed, they tended to buy far more than they needed to found a landed family, often acquiring estates dispersed around the countryside in half a dozen counties or more, many of which they probably never visited. As the period wore on, moreover, the increase in the number and prosperity of the lawyers, the enlargement of the apparatus of government under the Tudors, the expansion of old forms of economic activity and the development of new ones, ensured that there was a more or less continuous increase in the number of people with the resources to buy land. There was also a long term increase in the scale of their resources. In the first half of the period the greatest estates were built up by royal servants like William Cecil Lord Burghley and his son Robert Cecil Earl of Salisbury, and by lawyer-politicians such as Sir Nicholas Bacon, Queen Elizabeth's Lord Keeper of the Great Seal, Lord Chancellor Ellesmere and James I's Attorney-General Sir Edward Coke. In the sixteenth century mercantile fortunes very rarely rivalled those ac-cumulated through office and the law; and particularly beyond the immediate environs of London and the hinterlands of the major provincial ports, merchants were very much less prominent than lawyers as buyers of land. Indeed as late as 1642 only one of the big new estates established in Dorset in the preceding eighty years, that of Humphrey Weld at Lulworth, owed its origin to trade (Habakkuk, 1981. Simpson, 1961, ch. II. Ferris, 1965).

As the seventeenth century progressed, however, the developments in overseas commerce discussed in Volume II Chapter 9, and the increas-ing involvement of leading merchants in the lucrative businesses of tax farming, lending money to the government and the exploitation of monopolies, meant a marked expansion in both the number and the size of business fortunes. By the 1620s and 1630s the age of estate building on a grand scale by city men had dawned as individuals like Lionel Cranfield, Sir Arthur Ingram, Alderman Cockayne, Sir William Craven, Sir Baptist Hicks and Sir Paul Bayning moved into the land market in command of resources which exceeded those of even the most successful lawyers.[7] At the time of his death in 1630 Bayning's purchases had made him one of the half dozen largest landowners in Essex, whilst the even more extensive acquisitions of Sir Arthur Ingram left his son, sub-sequently created Viscount Irwin, with an estate worth £9000 a year, the biggest in Yorkshire outside the ranks of the established peerage. By this stage even a merchant financier who was clearly not in the same bracket as these moguls, Sir John Wolstenholme (d. 1639), was able to build up an

---

[7] Cranfield, Ingram and one or two others were apparently worth £250,000 or more at the height of their careers (Grassby, 1970).

estate, again in Yorkshire, which was larger than all but a handful of seventeenth century political and legal office holders ever acquired. The latter were no less rich than they had been, but the businessmen had now surpassed them and their dominance of the land market, at all levels, became increasingly apparent as the period drew to a close (Habakkuk, 1981. Hull, 1950, ch. VII. Cliffe, 1969, pp. 30, 353).

The volume of buying and selling seems to have increased continuously from the early part of the sixteenth century until it reached a peak at some time in the early seventeenth. Professor Stone has compiled an index which suggests that the number of transactions was more than twice as high in the 1610s as it had been in the 1560s, and in the seven counties studied by Tawney, one manor out of three changed hands at least once between 1560 and 1600, and an even higher proportion in the succeeding forty years (Stone, 1965, pp. 36–7, 754. Tawney, 1941). Some properties of course changed hands very much more often than once: Cotesbach in Leicestershire, for instance, after belonging to the Devereux family for 150 years had six different owners between 1591 and 1626 (Parker, 1948). The effects of all this land market activity were, moreover, superimposed upon changes in ownership brought about by transfers that took place independently of the market. It was common, despite a general climate of opinion favouring primogeniture, for the wealthier landowners, especially if they had themselves added to their inherited estates, to endow their younger sons with land, thereby establishing one or more cadet branches with estates of their own.[8] In some cases, indeed, the continuation of this practice in successive generations resulted in there being eight or even a dozen landholding branches of a single family. In Kent, for instance, there were ten distinct branches of the Boys family in the mid seventeenth century, and in Yorkshire thirteen of the Constables (Everitt, 1966 (1), p. 35. Cliffe, 1969, p. 6). On the other hand, when families died out entirely in the male line, as they did very frequently indeed, their property necessarily passed by inheritance into the hands of another. The net result was a very great change in the composition of the landholding élite. For reasons that are by no means entirely clear this was very much less pronounced in some parts of the country than in others. In Kent and Cheshire, for instance, there was little turnover amongst the landowners, and relatively few newcomers from outside. In the former county, despite an active land market in the districts nearest London, only a quarter of the gentry established

---

[8] Such endowment of younger sons often took the form of a long lease on favourable terms of part of the paternal estate, rather than an outright grant of the freehold. But in a period when conditions were highly favourable for commercial farming this often provided sufficient income for the recipients, if they were able and energetic, to buy lands of their own.

there in 1640 had appeared since the late fifteenth century, and in the latter the proportion was only one fifth (Everitt, 1966 (1), p. 36. Morrill, 1974, pp. 2–3). Such stability was, however, unusual. In Yorkshire, Leicestershire and Norfolk about 60 per cent of them were new since that time; in Suffolk and Northamptonshire 70 per cent or more; and in the extreme cases of Essex and Hertfordshire 85 per cent and 90 per cent respectively.[9] Moreover even these figures conceal the full extent of the change amongst the landowners, for many of those who had arrived in the sixteenth century had already died out or sold up before the middle of the seventeenth (Cliffe, 1969, pp. 13–19. Everitt, 1969 (2), pp. 20–1. Holmes, 1974, Appendix 3).

How these changes affected the structure of landowning in the country as a whole is a question which, because of its implications for the distribution of political power, has given rise to much discussion amongst historians, especially those interested in the origins of the English Revolution of the 1640s.[10] Unfortunately, however, there are severe difficulties in the way of any attempt to resolve this issue. These arise in part from the impossibility of any statistical measurement, and in part from the problem of how to establish appropriate categories for analysis in a society whose own terminological distinctions were either related to legal status and titles of honour, or to imprecise and well before the end of the period, partly subjective social differences, such as those between esquire and plain gentleman, and between gentleman and yeoman. At the top of the social pyramid the wealthiest of the peerage were always the greatest landowners of the day, but the peerage as a whole were never a class apart in a social sense, nor indeed in an economic one, for many families without hereditary titles of nobility possessed estates which were as large as those of all but a handful of the peers. This was particularly true in the later sixteenth century when there were only between fifty and sixty members of the peerage, but it remained the case even after the numerous promotions of the period 1603–28 had increased the number to approaching 130. All other landowners above the level of the working yeoman farmer, collectively referred to both by contemporaries and historians as the gentry, certainly shared common social values

[9] It is true that the percentages for the various counties are not strictly comparable because they do not all relate to the same portion of the gentry, but there is no doubt that the differences suggested by the figures were real enough.

[10] How relevant these matters *really* are as 'causes' of the Civil War and the events that followed is, however, questionable. Many historians are now inclined to see the conflict of the 1640s, not as the inevitable outcome of the social changes of the previous hundred years or of the long term polarization of politics between 'court' and 'country' over the previous fifty, but as something that developed out of the political events of 1640–2, and which was in no sense inevitable before late 1641 at the earliest (see for instance Fletcher, 1981, esp. pp. 407–19).

and a common outlook, but included families which varied in wealth and standing from the great proprietor with an estate of many thousands of acres in several counties down to the relatively humble owner of a handful of farms, whose horizons barely stretched as far as the shire town. Thus in Yorkshire in 1642 there was a small handful of families, notably the Ingrams of Temple Newsam and the Saviles of Thornhill, with incomes of several or many thousands of pounds a year, whilst at the other end of the scale the annual receipts of more than one third of those styled gentleman were less than £100 (Cliffe, 1969, pp. 28–30). Any economic and social distinctions are bound to be arbitrary and in some respects unsatisfactory, but it is probably reasonable to set on one side those great landed magnates who, whether or not peers themselves, were of comparable wealth, lived a similar way of life in a great country seat and whose families inter-married with the peerage, and on the other side the remainder of the gentry. The dividing line between them might be roughly set at a landed income of some £4000–£5000 a year in the mid and later seventeenth century, implying ownership of an estate of 10–15,000 acres or more (Mingay, 1963, pp. 19–21).

The first group, which included all but a minority of impoverished peers, many but not all of the knights and baronets[11] and some esquires and gentlemen, does not seem to have increased very markedly in numbers, and probably never exceeded a few hundred families altogether. Nor, if any reliance can be placed upon the estimates which have been attempted, was there much increase in the proportion of the landed property of the country that they controlled: indeed the latter may have been somewhat less in 1640 than it had been in the mid fifteenth century when, according to Mr Cooper's estimates, it was some 15–20 per cent. Certainly there was no striking increase in either the number or the size of the very large estates, despite the huge amounts of land which passed from the hands of the Church, the crown and the peasantry, into those of private estate owners in general (Cooper, 1967). Great new agglomerations of property were continually being created, by one family inheriting the estates of another or several others, and by the purchases of the wealthiest politicians, lawyers and merchants. However, only a very few purchasers could ever buy enough land to create a territorial magnate's estate in a single generation. Fewer than forty of those who held government office between 1625 and 1642 were able to buy land worth even £1000 a year, and in total the acquisitions of the small scale buyers must have been far greater (Aylmer, 1961, pp. 313–14). This on

[11] The baronets were a new 'order', established by James I in 1611, mid way in status between peers and knights, having hereditary titles but not entitled to a seat in the House of Lords.

its own would have tended inevitably to shift the balance of property ownership away from the great estates. But in addition the tendency for large estates to be created by means of inheritance seems, in this part of the period, to have been at the very least counter-balanced by the sales of those who were in financial difficulties, for the vice of over-spending was particularly prevalent in the very highest social circles. According to Professor Stone's study of the peerage, a substantial fraction of the group, nearly one third of it and including some of the greatest magnates of all such as the Earls of Northumberland, Cumberland, Rutland, Huntingdon and Bedford, experienced a severe financial crisis around the turn of the sixteenth and seventeenth centuries. Indeed even after extensive sales of land raising £173,000 they were still massively in debt to the tune of more than £150,000.[12] Altogether out of forty-one peerage families whose history could be traced over the period 1558 to 1602, thirteen had lost at least half their manors by the latter date and twenty-five had lost a quarter or more, whilst between 1602 and 1641 out of thirty-seven families fourteen lost half or more and twenty-two a quarter. Manors varied greatly in size and value and these figures are not necessarily a good guide to the proportion of their estates which they had disposed of, but there is no reason to doubt that they represent a considerable shrinkage of their landholdings, nor to suppose that such sales were confined only to those magnates who happened to have hereditary titles (Stone, 1965, ch. IV, esp. pp. 156–60, and 765–6, 778).

By contrast with the experience of the territorial magnates both the numbers of middling and lesser gentry, and the extent of their landed possessions, increased very greatly in this period. According to Mr Cooper they probably did not hold more than 25 per cent of the land in the fifteenth century, but by the middle of the seventeenth they must have had nearly half (Table V on p. 143). At this time the group numbered perhaps 15–20,000 families, or around 2 per cent of the total population. How large it had been at the beginning of the sixteenth century is uncertain, but the evidence of the subsidy assessments of the 1520s leaves no doubt that a resident squire was not yet a typical figure in the English countryside. In Suffolk and Rutland, for instance, only one village in five had one, in Leicestershire only one in six or seven. In most places at that time there was one predominating landowner, but it was much more often an ecclesiastical institution, the crown or a great territorial magnate, than a gentleman with strictly local interests. By the 1680s, however, the

---

[12] This financial crisis, which is only one aspect of a more general 'crisis of the aristocracy' discussed by Stone, was made much worse by Queen Elizabeth's notorious parsimony. This largely interrupted the flow of royal largesse, which at other times added considerably to the incomes of the nobility and partly financed the extravagant way of life of those in court circles.

proportion of villages with one or more resident gentlemen – and many had several – had risen to two thirds or even three quarters (Cooper, 1967. Cornwall, 1965. Hoskins, 1950, p. 127. Laslett, 1965, p. 63). In the case of Somerset Mr Havinden has estimated that between 1502 and 1623 the number of families accounted gentry had perhaps quadrupled, without there having been any perceptible change in what constituted gentility.[13] And certainly by the mid seventeenth century large and wealthy shires supported many hundreds of gentry families: in 1640 there were around 750 in Suffolk, rather more in Lancashire, at least 850 and perhaps as many as 1000 in Kent, whilst smaller counties like Northamptonshire and Buckinghamshire had about 330 and 200 respectively (Everitt, 1966 (1), pp. 33–4; 1969 (2), pp. 6–7. Johnson, 1963, pp. 7–15). The larger increase in gentry numbers than in the amount of land they controlled[14] obviously meant that the average size of their estates must have decreased, and in view of the very large numbers of yeomen who prospered sufficiently on the basis of commercial farming to rise into the lower ranks of the gentry this is not surprising. However because of the assault on customary tenures; because of higher fines and rack renting; because those who farmed on a substantial scale themselves, as most of the lesser gentry did, were exploiting their land more effectively; and because agricultural prices had risen relative to other prices, average real incomes had not necessarily declined by much or even at all. Nevertheless the overwhelming mass of the seventeenth century gentry clearly were landowners on quite a modest scale, with estates of 1000 acres or less, and incomes of only a few hundred pounds a year. In Buckinghamshire in 1640, for instance, only about thirty gentry families out of 200, that is 15 per cent, had landed incomes of £1000 a year or more, and in Yorkshire only seventy-three out of 679, or 10.8 per cent. By contrast more than half the Yorkshire gentry, and very much more than half of those in the poorer county of Lancashire received less than £250 a year from their estates, whilst dozens of backwoods gentry had incomes in only two figures (Johnson, 1963, pp. 7–15. Cliffe, 1969, pp. 28–30. Blackwood, 1976).

iii Landed society, 1640–1700

By the later seventeenth century the number of landowning gentry families was already beginning to diminish once more, and the average

---

[13] Unpublished paper read by M.A. Havinden at Bristol in 1979.

[14] The amount of land cannot be estimated with any pretence of accuracy, but even if they doubled their proportion, from 25 to 50 per cent, of a cultivated acreage increased by one quarter (see above Table V at the beginning of this chapter; and pp. 107–11), this would be a smaller increase than the likely three or four fold increase in the number of gentry families.

size of estates was tending to increase (Habakkuk, 1940. Everitt, 1969 (1), pp. 50–1). One important reason for this was demographic. As happened to the population in general, the rate at which the landowners were able to reproduce themselves gradually declined until by the last third of the century they were failing to do so by an increasing margin. In fact, even in the sixteenth century only a minority of families lasted more than three or four generations before becoming extinct in the male line, but by the end of the period they were failing biologically in greater numbers than ever, and property was passing from family by marriage and inheritance at an accelerating rate (Cooper, 1956. *A.H.E.W.* v, Part ii, 1984, pp. 165–70). Other things being equal the greater landowners tended to do better out of this process than the lesser, since it was naturally they who obtained the wealthiest heiresses as wives, but we have noted that down to the early seventeenth century their high propensity to sell land very largely or even entirely off-set this. As the century went on, however, this propensity became less marked.

The continued expansion of both London and provincial money markets, the long term fall in the rate of interest represented by successive reductions in the legal maximum from 10 per cent to 8 per cent in 1624 and 6 per cent in 1651, and the conversion of the mortgage from a short to a long term security, had a good deal to do with this. These related developments made it both easier and cheaper to borrow money; but most importantly the last, which, as we have noticed in another context (see above pp. 124–5), depended on the evolution of the legal concept of the equity of redemption, rendered it possible from the 1620s onwards for debts on the security of land to be left outstanding indefinitely. It was undoubtedly the ready availability of mortgages on these terms which enabled most landowners to emerge from the traumatic experiences of the Civil War without suffering economic catastrophe. Despite the unprecedentedly heavy taxes, the heavy losses of income resulting from the economic dislocation which affected all areas where there were military operations, the sequestration of many estates for years on end and the composition fines imposed on those who had sided with the king, few of the aristocracy and gentry had to sell on a large scale, unless they had already been in financial difficulties before the war began (*A.H.E.W.* v, Part ii, 1984, pp. 145–50). In the longer run, however, the importance of long term mortgages was that estate owners could now run up considerable debts as a result of over-spending, and could raise large capital sums to provide marriage portions for their daughters, without almost automatically being obliged to realize part of their assets in land. The future income available to the family would, of course, be reduced by the need to meet interest charges until the debt was somehow paid off, but its landholdings could remain undiminished. Although they did not by any means avoid sales altogether, the survival as major landowners of the Fitzwilliams of Milton (Northants.) and the Temples of Stowe (Bucks.), despite the enormous debts they contracted in the second quarter of the century, contrasts strikingly with the ruin that befell no more seriously encumbered families even a generation earlier (Finch, 1956, pp. 129–34. Gay, 1939; 1943).

Also there was a significant change of ethos amongst the landowners. Conspicuous expenditure upon houses, clothes, entertaining and the like long remained a characteristic of the greater landowners, but perhaps because of the influence of Puritanism and a complex of other factors belonging as much to cultural as to social or economic history, even by the time of the Civil War it was rarely taken to such damaging extremes as it had been a generation and more earlier (Stone, 1965, pp. 583–4). Besides, as an increasing proportion of those who had acquired their estates in the decades after 1540 were transformed, by the passage of time, from first generation new-comers into established family dynasties with firm roots in their localities, so traditional attitudes to land which had been partly eclipsed during much of the sixteenth and early seventeenth centuries, began to reassert themselves. The belief became more widespread that land was not a commodity to be disposed of at the whim of an individual, but was the collective possession of the family, past, present and future, to be retained at all costs so that succeeding generations would continue to inhabit the same place, and fulfil the same social rôle, as previous ones had done. One reflection of this was that it became increasingly unusual for owners to provide for younger sons by granting them lands carved out of the family inheritance, thereby simultaneously reducing the number of new gentry estates being created and lessening the attrition of the large estates which the practice had involved. Another reflection of the changing attitude towards land, so it has been argued, was the evolution of the strict settlement.

Even in the sixteenth century many of the established landowners held their property under the terms of a settlement which made them in law no more than tenants for life, the legal ownership being vested in trustees whose duty it was to protect the interests of subsequent genera-tions. However until the 1640s it was usually possible for an heir, if he was so minded, to break any entail that had been created, to convert his life tenancy into full ownership, and thereby acquire the freedom to sell. Strict settlements, however, incorporated an ingenious new legal device known as 'trustees to preserve contingent remainders' which made this very much more difficult: indeed it was impossible, unless a private act of parliament could be obtained, until the life tenant's eldest son had come of age and was prepared to co-operate in performing the necessary legal technicalities. Even with strict settlements there was nothing anyone could do to prevent an extravagant life tenant from ruining himself personally, but he could no longer destroy or fatally weaken his family's position for all time, since he could neither mortgage nor sell without the co-operation of his trustees and then only for purposes specifically permitted in the settlement, such as the raising of marriage portions. Probably stimulated by the events of the 1640s, when estates had been sequestrated by both sides and the victorious parliamentarians had actually confiscated and sold those of several hundred royalists but had invariably respected the terms of family settlements, during the third quarter of the century the greater and middling landowners rapidly adopted the new forms so as to provide their property with the best possible protection for the future. However, whether strict settlements deserve the importance which has traditionally been attributed to them has recently been called into question. It seems that they represented a natural evolution from the forms of settlement employed in the earlier part of the century rather than a radical departure from them, and that the reasons why the landowners came to favour them may have had less to do with the restrictions they placed upon the heirs' freedom to alienate, and more with other aspects of inter-family financial arrangements than was formerly supposed. And in any event strict settlements certainly did not prevent the families who adopted them from ever selling land. They had to be remade in each generation and this might for some reason not be done,[15] nor did the settlements necessarily cover a family's entire property. Besides in some cases an accumulation of debt, which was inevitably the fate of a proportion of families who by bad luck or bad management committed themselves in successive generations to paying out heavier marriage portions than they themselves received with their own brides, created so heavy a burden of interest charges that sales became unavoidable, with resort being had to an act of parliament if necessary (Habakkuk, 1940; 1950. Stone, 1965, pp. 178–83. Cooper, 1976, pp. 200–33. Bonfield, 1979; 1981). There was, moreover, always a good deal of buying and selling of outlying estates as landowners rearranged amongst themselves, in a mutually more convenient pattern of ownership, the various properties they acquired by means of inheritance from other families (Clay, 1981). It may, therefore, have been less the strict settlements themselves, than the new set of attitudes which accompanied their introduction that explain why, by the later seven-

---

[15] It was most commonly done when the heir married: if he remained single the making of a new settlement might be postponed indefinitely.

teenth century, the larger owners had ceased to be so conspicuously net sellers of land as they clearly had been in the few decades on either side of 1600.

Among the small estate owners, on the other hand, the propensity to sell remained high throughout the seventeenth century and beyond. With their smaller resources, their smaller credit base and their lack of rich and influential friends and relatives, there is no doubt that they suffered more severely from the disasters of the 1640s than did their wealthier brethren (*A.H.E.W.* v, Part ii, 1984, pp. 146–7). Then came the long periods of low agricultural prices, with their concomitants of falling rents, mounting arrears and untenanted farms which characterized much of the later seventeenth century. As is discussed elsewhere some districts suffered very much worse from these depressions than did others, and some producers successfully met the challenge of falling profits by adopting methods which increased their productivity. (See above pp. 92–3, 130ff.) However almost all landlords experienced some loss of income in the 1670s and 1680s, and some, especially those who depended directly upon farming profits and had few or no rent paying tenants to absorb the impact of falling prices, lost very heavily indeed. The late seventeenth century, especially the war years of the mid 1660s and after 1689, also saw very much heavier taxes on land than had ever been levied before 1640, taxes indeed which after 1692 were annually absorbing one fifth of the income of many of the gentry of the South, the East and the Midlands. Again these economic burdens bore with disproportionate effect upon those with the slenderest resources, forcing many of those on the lower fringes of the gentry to part with their land. Strict settlements were less often adopted by landowners at that level, but settlements apart from the owners of the more substantial estates usually had a sufficiently wide margin between income and expenditure to ride out the difficult periods (Habakkuk, 1940. Bonfield, 1981. Clay, 1981.).

The balance within landed society between large estates and small was also affected by the gradual retreat from the land market of those who had only moderate resources, a development which became particularly marked in the eighteenth century but which was already apparent by the later seventeenth. The volume of buying and selling had reached a peak, probably in the 1610s, and then began slowly to decline, although if the index of land market activity compiled by Professor Stone can be relied upon, even at the end of the period it remained considerably greater than it had been in the mid sixteenth century (Stone, 1965, pp. 36–7, 754). It was not that the smaller buyer was priced out of the market because there was less land for sale, for in fact the movement of land prices suggests that if anything demand for land from all quarters declined more markedly than did the supply of land for sale. Rather the greater difficulty of making profits from farming in the last third of the century meant that in most areas fewer yeomen were able to buy their way into the gentry, and fewer farming gentry had the funds with which to expand their estates. Large estate owners, on the other hand, could usually find the funds to buy land in order to expand if anything suitable came up in their immediate neighbourhood, and they tended to do so for reasons of social prestige and, sometimes, to facilitate enclosure or the reorganization of farms (Clay, 1974. *A.H.E.W.* v, Part ii, 1984, pp. 175 ff.). Besides at the very time when agricultural depression and increased taxation were reducing the attractiveness of land as an income yielding investment, there appeared a new range of alternative outlets for savings. Long term mortgages from the 1620s onwards, interest bearing deposits with goldsmith bankers from the 1650s, the bonds of the East India and other joint stock trading companies, and at the very end of the century Bank of England stock and the first of the new forms of government securities (see below II, pp. 274–6, 279–80), all offered a significantly higher rate of return than did land. Many of those who lent to the bankers burned their fingers in the financial crisis of 1672, but in general these opportunities were perceived by investors as being sufficiently safe to divert a growing proportion of the surplus capital generated in economic activities other than agriculture away from the purchase of land. Inevitably those who could least afford to purchase the social advantages a landed estate conveyed by accepting a lower rate of return on their capital, were most strongly drawn to these new forms of investment, especially so as by the later seventeenth century there was developing, both in London and many of the larger provincial towns, a social milieu in which a man of means could live something like the life of a gentleman in an urban as opposed to a rural setting. Many professional men, merchants and the like, still settled their families on the land in the traditional way, but a rapidly increasing proportion were content to remain as members of what has been called the pseudo-gentry. Such people either acquired no landed property at all, or did no more than buy a house in a country setting within easy reach of town to provide themselves and their families with access to rural amenities: Londoners in Hampstead, Chiswick or Clapham for instance, or Bristolians in Clifton. There was thus by 1700 a significantly reduced rate of recruitment to the lower ranks of the gentry proper, compared to that of 1600 or 1640. As for those who had accumulated very large fortunes in professional, mercantile or political careers, if they had social ambitions as they almost invariably did, they could afford to accept the reduced rate of return on their capital, and although the wider choice of investment outlets did affect the timing, and to some degree the extent, of their land purchases,[16] it did not deter them from buying as much as they needed to establish themselves as great landed magnates (Habakkuk, 1960; 1980; 1981. Everitt, 1966 (2)). Thus between the 1650s and his death in 1684 Sir John Banks, and in the 1670s and 1680s Sir Stephen Fox, two of the most successful financiers of that age, both built up estates sufficiently large for their descendants to support Earldoms, respectively of Aylesford and Ilchester (Coleman, 1963, chs. 3 and 9. Clay, 1978, chs. VIII and XIII). At the higher levels of landed society, therefore, as many new large estates were being created as ever, and indeed in view of the rapid increase in the wealth of city men in the last few decades of the century, perhaps more.

Well before 1700, therefore, the multiplication of the gentry, which had been so marked a feature of English society between about 1540 and 1640, had ceased. No longer increasing in numbers the landlord class was getting smaller, and the average size of estate was growing larger, but these were tendencies which were to become more marked in the eighteenth century, and even then their extent is immeasurable, remains a matter of some controversy and probably varied from region to region (*A.H.E.W.* v, Part ii, 1984, pp. 162–4). Certainly by the end of the seventeenth century they had not yet gone far enough to modify seriously the pattern of landholding which had developed in the century after the Dissolution of the Monasteries. The great landed magnates probably still owned no more than 15–20 per cent of the land, which was about the same proportion as they had enjoyed before the period opened (Table v on p. 143), and in most parts of the country the characteristic unit of ownership was the estate of between a few hundred and a few thousand acres, owned by men who resided upon them, farmed part of them personally, paid close attention to the management of the remainder, and played an active rôle in the social and political life of their local communities.

---

[16] The wider choice of investments available tended to deter men from purchasing land until later in their career than had been normal earlier; it meant that they no longer bought more land than they required to establish a landed dynasty; and it meant that they tended to concentrate their purchases in just one or at most two districts.

6

THE TOWNS

i Urban growth in the sixteenth and seventeenth centuries

We have seen that England at the end of the Middle Ages was an overwhelmingly rural and agricultural society, and she remained so throughout the sixteenth and seventeenth centuries. Most people lived in the countryside, in villages, hamlets or isolated farms, according to the settlement pattern of the district, and worked on the land for most of their time, even though they might devote part of it to other pursuits. Nevertheless the proportion of the population who were primarily employed in agriculture certainly declined over the period. There is no means of knowing precisely what this proportion was at the beginning of the sixteenth century, though it is hardly likely to have been less than 80 per cent and may well have been even larger, but two hundred years later it was certainly no more than about 60 per cent and may have been less than half (Lindert, 1980). It is equally clear that the proportion of the population living in towns of any substance rose markedly, from about 10 or 12 per cent in the early part of the period to a little less than a quarter, perhaps 22 or 23 per cent, at the end of it (Chalklin, 1974 (1), p. 16. Clark and Slack, 1976, p. II).

In the early sixteenth century indeed England seems to have been no more, and in all probability rather less, urbanized than it had been two hundred years before. The epidemics of the later Middle Ages had struck the towns with particular ferocity, whilst improved economic prospects in rural areas, as a result of reduced pressure of population on resources, had reduced the rate at which immigrants came to fill the gaps. The populations of all the principal towns fell heavily in the fourteenth century, and taken together they probably fell by a greater proportion than did the total population of the country. A reduction in size did not, however, necessarily imply economic decay, and many of them, especially the larger ones, seem to have remained remarkably prosperous well into the fifteenth century. From the second half of that century, however, there is a growing body of evidence to suggest that many of the leading urban centres, though by no means all and certainly not including London, were suffering from a renewed shrinkage of population and an economic malaise that was not reversed until well after the start of our period. The evidence, however, is often difficult to interpret, so that the cause, and indeed the very existence of this late medieval urban 'crisis', are controversial. Certainly both its extent and severity may have been exaggerated by the excessive attention paid to places, such as Coventry, whose staple textile industry was in serious difficulties, and ports like Bristol and Southampton which were losing overseas trade to London, where particular circumstances caused an exceptionally acute contraction in both size and economic activity. Nevertheless it is probably true that the stimulus the economy derived from the early stages of population growth at home, and the expansion of the overseas market for cloth, brought disproportionate benefits to the countryside as opposed to the towns. In due course most towns did come to share in these benefits, but during the first half or even two thirds of the sixteenth century the growth of commercial farming and rural cloth manufacture was not matched by a corresponding expansion of urban economic activity, although those places with rapidly developing hinterlands and well situated to handle the expanding trade in agricultural produce and exported textiles prospered satisfactorily enough.[1] Elsewhere, however, contemporary urban records are full of references to empty and derelict houses, to municipal finances dislocated by shrunken rent rolls and to the inability of local businessmen to shoulder the financial burdens of local office holding (Dobson, 1977. Phythian-Adams, 1978. Bridbury, 1981).

The enquiries of the government into the taxable wealth of the country in the 1520s and the tax assessments levied in consequence of those enquiries provide a reasonably sound basis for a survey of the state of the towns in the early part of the period. There was then only one provincial town whose population was clearly over 10,000, and almost certainly no more than half a dozen with over 5000. Norwich may have had about 12,700 inhabitants, but Bristol was the only other city whose population approached five figures, although it is unlikely quite to have reached it. Exeter and Salisbury had about 8000 people each, York rather fewer, Coventry some 6600, and a handful of other places, including Ipswich, Lynn (King's Lynn as it was later to become known), Canterbury, Colchester and Worcester, may have approached 5000. But even major provincial towns like Newcastle, Gloucester, Shrewsbury, Leicester or Lincoln, which acted as markets for a wide area and as centres of county

[1] London was the principal beneficiary from the expansion of exports at this time: see also below sec. vi of this chapter; and ii, Ch. 9 sec. ii.

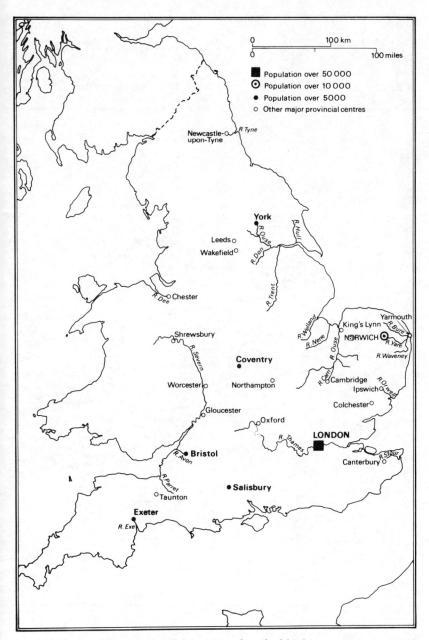

Map 3 Principal English towns and navigable rivers, *c.* 1520.

Map 4 Principal English towns and navigable rivers, *c.* 1700. (Rivers after
Willan, 1936, map on p. 32.)

government and often of ecclesiastical administration as well, had no more than 3000 or 4000 people, and anywhere with as many as 2000 would have been of considerable local importance (Hoskins, 1956. Corfield, 1976).

By the end of the following century Norwich had about 30,000 people; Bristol about 20,000; Newcastle and Exeter perhaps 16,000 and 14,000 respectively; York possibly over 12,000; Great Yarmouth about 10,000; whilst there were probably at least twenty-five other places with between 5000 and 10,000 inhabitants. Nevertheless of those mentioned only Newcastle (thanks to the rapid development of its coal trade with London), Norwich and its outport Yarmouth had grown more rapidly than the two and a quarter fold increase recorded by the population of the country as a whole, and even Norwich had barely exceeded that rate of growth. Some of the towns which in 1700 were still smaller than these, notably places like Birmingham, Manchester, Leeds, Sheffield and Tiverton, which lay at the heart of areas where there had been a substantial development of rural industry over the preceding two centuries had, it is true, expanded much more rapidly. So had a number of other places where there was some special factor at work, such as Bath whose development as a health and holiday resort was well under way by the end of the period; Chatham and Portsmouth, with their naval dockyards; and Liverpool, an ancient but obscure port which was beginning its rapid rise to prominence as the basis of trans-Atlantic trade in the later seventeenth century. So, too, had some of the smaller market towns like Farnham in Surrey and Stowmarket in Suffolk, which had flourished on the steadily rising internal trade in agricultural products.[2] On the other hand there were probably almost as many towns, which had been important at the beginning of the period, whose populations had grown by much less than the national total or indeed, like those of Salisbury, Coventry, Beverley and Southampton, had hardly increased at all, either because the decline of old established manufactures had not been compensated by the development of new ones, because of the shifting of domestic or international trades routes, the relative economic stagnation of their hinterland, or some other less readily identifiable cause. All in all the population of the provincial towns taken together had grown impressively in absolute terms, but they did not comprise a very much larger fraction of the whole nation at the end of the period than they had done at the beginning. Most, perhaps as much as two thirds, of the increase in the proportion of urban dwellers in the two centuries with

---

[2] Many others, however, after a period of rapid growth between the late sixteenth and mid seventeenth centuries, had begun to shrink again after about 1640, and were smaller in 1700 than they had been fifty years before. For some reasons for this see below secs. ii and iv of this chapter.

which we are concerned was accounted for by the growth of the capital. From the 1520s when its 60,000 people made up some 2.5 per cent of the national total of 2.3 million, London grew to reach about 200,000 by 1600 and perhaps 575,000 by the end of the seventeenth century, by which time its population was equivalent to about 11.5 per cent of England's 5.06 million. The expansion of non-agricultural forms of employment thus mainly occurred, on the one hand in London, and on the other in the countryside: it was not associated with any general advance of urbanization as it was in the period after 1750 (Clark and Slack, 1972, pp. 30–2; 1976, p. 83. Chalklin, 1974 (1), pp. 3–25. Corfield, 1976).

With the exception of London, England remained a country of small towns by the standards of contemporary continental Europe, and indeed most English market towns were very much smaller than those places with which we have been mainly concerned so far. The problem of defining exactly what constitutes a town makes it difficult to be precise as to how many there were, but at the beginning of the period there were at least 500 settlements, possibly nearer to 700, to which the term could reasonably be applied, and about 600 by the end of it (Clark and Slack, 1976, pp. 7–8. Patten, 1978, p. 54). In most counties one or two relatively obscure villages throve sufficiently to develop urban characteristics during the course of the sixteenth and seventeenth centuries, but in general those places which possessed these in 1700 already had them in 1500. On the other hand some which had possessed at least rudimentary urban characteristics at the earlier date dwindled away to total insignificance during the course of the following two centuries, especially perhaps in the mid and later seventeenth century. This was because by that time the total volume of internal commerce was no longer growing as fast as formerly, changes in commercial practice were adversely affecting urban markets, and improvements in transport were beginning to concentrate business in the larger centres. Right throughout the period the great majority of these numerous towns were tiny by later standards, and particularly in the early part of it places of any real substance were so few that even in the South and East, where urban settlements were most numerous, there were whole counties with only one or two, or even with none at all. Thus in Sussex in the 1520s Chichester and Rye with about 2000 people each, and Lewes with 1500–1600, were the biggest towns, whilst in Buckinghamshire there was nowhere larger than High Wycombe which had about 900–1000. The average market town at that time seems to have had only 500 or 600 people, that is perhaps 100 to 150 houses strung out along a single street with a few alleys behind it, or grouped around a market-place or crossroads. Even by the middle of the seventeenth century such places commonly had no more than 900–1200 inhabitants: certainly in the case of East Anglia only twenty out of the forty-seven places classifiable as urban clearly exceeded the latter figure (Cornwall, 1962. Patten, 1978, pp. 251, 292).

The main reason why towns were at once so numerous and yet so small was that, because travel and transport remained slow, difficult and expensive, the provision of both marketing facilities and basic services remained highly decentralized. Inability to get to a market town and back within a single day, which meant a journey of not more than ten or a dozen miles in each direction, imposed a severe burden on small agricultural producers, and the shorter the distance they had to travel the less the cost to them in effort and time. For this reason in the more densely populated parts of the country, such as most of the Home Counties, Suffolk, Gloucestershire and Somerset, market towns were very thickly spread indeed, each with a correspondingly small hinterland. It was only in the more sparsely inhabited areas of the North that there were many communities for whom the journey to a town meant a night away from home, but although the towns there had much larger areas dependent upon them in geographical terms, they were no larger in terms of population. Of course people did not go only to the town nearest to them and might go regularly or occasionally to a more distant one if it suited their purpose better, and as we shall see some quite small places developed specialist markets which attracted the agricultural produce of an unusually large district, but even so it is probable that the average small market town in the South and East relied largely on custom generated within a radius of five or six miles. Larger towns naturally had a more extensive catchment area, and the wider choice of goods available in their shops and markets, and the specialist services they offered, might draw people from considerable distances, but it seems that even the market of an important provincial centre such as Worcester was not, in the sixteenth century, often visited by people who lived further than twelve miles off (*A.H.E.W.* IV, 1967, pp. 496–502. Dyer, 1973, p. 68).[3] The second important factor which limited the size of towns was that within their hinterlands the subsistence orientation of most small producers, relatively low agricultural productivity and unequal distribution of income ensured that most of the rural population had very limited purchasing power, so that their custom was unable to support more than a very few craftsmen and traders. As for those with more money to spend, the larger landowners and the successful commercial

---

[3] The table of market areas given by Everitt in *A.H.E.W.* IV, 1967, p. 498, suggests that market areas were rather larger than those mentioned in the text, but his findings would seem to be based mainly on evidence deriving from the activities of the larger farmers, who are likely to have gone further afield than most country people.

farmers, they were not sufficiently numerous, nor was the effective demand they exerted for luxury goods and services sufficient, to support more than a small number of larger towns, especially as the wealthiest of them concentrated much of their expenditure on such things in London. (See below sec. vi of this chapter.)

In some respects these small towns were almost indistinguishable from the villages all around them, and the majority of their inhabitants followed a way of life which differed little from that of the countryman. Even the larger ones, which as chartered boroughs enjoyed the full panoply of municipal institutions, still had something of a rural air about them in the sixteenth century. In none of them, save London, was it more than a few minutes' walk from the centre to the open country. Pigs might commonly be met with wandering their streets, and cows grazing in the churchyards. Thus in late sixteenth century Manchester, a place of 2000 people or more, the authorities found it necessary to ban pig keeping by those without their own back yards, and to forbid both the erection of pig sties in the streets and the practice of allowing swine 'to go at large either in the church or churchyard, market place or in the streets ... unringed and unyoked' (Willan, 1980, pp. 39–41). There were still large gardens and orchards inside the walls of most towns, and outside them there was often a set of arable fields, pastures and meadows belonging to the townsmen as individuals or to the community. Leicester, a town of about 3000 people in the second half of the century, had open fields extending over 2600 acres (Hoskins, 1955). As for the lesser places, few of them had any pretensions to rank as boroughs, and most of those that did had only the most shadowy of burghal institutions, so that their affairs were very much under the control of a manorial lord, a situation symbolized by the way in which towns like Petworth, Arundel, Corfe and Alnwick were physically dominated by the great house or castle which loomed over them. Many, even most, of the inhabitants were farmers, and the houses in the main streets were as likely to be farmsteads as the premises of shopkeepers or artisans. At Oakham, a town of about 600 people in Rutland, traders and craftsmen made up only a quarter of the working population in the 1520s and almost all of them were also part-time agriculturalists, whilst in most of the small towns of Gloucestershire early in the following century between a third and a half of the inhabitants were primarily employed on the land. Even at the very end of the period rural occupations absorbed between a fifth and a half of the employed population of the inland towns of Sussex. Besides, many of those that did pursue crafts were in occupations such as tailoring or shoe-making, which could often be found in places which were unquestionably country villages (Cornwall, 1962. Tawney and Tawney, 1934. Patten, 1978, pp. 170–1).

But for all the small size of most towns in the sixteenth and seventeenth centuries, and the limited extent to which many of them had developed urban characteristics at all, taken together they performed functions crucial to the operation of the economy, even at the beginning of the period. First and foremost they acted as centres of exchange where the people of the surrounding rural areas were able to sell their surplus production and to buy what they were unable to produce for themselves. Secondly they provided a range of services, some of which were almost equally indispensable in nature. It was mainly the scale on which a town functioned as the former, and the scope and volume of the latter, which determined its size, but in essence there was no fundamental difference in the nature of the rôle played by a minor market town on the one hand and a great regional capital like Norwich or York on the other. In many respects London, too, fulfilled for the country as a whole the same rôle as lesser towns did for more limited geographical areas. However, London grew so much larger than any other city that it may be regarded as having become, at least by the second half of the sixteenth century, different not only in degree but also in kind. We shall therefore first consider the provincial towns collectively, and then deal with London on its own.

ii The provincial towns as market centres

Throughout the sixteenth and seventeenth centuries the public markets of the towns provided the chief means whereby not only the surplus agricultural output but also, to a lesser extent, the industrial production of the countryside found a buyer, and whereby country people were able to obtain such necessities and luxuries as they had money to pay for. They did not, however, have a complete monopoly of this function at any time. There was always some buying and selling between neighbours, and landowners who maintained large country establishments sometimes supplied them with food-stuffs by buying direct from their tenants. Besides, even in the early part of the sixteenth century, the larger villages received occasional visits from travelling chapmen offering for sale such goods as knives, pots and pans, pottery, glass, lace and ribbons.

There were also organized markets in some quite small villages, and although most of them probably had an extremely small turnover and were attended only by people from the immediate vicinity, they were often of some local significance. More important was the existence in every part of the country of fairs, usually held yearly or twice yearly.

Some of these were conducted under the aegis of a town, and indeed most market towns had a fair of some sort, but many were not. A considerable number of the most important fairs, indeed, were held in otherwise obscure villages, or because of their exceedingly ancient origin and because plenty of space was essential, on uninhabited downland or a moorland hill-top, far from any settlement at all. Fairs are often thought of as characteristically medieval institutions, which indeed they were, and already in decline by the sixteenth century, which however they were not, for most of them continued in full vigour well into the eighteenth century and beyond. They were particularly important in the sale and purchase of livestock, above all cattle, with which many of them were exclusively concerned, and although there were fairs which concentrated on other commodities such as cheese, cloth and yarn, leather goods and agricultural implements, and which carried a variety of manufactured goods, they were not numerous by comparison. Some of the better known cattle and horse fairs of the North, such as that held on Bowes Moor in Yorkshire, of the Welsh border and of the Midlands had a national reputation and conducted business on a very large scale indeed. The same was also true of some of the biggest sheep fairs of the South, like Weyhill fair in Hampshire, and perhaps above all the famous Stourbridge fair near Cambridge which dealt in a wide range of goods, including hops, wool, cloth and manufactures. Hundreds of horses, thousands of cattle, and many thousands of sheep might change hands in a few days at the largest fairs. However, these were by no means typical of the very much larger number of small gatherings which were rarely attended by anyone from further than a few miles away. The county of Somerset alone had 180 fairs a year by the end of the period, most of them of strictly local significance. The major livestock fairs played a crucial rôle in the long distance trade between the areas where cattle, and to a lesser extent sheep, were raised, and those where they were fattened for the butcher, but taking internal commerce as a whole neither the volume nor the value of the business they handled rivalled that conducted in the markets of the towns (*A.H.E.W.*IV, 1967, pp. 532–43).

First and foremost the towns provided markets for agricultural produce, but where there were small scale rural industries the peasant-craftsmen were equally dependent on them for the disposal of what they produced. However in areas where such industries outgrew a strictly local demand, came to produce for customers living in distant parts of the country, or even overseas, and to rely heavily on raw materials from distant sources, the mechanisms whereby materials were supplied to workers, and their output was disposed of, frequently by-passed the local markets. For instance the employing clothiers who organized production of woollen cloth tended to obtain their wool in bulk direct from the growing areas, and to take or send the finished product direct to London, or to some other large town or port without offering it for sale locally. Nevertheless even in the woollen manufacturing areas of Gloucestershire, Wiltshire and Somerset, where these developments were already well advanced in the early part of the period, many of the spinners and weavers continued to remain independent of any employer and relied on buying their wool, and selling their yarn or cloth, in the markets of the nearby towns. Indeed as late as 1615 it was estimated that half the output of the West Country industry derived from yarn which had thus passed through the market place. In areas of less precocious industrial evolution, such as the West Riding of Yorkshire where woollen cloth was also made, and South East Lancashire where woollens and linens were produced and, in the seventeenth century, linen-cotton mixtures known as fustians, the families of smallholders and cottagers generally retained their economic independence even longer. They therefore continued to rely heavily, if not exclusively, on the open markets until very late in the period, and in some cases until after the end of it. (See also below II, Ch. 8 sec. xi.)

In the smallest places the markets remained unspecialized throughout the sixteenth and seventeenth centuries, handling a relatively wide range of commodities in small quantities and serving a very limited district. The bigger towns, however, whose sphere of influence was correspondingly more extensive, already had separate markets for the more important classes of goods produced in the surrounding area even at the beginning of the period. At Worcester there were, before 1500, physically separate markets for English cattle, Welsh cattle, sheep, wheat, barley, oatmeal and salt. York in the early sixteenth century had them catering for malt, leather, sea fish, fresh-water fish, pigs, meat and cattle, in addition to two general purpose markets held three times a week. As the period wore on, and particularly after about 1570, the growing commercialization of agriculture and the development of rural industry meant an increasing tendency towards greater market specialization. Thus at Worcester separate sites were set aside for dealings in garden produce, ironmongery, leather and wooden goods during the course of the sixteenth century, and at York a new market for Kendal and West Riding cloth was established in 1546. Specialist markets also began to appear in many towns of lesser importance, especially those that lay on the main lines of communication or were in districts where there was a substantial growth of rural industry. It has been calculated that by 1640, out of a total of nearly 800 market settlements, over 300 specialized in one or more products, and some quite small towns had developed highly important rôles in internal commerce by acting as the collecting points for the production of a considerable region which was thus funnelled through them towards London or some other centre of consumption. Thus vast quantities of grain destined for the metropolis passed through the market of the little Surrey town of Farnham, whilst in the West Country, Bruton and Wincanton drew grain from the sheep–corn areas of Wiltshire and Dorset and supplied it to the heavily populated clothing villages of East Somerset (*A.H.E.W.* IV, 1967, pp. 490–6. Dyer, 1973, p. 73. Palliser, 1973 (2)).

Before the end of the period, however, the open markets, carefully regulated by the municipal authorities partly in the interests of the income from tolls they yielded, and partly in the interests of the urban consumer, were beginning to lose ground to new ways of conducting business. These developments did not lessen the significance of towns in general as centres of exchange, and like increasing market specialization they represented an adjustment to the growing scale and complexity of the country's internal commerce. They did, however, enhance the importance of some places at the expense of less well situated neighbours, and especially after the mid seventeenth century, many of the smaller market towns, such as Ashby de la Zouch (Leics.) and Wickham Market (Suffolk), were clearly declining in size and importance, in some cases to the extent that by 1700 they were well on the way to losing their urban characteristics altogether (Clark and Slack, 1976, pp. 24–5. Chartres, 1977 (1), p. 48. Patten, 1978, pp. 206–7, 218–20, 292). From the later sixteenth century onwards, and particularly in the last third of the seventeenth, those people dealing with large volumes of grain, sheep and wool, but to a lesser extent other forms of country produce, including cattle, hops, cloth and leather began to forsake the publicity of the market place and to make private deals behind closed doors, away from the prying eyes of neighbours and market officials. Buyers and sellers often thus established long lasting relationships, which guaranteed the one a regular source of supply and the other a regular customer, so that both ceased to patronize the the market at all. Urban inns were the main meeting place of the private traders, and many of these came to provide not only accommodation for the large numbers of men and horses who were travelling in pursuit of trade, but also extensive storage facilities for goods, pasturage for livestock and even a commercial information service in the form of landlords who would put parties who might be able to do business in touch with each other. With increasing speed after 1660, therefore, the commercial heart of large numbers of towns was moving from the market streets and squares to the back-rooms of the principal hostelries, where methods of dealing, often on the basis of samples, frequently making use of credit, and sometimes involving very large sums of money, became increasingly more elaborate than those used in the market place (*A.H.E.W.* IV, 1967, pp. 543–63. *A.H.E.W.* V, 1983, pp. 416–18, 471–2. Chartres, 1973).

Whilst the open market was losing much of the wholesale trade, particularly in the most important primary agricultural products, to inns, it was also losing a growing proportion of the retail trade in manufactured goods on the one hand to permanent shops, and on the other to travelling chapmen. Goods obtained from outside the town and its immediate hinterland were the province of merchants who were traders pure and simple and themselves undertook no production processes, although even in medium sized market towns they might be part-time farmers. Such people most often called themselves mercers, drapers, haberdashers or grocers, although it was generally only in the larger towns that the volume of their business warranted specialization in particular classes of goods. Their main stock in trade was textile fabrics, in smaller places doubtless mainly the cheaper varieties of English cloth, but even there they also stocked small quantities of imported items such as French linens and canvas, and by the end of the period Indian calicoes and muslins. In addition they kept a wide range of miscellaneous manufactures from cutlery and cooking utensils to dried fruits, pins, buttons, paper, wine and medicines, and in the seventeenth century, sugar and tobacco. In the early part of the period they still made most of their sales through markets and fairs, but as the period wore on they tended to rely increasingly on selling from shops which remained open the week long and which, especially by the later seventeenth century, were fitted up with considerable elaboration and concern for the visual appeal of the window display. This development of course occurred earliest in London, where indeed it was well under way by the mid sixteenth century, and then in the larger provincial towns. However, during the course of the later sixteenth and seventeenth centuries shops began to appear not only in the smaller towns, but in many villages too. As early as 1578 the little town of Kirby Lonsdale near Kendal had a shop-keeper, James Backhouse, whose stock in trade covered almost every conceivable type of cloth from sackcloth to Spanish silk, an impressive range of fashion accessories including both felt and silk hats and French garters, besides all the usual grocery wares, paper, ink-horns and books, mainly of a religious and educational nature. However, these developments in retailing were especially marked in the economically more advanced areas such as East Anglia and the Home Counties. Thus by the end of the period grocers are recorded in thirty-five out of East Anglia's forty-seven towns, and in as many as seventy-seven villages, so that no one in the region can have lived very far from a retail shop. This multiplication of village shops reflects both an increase in the variety of the goods available for sale (see below II, Ch. 8 sec. V; and pp. 164–9), and a growth in demand for them to the point where people were no longer satisfied by weekly visits to the nearest town. The same developments lay behind the increase, particularly noticeable after the middle of the seventeenth century, in the number of pedlars and chapmen who carried light weight consumer goods from door to door as they travelled amongst the villages. But although both village shops and chapmen were a symptom of the growing volume of internal commerce, they clearly did actually draw trade away from the smaller market towns and contributed to the economic eclipse which we have noticed that some of them experienced in the later seventeenth century (Willan, 1976, chs. II–III. Thirsk, 1978, pp. 120–4. Patten, 1978, pp. 186, 222–4, 278, 289–90).

The shopkeepers of the smaller towns, who thus made available to country people a widening range of manufactured goods made in other parts of the country and abroad, received part of their stocks from itinerant tradesmen specializing in particular classes of goods, such as Yorkshire kersies, Wealdon glassware, Norwich stuffs, Sheffield cutlery or, by the end of the period, Staffordshire pottery. They would collect supplies in the district of origin, buying them in the markets or direct from the manufacturer, load them onto pack-horses and travel from place to place, probably following a regular route, offering them for sale. To a considerable degree, however, and especially in the case of commodities from distant regions or abroad, smaller towns were supplied by the wholesale merchants of the larger ones. The latter thus acted not only as markets and centres of exchange for the area immediately surrounding them, but also as centres of distribution for a very much wider hinterland, a rôle which they had acquired as a result of being well placed in respect of transport and communications, particularly navigable rivers. London was, of course, pre-eminent as a distributive centre, particularly of imported commodities, for so much of the country's overseas trade was concentrated there. However in the sixteenth century, although not in the seventeenth, the provincial ports had a larger share of imports than of exports, and several of them, notably Bristol, Exeter, Hull, Chester and Newcastle, played an important part in their distribution. So also did places which were able to carry on foreign trade through them, as in the early part of the period Salisbury did through Southampton, and until towards the end of it York did through Hull. In all major distributive centres, whether or not they were ports, there was a class of wholesale merchants who purchased in bulk at the distant source of supply, arranged for transport back to their base of operations and then sold in smaller lots to the retail dealers who depended on them. Such merchants were usually the richest and most influential men in their communities, and though outside London they often engaged in retail trade as well, for the more successful of them it was normally only a subordinate part of their business.

Of all the provincial towns which fulfilled the rôle of distributive centre, Bristol probably served the largest region, for the Bristol Channel and the river Severn made it possible for boats from there to reach as far as Minehead or Bideford and beyond in one direction, the ports of South Wales in another and Worcester and Shrewsbury in yet another, whilst the opening of the Warwickshire Avon to navigation in the late 1630s extended the area readily accessible to its merchants deep into the Midlands. To take another example the wholesale dealers of York in the later sixteenth century handled grain from Holderness, Lincolnshire and Norfolk; salt and fish, both from the north east coast and imported, the former from France, the latter from North Germany, Holland and Scotland; coal from the Tyne and Wear; cloth from the West Riding of Yorkshire and Westmorland; and manufactures and imported luxuries such as wine, dried fruits and spices, obtained from London or direct from abroad through the port of Hull. These goods were then supplied to the large part of the North East and North Midlands to which the rivers Ouse, Humber, Trent and their tributaries gave access (Palliser, 1973 (2)). Bristol and York, along with Exeter in the South West and possibly Chester in the North West, were the most important of the regional centres of distribution, but every county had one or two towns which acted in the same way for a smaller area.

iii The provincial towns and the provision of services

Even the smallest towns of the sixteenth and seventeenth centuries offered the services of a range of craftsmen, many of whom were craftsmen-retailers who worked in a shop where, for the most part, they made goods to order but where they might also keep a modest stock of finished work to sell on the spot. In the less important places the range of craftsmen was restricted, the extent of their business small, and most of them would be in trades which catered for the basic needs of the surrounding countryside and those of the townspeople themselves. Trades found most commonly in such places were those concerned with processing the agricultural produce of the neighbourhood, butchers, chandlers, tanners, millers, bakers, maltsters and brewers. There would also be tailors and shoe-makers to provide clothing and footwear;

carpenters, bricklayers, masons, tilers and thatchers to undertake building work; smiths to make and repair metal objects such as locks, hinges, chains and the fittings of agricultural equipment; and perhaps saddlers to make the harness for draught animals, and cartwrights or wheelwrights to make the few wheeled vehicles used for local purposes.

In the larger towns not only were there greater numbers of craftsmen in the common trades but also there appeared those who depended on the patronage of more affluent customers, particularly local gentry land-owners and members of the urban élite, and those whose services were of a specialist nature. Thus in Sudbury, a locally important town in Suffolk, in the 1520s such occupations as glover, plumber, pewterer, goldsmith, armourer and fletcher or arrow-maker, appear alongside the more run of the mill crafts. In mid sixteenth century Norwich, the largest city outside London, an even more varied assortment is found including ones with such limited appeal as sieve-maker, fingerbread-maker, embroiderer, parchment-maker, and book-binder. Altogether 171 different occup-ations are recorded at Norwich in the early seventeenth century, compared to between fifty and a hundred at middle sized cities like Yarmouth, Ipswich, Winchester and Lichfield, and twenty-five or less in the generality of small market towns. As the period progressed some crafts, such as the fletcher's, disappeared altogether, but they were replaced by others whose evolution reflects the availability of new products and the increasingly sophisticated lifestyle of the better off members of the community. Thus in the later sixteenth century glaziers became established in one town after another as the use of glass in the windows of domestic buildings became increasingly common. Likewise in the seventeenth century chair-makers, cabinet-makers and up-holsterers increased in numbers as the wealthy began to fill their houses with furniture; clock-makers and book-sellers multiplied; and map-makers, tobacco-pipe makers and confectioners appeared for the first time (Pound, 1966. Patten, 1972; 1978, pp. 166–7, 252ff).

Another important service which the towns provided for the countryside was long distance transport. Throughout the sixteenth and seventeenth centuries, and indeed until the coming of the railways in the nineteenth, conveyance of bulky freight was undertaken by water whenever possible and this was especially true of anything with a low value in relation to its volume, such as coal, minerals or grain. It was so because, given the prevailing technology, it was very much less expensive, rates per ton mile being anything up to ten or twelve times greater if goods had to be taken by road. As may be seen from Map 3 on p. 167, most of the important towns of the period stood on navigable rivers, indeed only three of the ten richest provincial towns in the 1520s did not,[4] and more came to do so as a result of the improvements made to a number of hitherto unusable streams from the 1630s onwards, for instance Oxford, Stratford-on-Avon, Guildford, Salisbury and Hereford.[5] It was thus not only those places which were on the sea coast from which freight could be despatched by water. At both sea ports and river ports the quays and warehouses were often maintained by the municipal authorities, and even in a place which lay as far from the open sea as did Worcester, a not insignificant proportion of the working population were employed in loading and unloading the boats which plied on the Severn, and in providing the crews and the gangs of hauliers for them (Dyer, 1973, pp. 60–6). A proportion of the vessels in the coastal and riverine trade were owned by merchants who used them mainly to carry their own merchandise, and some indeed were designed and operated for a highly specialized purpose, most notably in the carriage of coal from the North East to London, but most were certainly operated by men who were prepared to take the goods of others upon payment of freightage.

As for transport by road, which it is now clear was much more important to the economy than historians once believed, much short and medium distance carriage was provided from within the farming community. Indeed for some of its members it was an important supplement to their agricultural incomes, for they regularly employed their draught animals in carting during those parts of the year when there was little work for them on the land. But over longer distances the business was mainly in the hands of professional urban based carriers, and in the case of livestock, professional drovers. By the early part of the seventeenth century, and probably well before, the carriers, using waggons or pack-horses as conditions dictated, were providing regular and scheduled services. Almost every significant town in the country was thus linked to London by weekly or fortnightly departures, even those as far off as York, Manchester and Plymouth. There were certainly also some cross country services between the provincial towns themselves, and many more appeared before the end of the century. Although far more expensive than river barge or coastal vessel, carriers were more reliable and quicker, and were thus preferred for the conveyance of high value goods like textiles and other manufactures, even for long

[4] The three were Coventry, Salisbury and Canterbury.
[5] As a result of improvements respectively to the Thames and Warwickshire Avon in the 1630s, the Wey in the 1650s, the Wiltshire Avon after 1660 and the Wye in the later 1690s. By the end of the seventeenth century schemes were afoot to make navigable the rivers on which a number of rapidly expanding northern towns stood, including Leeds, Wakefield and Sheffield, although these were not implemented until after 1700 (Willan, 1936, ch. II). For the navigable rivers *c.* 1700, see Map 4 on p. 168.

distances (Chartres, 1977 (2)). Cloth from both Norwich and Devonshire, for instance, invariably reached London by waggon. However, for passengers and mail, road transport was still agonizingly slow in the early seventeenth century. But the 1630s saw the introduction of a relatively rapid postal service between London and the most important provincial towns, and those places that lay on the roads thither. It also saw the appearance of the earliest passenger coaches, which at first plied only between London and towns within about thirty miles, but which by the middle of the century were going to all parts of the kingdom. The urban inns provided the termini of these carriers' and coaching services, and also the many resting places along the way that were required on the longer journeys, for even the coaches could not manage more than twenty-five or thirty miles a day. Thus they fulfilled a vital rôle as links in the web of communications which made it possible for men and goods to move from one part of the country to another. Those towns which lay at the centre of a network of roads, or on important through routes, thus came to develop very extensive hostelry facilities indeed. The little town of St Albans in Hertfordshire, on the road between London and North West, had as many as twenty-seven inns as early as 1577, whilst by the early eighteenth century the more important town of Northampton had about sixty, which between them must have been able to provide accommodation for 4000 horses. The number of inns increased almost everywhere during the sixteenth and seventeenth centuries and the largest of them were elaborately, even lavishly, equipped establishments, managed by men of substance who, by the latter part of the period, were often among the wealthiest men in their communities. The wealth and standing of the whole inn-keeping profession indeed improved markedly, especially from the later sixteenth century onwards, as the volume of their business expanded and they began to assume new functions, both commercial, and as we shall see, as providers of organized entertainment for county society (Everitt, 1969 (1), pp. 25, 38–41; 1973).

Towns also provided financial services for the surrounding rural areas. There were no banks established anywhere in England outside London before the eighteenth century, and there is no question that the London money market was by far the largest source of loan capital throughout the period, and those who wanted to borrow really large sums would be unlikely to obtain them anywhere else. Nevertheless, from quite early in the seventeenth century and even before, there were individuals in the provincial towns, whose main activity lay in other fields, who were acting as financial intermediaries and fulfilling some of the functions of bankers. Attorneys and others who handled the legal affairs of clients both affluent and needy were well placed to put those with surplus capital to invest in touch with those who wanted to borrow, and to arrange loans secured by bond or mortgage between individuals who might otherwise never have come together. Some of the loanable funds thus made available will have come from the coffers of townsmen, but as much and probably far more would have been from those of the gentry and successful farmers, and it is very unlikely that even medium sized towns were a more important source of capital for would-be borrowers in the countryside than were other members of the rural community. However there is no doubt that the major regional centres, Norwich, Bristol, Exeter, York, Newcastle, and by the mid seventeenth century Manchester and perhaps Birmingham too, particularly the merchants in those places engaged in overseas, wholesale and distributive trades, did contribute very largely to the capital requirements of landowners and others in the regions where they lay. At York, for instance, where usury was reported in the later sixteenth century to be practised 'as well by merchants as by artificers and men of all sorts', the war waged against it by the ecclesiastical authorities provides an indication of the city's importance as a local money market (Palliser, 1979, pp. 280–1).

Merchants certainly used such lending as one means of investing the fortunes they themselves had made, and it is probable that they also offered an outlet for the savings of others by accepting deposits from them and using the funds so acquired to expand their own businesses or even re-lending them at a higher rate of interest, the latter representing an important step towards true banking. But even in quite small towns there was one financial service which wholesale traders commonly provided, that of remitting funds from place to place without incurring the risks necessarily involved in actually transporting cash. They were able to do this because throughout the period those involved in internal commerce on a large scale made extensive use of credit, and balances due between traders resident in different places were settled by means of inland bills of exchange. Great landowners, many of whom lived for much of the year in London, often wanted a large part of the proceeds of their country estates made available to them there, but many others might need to transfer money to the capital or some other large town, for instance to defray the cost of a visit, to pay an apprenticeship premium or to support a son at school or at one of the universities or Inns of Court. Provided that there was a sufficient volume of trade between some nearby market town and the desired destination, it was possible for them to buy bills from a trader involved in commerce, bills which would be drawn on someone who owed that trader money, and in effect gave the purchaser the right to collect from him a specified part of the debt upon presentation on or after a stated date. The butchers and graziers of Buckingham and

Leighton Buzzard, who sent beef cattle to London but who needed to
have the proceeds available in the country in order to buy more stock,
were, for instance, the main channel whereby the leading gentry families
of Buckinghamshire remitted their rent income to the capital in the
second half of the seventeenth century. In other areas, where local
commerce was far less dominated by the livestock trade, wholesalers
dealing in such commodities as corn, cloth and ironmongery seem to have
acted in the same capacity (Davies, 1971).

There was also a range of other services which towns provided that
were less strictly economic in their nature, but which had economic
implications for those who used them, and which certainly made their
contribution to the prosperity of the towns themselves. Legal services in
the provinces were mainly provided by attorneys and scriveners, who
were mostly to be found in the county towns where Quarter Sessions and
Assizes were held, especially if these were cathedral cities where there
were also church courts generating legal business and posts in the
diocesan administration for them to fill. They were available, to that very
small section of the community who had both the occasion and the means
to employ them, to provide legal advice, draft wills and draw up the
bonds which were much used in commercial transactions where one
party allowed credit to the other, besides acquittances, leases, con-
veyances and settlements of property. Landowners in particular provided
them with a steady flow of such business, and attorneys and scriveners
also came increasingly to provide estate management services for
absentee owners of property, acting as manorial stewards, holding courts
and keeping court records, collecting rents and fines and generally
supervising tenants. On the other hand virtually all the vast amount of
litigation in which Englishmen engaged in the sixteenth and seventeenth
centuries took place in London, owing to the concentration there of the
common law and equity courts and to a lesser extent, until their abolition
in 1641, of the prerogative courts also. The legal work thus generated in
the capital, and it was not only the largest but also the most lucrative part
of the whole, was virtually monopolized by metropolitan lawyers, and
this served to limit the extent to which the profession was able to develop
in other parts of the country. Among the principal towns only York could
in any way rival London as a legal centre. This was because of the
permanent presence there of the Council of the North from 1561, and of a
unique concentration of ecclesiastical courts, of which the former in
particular handled a large volume of cases and attracted not only a large
legal fraternity, but also their numerous clients, and had a good deal to do
with the revival of the city's prosperity in the later sixteenth century
(Palliser, 1978; 1979, pp. 146, 261–5).

As for medical services, licensed physicians, surgeons and apothecaries (who not only prescribed and sold drugs but increasingly acted as practitioners of medicine in general) mostly lived in the towns. So did a large proportion of the many unlicensed, but not necessarily unqualified or incompetent 'empirics', who practised illegally alongside them. At the beginning of the period the number of such people was relatively small, and they were found mainly in the larger places, but from the later sixteenth century they became considerably more numerous and began to appear even in quite small market towns. This increase in numbers coincided with a marked improvement both in their social status and their professional understanding, although probably not in their ability to cure the ailments of their patients. The growth of the medical profession seems to have been in response to a growth in demand for treatment and to a considerable degree this, like the demand for legal services, came from the gentry and their families, although those lower down the social scale clearly also provided much business, especially for the unlicensed. For the very best doctors it would be necessary to go to London, but few, even among the gentry, could afford to do so, and the rest would have to consult those nearer at hand. At any rate there is ample evidence that many urban doctors had considerable rural practices. At least seventy-three medical practitioners of one sort or another have been identified in Norwich between 1570 and 1590, and over a rather longer period in the later sixteenth century twenty-four in Ipswich and fifteen in King's Lynn. Many of these must have relied heavily on the patronage of patients living in the surrounding countryside (Roberts, 1962. Raach, 1962. Pelling and Webster, 1979). Another professional group whose members were mainly located in the towns, especially London, were the astrologers, and although the science they pursued had come to be regarded as spurious by educated opinion by the end of the period, as late as the 1650s they were numerous, their advice was still sought by all classes and the value of it was as great or greater than that dispensed by the majority of physicians (Thomas, 1971, pp. 300–22).

Educational facilities were less centralized than was medical advice: village doctors, at any rate doctors with any form of training, were rare in this period although midwives, 'cunning men' or the local clergy might try their hand at healing. Village schoolmasters, on the other hand, were common, at least in the South and East, although probably less so in the North. Especially in the later sixteenth century and the first half of the seventeenth a surprisingly large number of villages in counties like Cambridgeshire, Norfolk and Leicestershire, had schools run by university graduates, providing a grammar education and capable of preparing boys for Oxford, Cambridge or one of the Inns of Court. Most of them were, of course, very small, with perhaps just a handful of pupils, and many were also ephemeral, depending for their continued existence upon a single teacher and dissolving when he obtained better paid employment elsewhere. There were also endowed grammar schools in some villages, but the great majority of the hundreds which were founded in this period, mostly in the century or so after the Reformation, were established in the towns. In Kent, for instance, there were twenty-one such endowed schools by 1700, fourteen of them urban. Towns also had their small unendowed schools, and there can be little doubt that the volume of educational provision at grammar level in the towns exceeded that available in the countryside, and did so by an increasingly wide margin as the number of village schoolmasters gradually dwindled in the later seventeenth century.[6] Some quite small market towns, such as Sevenoaks and Tonbridge in Kent, had disproportionately large endowed schools, and the major cities, especially regional capitals like Exeter, Salisbury, Norwich and York, often had two or three by the middle of the seventeenth century, all of them catering not only for the sons of urban tradesmen but also for those of the gentry and farmers of the countryside (Stone, 1964. Spufford, 1970. Simon, 1968, chs. 1 and 2. Chalklin, 1965, pp. 262–4).

Yet another service which towns provided for their rural hinterlands was that of social centres and places of entertainment. At the most rudimentary level market day was, as it still is in peasant societies to this day, not only a commercial but also a social occasion, and many of those who attended did so as much for the sake of a day's outing, to exchange gossip and to hear the news, as they did to buy or sell. Every market town had its alehouses, which offered the opportunity for singing, dancing and gambling, as well as drinking, and in the larger ones these were astonishingly numerous. Worcester in 1590 had fifty-eight licensed alehouse-keepers, and apparently Derby in 1693 had 120, far more than could have been kept in business by even the most bibulous urban communities. Alehouses were mainly patronized by poorer people, and those with more money to spend went to the inns, which catered for the respectable elements of society and offered refreshments and other diversions in a form even the gentry found acceptable. Indeed by the later sixteenth century inns were increasingly being used by the local gentry

---

[6] Village schoolmasters seem to have been so numerous in the late sixteenth and early seventeenth centuries because the expansion of the universities had produced a large number of graduates, trained for the ministry but unable to find benefices, who were thus forced to take any appropriate employment available. As the number of those going to the universities ebbed after the mid seventeenth century, so did the number of those willing to teach in the countryside (Spufford, 1970).

as meeting places, where the administrative problems of the shire, and at times their political grievances, could be discussed. To attract further custom the landlords of the bigger inns began to organize social functions such as cock-fighting, bear-baiting, card parties, plays performed by visiting companies of actors, banquets, balls, and by the very end of the period even concerts and flower shows, which came to play an important part in the social life of the better off members of local society (Everitt, 1973. Dyer, 1973). Other enterprising property owners, or even the municipal authorities, began to provide such amenities as cock-pits and bowling greens, and to organize horse races, whilst in a number of places what had survived of later medieval civic ceremonies and processions came to form something of a tourist attraction for county society.

In at least one of the larger towns in each county the business of providing entertainment for the gentry, and the well-to-do generally, developed to a marked degree, and indeed became an important industry providing considerable employment. This happened earliest in the major provincial capitals: at York, for instance, which had no fewer that sixty-four inns in 1596. Here horse racing for a trophy was recorded as early as 1530, there was regular cock-fighting from 1568 and almost annual visits from companies of actors in the later sixteenth century (Palliser, 1979, pp. 20, 167. *V.C.H. City of York*, pp. 157–8). Elsewhere the development occurred somewhat later and seems to have owed much to the invention and growing popularity of the coach which enabled a man to travel with his whole family. The really wealthy landowners went to London to find amusement, but those who were unable to afford the capital made do with the local assize town, began to acquire houses there, or more often to take lodgings or rooms in an inn for a few weeks every year. Thus gradually during the first half of the seventeenth century in towns such as Maidstone, Bury St Edmunds, Northampton and Preston a definite winter 'season' of organized social events began to emerge. The second half of the century saw a further acceleration of this development, and by the end of the period it had begun to call into existence new facilities and institutions to supplement those provided by the inns, many of which were being rebuilt on a truly enormous scale. Assembly rooms were constructed, coffee houses appeared, and in the first few years of the eighteenth century the first purpose built theatres outside London opened in Bath and Bristol.

iv The provincial towns and immigration from the countryside

In all towns, save the smallest, living conditions for the majority of the population were very bad. The well-to-do might have spacious houses facing onto wide streets, with gardens behind them, but most people lived in tiny and frequently ramshackle dwellings closely packed along cramped alley-ways or around foetid courtyards, or crammed into larger houses sub-divided to accommodate as many families as possible. The disposal of waste, sanitation and water supply posed perennial difficulties, and ones that few municipal authorities were able to solve with much success, although they often devoted much time and effort to the attempt. Particularly noisome activities, like tanning and the slaughtering of livestock, were usually banished to the edge of the town, or confined to particular quarters, but even so mountains of animal manure and other forms of rubbish piled up to rot malodorously in immediate proximity to human habitations. Privies often discharged directly onto the street, chamber pots were emptied unceremoniously from upper windows, and even those householders who kept barrels in their closets would eventually tip the contents out into a public place or at best into a nearby stream, as the citizens of Manchester did from Salford bridge over the Irwell (Willan, 1980, pp. 121–2). Only the wealthy had their own wells and pumps, and everyone else had to rely upon public ones drawing upon sources of water almost inevitably contaminated by seepage, or upon supplies brought round in leather sacks slung across the back of a horse, as was still normal in York in the 1680s (Palliser, 1979, pp. 161–2).

The consequences of such conditions for the health of town dwellers has already been alluded to: the incidence of endemic disease was so high, and epidemics so frequent and so destructive, that death rates were markedly higher than in rural areas. (See above pp. 7–8, 20–3.) Especially was this true of infant death rates which in some poor parishes in large cities, at least at some periods, clearly exceeded 250 per 1000 (Palliser, 1979, pp. 119–20). The demographic consequences of this were compounded by the fact that the presence of large numbers of apprentices and living-in servants, domestic or otherwise, produced a society in which there were an abnormally high proportion of unmarried people, and in consequence a low birth rate. There were, therefore, few towns of any size which were able to maintain their numbers for long periods by means of natural increase alone, unless they were exceptionally fortunate in escaping major epidemics. A few were. York experienced no major mortality crisis between 1559 and 1603, and although plague broke out a number of times in Worcester in the later sixteenth and early seventeenth centuries, only in 1637 did it claim as many as one tenth of the population (Palliser, 1979, pp. 124–7. Dyer, 1973, pp. 44–7). Other places, however, suffered dreadfully. At Colchester there were serious outbreaks of plague or typhus in 1579, 1586, 1597, 1603, 1626, 1631, 1644, and finally in 1665–6 when nearly half the population died, whilst Norwich was struck by plague six times over the same period (Doolittle, 1975. Clark and Slack, 1976, p. 89).

The majority of towns, therefore, depended on immigration even to maintain a stationary population, and in order to achieve substantial growth it was necessary that the inflow should be continuous and sustained at a high level. Most movement from one locality to another occurred because people felt that their economic prospects would be better if they went elsewhere. At one end of the scale there were those for whom a move was a deliberate and considered step, such as taking up an inheritance, entering an apprenticeship or commencing a business partnership with a friend or a relative, in which the emigrant was taking advantage of a specific opportunity for advancement which he had been offered or which he had sought out for himself. Such people did not, in general, move very great distances, and most provincial towns recruited their respectable immigrants from the immediately surrounding countryside, few coming from further than thirty or forty miles distant. Thus over 70 per cent of those taking up apprenticeships in Maidstone in the later sixteenth century came from within eleven miles of the town, and even a much larger place such as Worcester did not admit many new freemen from further than twenty-five miles off. It is true that the largest provincial centres attracted people from further afield: there was, for instance, a small but steady flow from the Yorkshire Dales to Norwich, from the upper and middle Severn valley to Bristol, and from Cumberland and Westmorland to York. But even in these places apprentices and freemen from far away were a small minority: at York in the mid sixteenth century not many more than a quarter, 28.5 per cent, came more than fifty miles (Clark, 1972. Patten, 1973, pp. 33–43. Dyer, 1973, p. 183. Palliser, 1979, pp. 127–31). Further down the scale there were those with some resources, contacts or marketable skills, but who were for some reason obliged to find somewhere new to settle and to make a living. And at the bottom of it were the workless, and more or less destitute, who wandered from place to place in the hope of finding some means of subsistence, whether it was only casual labour or at worst merely the hope of charity or poor relief. (See below Ch. 7 sec. i.) In general, at least before the mid seventeenth century, the poorer immigrants seem to have travelled further from their original homes than the more respectable ones, perhaps because necessity so often forced them to move repeatedly. By the end of the period, however, reduced population pressure, the development of new urban centres in the highland zone of the North and West, and increasing official interference with the freedom of poor people to move as they wished (see below Ch. 7 sec. iii), had apparently reversed this situation (Clark, 1972; 1979).

The period of increasing population in the sixteenth and seventeenth centuries inevitably witnessed an increase in all types of migrant, and since there was also a considerable reverse flow out of the towns back to the countryside, and much movement between different towns, the populations of most urban centres were constantly changing in composition. Naturally, however, the number of immigrants in the middle and lower reaches of the spectrum rose faster and further than did that of those at its higher end. Indeed it was probably only they whose movement was on a large enough scale to make an appreciable difference to the geographical distribution of the population, and whose arrival or non-arrival determined the rate at which urban population grew. Had all, or even most, of those who found it necessary to leave their places of origin to make a living gravitated towards the provincial towns and stayed there, the latter would have exhibited a very much faster collective rate of growth than in fact occurred. They did not do so because, throughout the period, the ability of most provincial towns to attract immigrants was relatively weak compared to that exerted by alternative destinations.

Many of those who left rural homes in the sixteenth and seventeenth centuries moved, not to urban areas, but to other country districts, particularly to those where the survival of large areas of forest, fen or moorland meant that there were still extensive commons. For most of the period the main lure of such areas was their relative emptiness which made it possible for incomers not only to find a place to live, albeit as unlicensed squatters, but to support themselves by some combination of small scale animal husbandry, casual or seasonal agricultural work in adjacent areas of mixed farming and the pursuit of a craft. (See above Ch. 3 sec. viii.) Besides, as the period wore on the abundance of cheap labour available in these districts encouraged entrepreneurs to develop local crafts into domestic industries producing for a wide market, and even to introduce quite new industries. (See esp. II, pp. 91–2 and Ch. 8 sec. v.) By the end of it once sparsely inhabited areas were supporting populations of a considerable density, and yet industry had taken hold to such a degree that demand for labour was beginning to outstrip supply, so that the continued inflow of people from other districts was no longer on account of under-utilized land, but almost entirely because of the prospects of industrial employment. Thus by 1700 or so wage levels in the areas of most rapidly expanding rural industry in the North, and probably in the West Midlands also, were still lower than those in the South and East, but they were showing much more of a tendency to rise (Gilboy, 1934, esp. pp. 219–27). The inhabitants of those areas still lived in country villages but a growing number of them were coming to depend primarily, sometimes almost exclusively, on their industrial earnings.

Of those who, out of choice or necessity, did migrate from the countryside to a town, a disproportionately large number ended up in London, either going there directly or perhaps more often after trying their luck for a while in one or more smaller places. For whether a man was drawn by the lure of starting a career in wholesale or overseas trade, or driven by the desperation of utter poverty, London beckoned more strongly than any provincial city. So much economic activity was concentrated in the capital that the demand for labour and the possibilities of getting employment were immeasurably greater than elsewhere. Besides in the sprawling suburbs, where the writ of the city authorities did not run, it was as easy for a new-comer to find somewhere to live undisturbed or even to start his own business if he had the wherewithal to do so, as it was in the Pennine valleys or the heaths of Staffordshire. So great indeed was the drawing power of the capital that it has been estimated that, during the decades on either side of 1700, immigration to London absorbed half the natural increase of the entire population of the country (Wrigley, 1967).

v The provincial towns and manufacturing industry

As the preceding section should have made clear, the limited extent of provincial urbanization was largely the corollary of the development of rural industries on the one hand, and the immense growth of London on the other. Both, in different ways, limited the scope of the economic activities carried on in the country towns, and thus the ability and indeed the willingness of most of them to attract and retain enough immigrants to do more than keep pace with the general growth of population. For sluggish growth in employment opportunities in the majority of provincial towns, though not, as we shall see, in quite all of them, was reflected in hostility to new-comers on the part of established townsmen and municipal authorities. There were attempts to discourage even respectable immigrants. For instance in Canterbury, Rochester, Maidstone and other Kentish towns in the late sixteenth and early seventeenth centuries, the fines which they had to pay for admission to the 'freedom', in effect a licence to carry on a business of their own, were steeply increased, and there were campaigns to deny them the right to acquire the freedom at all (Clark, 1972). As for poor immigrants coming in search of work they were widely regarded as a liability rather than an asset, as indeed they were in places where there was no work for them.

Nevertheless, the degree of economic 'push' generated in those parts of the countryside where population was growing faster than employment opportunities was such that they continued to come, giving rise in many places to an acute poverty 'problem'. As we shall see in Chapter 7, the urban authorities were therefore forced to make strenuous efforts to keep them out and to expel many of those who had established themselves. (See below Ch. 7 sec. i.)

The growth of London will form the subject of the final section of this chapter, but we must first consider why it was that so much industrial output came not from the towns but from the countryside. There were certain types of manufacturing process which were usually carried on in urban locations. These included those which depended upon highly skilled workers for whom industry was a whole-time, rather than a part-time, activity; those for which close proximity to customers was advantageous, for instance because transport of the finished product was excessively costly in relation to its value, or excessively difficult; and those which used bulky raw materials imported from abroad, and for which a port was the obvious site. However, in the principal consumer goods industries – textiles, metal goods, leather goods and articles of wood – most and in some cases all the processes of production could, given the techniques of the period, be performed by the workers in their own homes. The main essential in these industries was for large amounts of labour, from whom only a limited range of easily learnt skills were required. (See also below II, pp. 87–9.) Employers seeking to take advantage of growing demand by expanding their output would therefore do so by tapping whatever reservoirs of unemployed or under-employed labour they could find. Sometimes towns might provide the work-people they needed, especially if some old established industry was in decay leaving behind it an economic vacuum. But in general labour was more abundant in the countryside, especially in areas where small scale pasture farming flourished and, as we have just seen in the preceding section, above all where ample commons and weak manorial control made possible unrestricted immigration.

It was also important that labour in the countryside was cheaper. This was partly because of the absence of gilds, whose control of the apprenticeship system enabled them to limit the number of entrants to particular occupations, thereby keeping the level of wages somewhat higher than it would otherwise have been. More important, however, was the fact that, at least in the larger towns, industrial workers were more completely dependent on wage earning for their livelihood and thus inevitably had to be paid more than part-time farmers and their families, who also had the resources of an agricultural holding or the livestock which access to common land enabled them to keep. Other aspects of gild and municipal regulation, for instance measures interfering with production methods with the intention of maintaining standards of quality, also tended to raise the costs of urban manufacturers. However the evidence does not suggest that this was a major factor in determining location, particularly as in the case of the woollen textile industry a national system of regulation, which applied to rural and urban areas alike, was established during the sixteenth century and enforced at least intermittently. (See below II, pp. 233–4, 245–8.) As for those forms of industry could not be carried on in the cottages of the work force, because they required a substantial amount of fixed capital in the way of powered equipment, elaborate apparatus or installations of other types, or buildings, different considerations governed the choice of site, but nevertheless more often dictated a rural than an urban one. For instance in the case of industries which used mills, whether to pulp rags for paper or to roll out metal bars into sheets, or which involved furnaces capable of very high temperatures as in the processing of metal ores or the making of glass, access to power and fuel, or both, were all important. Few towns could provide more than a handful of water-power sites, and any plant which required large amounts of heat was clearly best established in a forested area if it burnt wood, or in close proximity to coal mines if, as became usual in an increasing number of processes in the seventeenth century (see below II, pp. 47–8, 86–7), it relied on mineral fuel.

These general considerations explain why, although the economic structure of many individual towns underwent considerable change during the sixteenth and seventeenth centuries, with some occupations losing relative importance and others rising to take their place, virtually all of them remained, throughout the period, primarily commercial and service centres and only very secondarily centres of manufacturing industry. Some of the service activity of the towns was, as we have seen, simultaneously industrial in nature, for it involved the making of goods for local consumption, but industries that aimed at supplying wide markets and distant consumers were of major importance in only a minority of places.

In small towns, indeed, their very existence was rare, except in districts where they had developed in the surrounding countryside and had been taken up by the under-employed poor in both village and town alike. Moreover in areas where the rural industry was the making of woollen cloth, or other forms of textiles, the final processes of manufacture, such as fulling, dyeing and shearing, tended to be carried out in centrally placed locations, convenient of access from the widely dispersed villages where the spinning and weaving were done in the homes of the work-people themselves. This meant that whether the processes were in the hands of independent craftsmen, or were carried out by the clothiers' own employees in premises provided by them, as was usually the case in the economically more advanced clothing areas, the mills and workshops were usually in the towns rather than the villages and hamlets. Thus from even before the beginning of the period the market towns of Suffolk and Essex, such as Sudbury, Lavenham, Long Melford and Halstead; of Gloucestershire, Wiltshire and Somerset, such as Stroud and Minchinhampton, Bradford-on-Avon and Trowbridge, Bruton and Shepton Mallet; of Devon and the West Riding of Yorkshire; acted not only as commercial and service centres, but also undertook some aspects of production. Likewise as the various textile industries of East Lancashire grew to importance from the mid sixteenth century onwards; towns such as Colne, Burnley, Bury, Rochdale and above all Manchester began to develop in the same way. Similarly in areas where the metal trades were established in the countryside, the making of items whose production processes were complicated and required a high level of skill, such as saddlery fittings, buckles and locks in the West Midlands, and good quality knives and cutlery in the case of South Yorkshire, tended to be largely carried on in the towns: Birmingham, Wolverhampton and Walsall in the case of the former, Sheffield in the case of the latter. Some of the most important of these towns which acted as centres for districts where rural manufacturing flourished were growing to a considerable size by the end of the period, notably Birmingham and Manchester, Tiverton and Leeds, of which the first two had populations of 8000–9000 by 1700, and the last two almost as many (Chalklin, 1974 (1), pp. 9–12. Corfield, 1976). But even in these places, which were undoubtedly developing something of an industrialized character, it is unlikely that manufacturing activities had come to be of greater importance than commercial and service ones.

Outside the areas where highly developed rural industries existed, manufacturing for non-local markets was more frequently found in large towns than small, but even there it did not often dominate their economies. Accurate statistics of the numbers of people employed in the various forms of economic activity found in sixteenth and seventeenth century towns are not available, and in particular it is difficult to know how the poorer inhabitants with few or no skills made a living. Some must have been employed in fetching and carrying within the town, others as casual labourers in trades where there were tasks which required physical strength but little training, as industrial outworkers, and as domestic servants. But many undoubtedly lived very much hand-to-mouth, finding work only intermittently, and constantly changing both employer and occupation.

For those rather higher up the social pyramid we are better informed because for some boroughs the records of those admitted to the 'freedom' – who can be equated with the more affluent quarter of the community, all of whom had some skill or training usually acquired by apprenticeship and many of whom were themselves employers of less skilled labour – provide some indication of the relative importance of different occupations. This evidence suggests that it was common, even usual, for the processing of food and drink, the making up of clothing and foot-gear, building, the provision of household necessaries and other forms of retailing and distribution to provide work for between about 60 and 70 per cent of the regularly employed population of medium sized and large towns. The use of such broad categories is not wholly satisfactory for it is not always clear how some crafts ought to be classified, and local historians have not adopted a uniform practice in this respect. Besides as in the countryside, so also in the towns, many people followed more than one occupation. But despite the difficulties implicit in the data it seems to have been demonstrated that typically over half the labour force, and often well over half, was engaged in service and commericial occupations, and in providing elementary necessities for those who actually lived in the town and who visited it from the surrounding countryside.[7] For instance at Leicester during the period 1580 to 1603 the proportion employed in the five occupational groups mentioned was 59.5 per cent. Of those admitted to the freedom in those years 19.5 per cent were in the first of the foregoing groups of trades, mostly as butchers, bakers and brewers; 22 per cent were in the second, mostly as tailors and shoe-makers; 6 per cent were in the building trade as carpenters, joiners, masons, glaziers and the like; 6 per cent were in the trades providing household goods, as cutlers, chandlers, ironmongers etc; and a further 6 per cent were merchants, carriers and others involved in distribution. At Norwich, a much larger city, roughly the same groups of occupations accounted for nearly 61 per cent of those admitted to the freedom during the sixteenth century as a whole, and at Exeter 65 per cent of those admitted between 1620 and 1640. At York the proportion rose from two thirds in the first decade of the sixteenth century to three quarters in the last, and was about 70 per cent in both the 1650s and the 1690s. By contrast the main 'industrial' occupations at Leicester and York, which in both cases were the processing of leather and the making of textiles, made a relatively small contribution to employment. In the former they accounted for only 16 per cent of those admitted to the freedom in the

---

[7] Of course not all practitioners of the trades in question catered exclusively for local consumers. For instance the shoe-makers of Banbury in the later sixteenth and early seventeenth centuries, and of Northampton in the mid and later seventeenth century, were certainly producing for a wider market (*V.C.H. Oxfordshire* x, pp. 63–4).

sixteenth century taken as a whole, and in the latter 15–16 per cent in the early sixteenth century, declining to between 13 and 14 per cent in the later sixteenth and seventeenth centuries, and the output even of these industries must have been partly for local consumption. Similarly at Exeter the finishing of cloth woven in the country areas of Devonshire was the most important industry orientated to a non-local market, and it provided the occupation of only 16 per cent of the freemen admitted between 1620 and 1640 (Hoskins, 1955. Pound, 1966. MacCaffrey, 1958, pp. 162–4. Palliser, 1979, pp. 154–9. *V.C.H. City of York*, pp. 166–8).

Certainly there were towns of a comparable size to these five where industry was considerably more important. For instance at Bristol in the 1530s there were four major industries, all of roughly comparable weight: textiles; leather; wood-working, especially the making of casks, barrels and chests, which was doubtless connected with the city's rôle as a port; and metal goods; and together these employed 45 per cent of those who enrolled as apprentices in that decade. However there do not seem to have been many places where such activities absorbed more than half the labour force. An example, however, is Coventry in the 1520s where almost exactly one third of the freemen were employed in making caps and hats, for which the town was famous, and in other branches of textile manufacture, whilst the processing of leather occupied a further 11 per cent and the metal trades 8 per cent, together 52 per cent (Hollis, 1949, pp. 199–200. Hoskins, 1956). What was most unusual of all was for a *single* industry to have predominant weight in a town's economy. Most of the so-called cloth towns were, as we have seen, mainly commercial and servicing centres which also undertook the finishing processes, but the earlier stages of manufacture *were* carried on in some of them instead of being dispersed through the surrounding country areas. In a number of places these genuinely urban textile industries decayed during the sixteenth century in the face of rural competition, for instance at York, Beverley, Reading and Newbury, but in a few they expanded rather than contracted and gradually provided a larger and larger proportion of total employment. Thus at Worcester the relative importance of cloth-making progressively increased, until by the period 1590–1620 it apparently occupied over half the labour force. A similar development occurred at Norwich, and perhaps Colchester, from the later part of the sixteenth century onwards, as a result of the establishment of the 'new draperies'. At the former the number of freemen admitted whose occupation was in the textile trades alone rose from 23 per cent of the total in 1600–19, to 44 per cent by 1660–79, and 58 per cent by 1700–19. If those admitted in the field of leather and metal manufacture are also taken into account these three industries accounted for over 56 per cent of new freemen in

1660–79, and approaching 70 per cent by the early eighteenth century (Dyer, 1973, pp. 81–3. Corfield, 1972).

Even more specialized in their nature were the economies of a small group of coastal towns where there were naval dockyards, and in some cases private shipyards alongside them. Each of the major foreign wars in which England was engaged from the 1540s onwards, led to an extension of the facilities for building, maintaining and repairing warships, and successive programmes of naval expansion called into being communities which depended overwhelmingly on the dockyards for their livelihood. The most notable of these were at Deptford, Woolwich, Chatham, Sheerness, Portsmouth and Plymouth, of which all save the first underwent their most rapid expansion during the last part of the period, when the three Dutch Wars of the third quarter of the seventeenth century were followed by the great war against France after 1689. The population of Chatham was said to have tripled in the forty years before 1686, and even in the mid 1660s 800 men were employed in the yards there, whilst at Portsmouth the number exceeded 1000 by 1700. Plymouth was also a port of some significance which generated a considerable amount of employment independent of the dockyards, but the others probably represent the nearest approach found before 1700 to the type of town, which became so common after the Industrial Revolution, in which the economy depended almost entirely on a single manufacturing industry (Coleman, 1953. Chalklin, 1965, pp. 140–6. Patten, 1978, pp. 175–6).

vi The growth of London

London was already by far the largest city in the country at the beginning of the period: in the 1520s with 60,000 inhabitants it had nearly five times the population of the greatest of the provincial towns, Norwich, and nearly ten times its wealth. By the end of the seventeenth century, as we have seen, the number of its people had risen to about 575,000, so that it was then nineteen times the size of Norwich, and more than twenty-five times that of Bristol, and accounted for nearly half the urban population of the country. In terms of taxable wealth it had likewise increased its advantage, and even in the 1650s its assessments were regularly twenty-five times those of Norwich (Wrigley, 1967. Hoskins, 1956. Firth and Rait, 1911, II, pp. 24–30ff.).[8]

Throughout the sixteenth and seventeenth centuries, as both earlier and later, London derived its predominance amongst English cities from the fact that it was both the country's greatest port and commercial

---

[8] The factors by which London's wealth exceeded that of the larger provincial centres would have been even greater but for the fact that Westminster and Southwark were separately assessed.

centre, and its political and social capital. In no other major European state were these functions performed by a single town, and it was this unique combination which explains why the difference in size between London and its nearest rival was so much greater than that between first and second cities almost everywhere else on the Continent. However at the end of the Middle Ages London had not yet come fully of age in either respect. It handled more trade than any of the provincial ports, but the value of its commerce was still rivalled by the combined total of the latter. It was clearly the political heart of the kingdom, the seat of some major organs of government and the centre of the legal system, although the monarchs of the fifteenth century did not yet have a bureaucracy of any great size or complexity. Nor did parliament yet meet very often, or for very long, and when it did it was not necessarily at Westminster. For the wealthy and powerful London was a place to visit only on business or for political reasons, not for pleasure, and few save the bishops and the greatest of the lay lords had houses there. The mass of the gentry probably did not go there once in the course of a life time. The ultimate dynamic behind the growth of the metropolis may have been the thousands of immigrants who kept streaming in, and this in turn, at least until the mid seventeenth century, in large part reflected the rise in the national population and the inability of the countryside to provide a livelihood for continuously increasing numbers. But it was the coming to maturity of the two rôles just discussed, together with their consequences, direct and indirect, which made London a sufficiently powerful magnet to attract such an influx, and to continue to do so even after the English population had ceased to grow.

The natural advantages of London's geographical position ensured that a substantial share of trade between England and the rest of Europe would always pass through it. It had good communications, both internally and externally. Transport to and from almost all parts of the country was relatively easy, for the road system converged upon it, the River Thames led deep into the heart of southern England, and standing as it did almost equidistant from the south western and north eastern extremities of the kingdom London's shipping had ready access to the whole of the south and east coasts. By the same token it was only a short sea voyage from the Thames to the ports of the Netherlands, in whose hinterlands lay the most densely populated and richest areas of western Europe, or alternatively to pick up the sea lanes which led to Scandinavia or the Baltic to the north, and all the regions bordering on the Channel, the Bay of Biscay and the Atlantic to the south.

The full value of these advantages, however, was only gradually becoming apparent during the last two centuries of the Middle Ages.

Until the later fourteenth century England's main export had been raw wool, and much of it was produced in areas such as Yorkshire and Lincolnshire whose natural outlet was through other ports, particularly Hull and Boston. Gradually, however, exports of raw wool were replaced by those of manufactured cloth, and the most important cloth-making areas, especially East Anglia, and Gloucestershire, Wiltshire and Somerset, were much more conveniently placed to ship through London. This tendency was reinforced by the increasing concentration, between the late fifteenth and mid sixteenth centuries, of the market for English cloth upon the great entrepôt city of Antwerp, where it was also possible to obtain a high proportion of the commodities required by importers. (See also below II, Ch. 9 sec. ii.) An increasing number of merchants who had thitherto traded from provincial ports thus began to transfer their base of operations to London, and the difficulties experienced by the ports of the South West, notably Bristol and Exeter, in their trade with southern Europe, mainly as a result of periodic wars with France, and deteriorating political relations with Spain from the 1530s onwards, added yet further impetus to the long drawn out process whereby London engrossed more and more of the country's overseas commerce. Besides, in the competition for trade with their compatriots in the outports, the merchants of London had more than just a favourable geographical situation. The accumulation of wealth in the city ensured that the financial resources available to them were greater, an advantage which was already considerable in the early part of the period, and which had become much greater still before the end of it with the emergence in London in the later seventeenth century of banks, a securities market, and other financial institutions. The wealth and the numbers of the London merchants enabled them to form powerful commercial organizations, whose ability to furnish the government with loans secured for them political support and the grant of trade privileges. Thus all the 'national' trading companies of the period, from the Merchant Adventurers which had already come into existence before 1500 to the East India and Royal African Companies of the seventeenth century, were dominated, if not monopolized, by Londoners, and pursued policies which were dictated by the interests of their London members.[9]

As a result of all these factors, from soon after the beginning of the sixteenth century not only the proportionate share, but also the absolute volume, of the trade handled by almost every provincial port was shrinking to London's advantage. Already in 1500 well over half of England's cloth and wool exports passed through London, and by the

---

[9] For the trading companies see also below II, Ch. 9 sec. vii.

middle years of the century the proportion sometimes exceeded 90 per cent of a very greatly increased total (Gould, 1970, pp. 120, 136).[10] Exports other than these were of relatively slight importance, and anyway a large proportion of them went from London too. The capital did not dominate the import trade to quite the same extent, but throughout the second half of the sixteenth century it accounted for between two thirds and three quarters of exports and imports combined, and sometimes even more. As new trades were opened up in the later sixteenth and early seventeenth centuries, with Russia, the Baltic, the Mediterranean, the Americas and the Far East, they too were principally conducted from London, and in the cases of the Mediterranean and the Far East, completely monopolized by her. (See also below II, Ch. 9 sec. iii.) The only branch of overseas trade in which she was not supreme was that with Ireland, which was mainly carried on from Bristol, Chester and other western ports. London's supremacy thus survived undiminished until almost the end of our period, for it was only in the later seventeenth century that the exports of cloth from Exeter, Hull and Newcastle came to attain substantial dimensions, and that Bristol and Liverpool began to encroach on trade with the American colonies. Nevertheless the absolute volume and value of London's trade continued to grow with every period of commercial expansion, increasing by at least a third between the 1660s and the end of the century, and in the years 1699–1701 she still handled 62.5 per cent of all exports of native products, 84 per cent of re-exports (which were mainly of colonial and Indian goods), and 80 per cent of imports (Davis, 1954).[11]

London was not only by far the largest distributive centre for imported goods, but also, because of her position in respect of interior and coastal lines of communication, for domestically produced ones. Her superiority in this respect was certainly less overwhelming, but it may have increased somewhat in the latter part of the period, since in the seventeenth century some progress was made towards improving the roads – mainly by bridge-building – and particularly the rivers, which linked the main provincial towns and the principal concentrations of industry to London. By contrast, before 1700 much less had been done to facilitate communication with either of the former. (See above n. 5 to this chapter.) The scope of London's distributive trade in the early 1680s, for instance, is indicated by the wide variety of goods found aboard outward bound vessels sailing coastwise, which included such agricultural products as hops, cheese, linseed oil and tallow, and such manufactures as paper, soap, glass, earthenware, haberdashery and lead shot, the bulk of which

[10] See also below II, pp. 107–8, 111–12.
[11] See also below II, pp. 181–2.

were certainly produced inside the country, as well as imported wine, brandy, tobacco, sugar, Mediterranean fruits, iron and timber. These shipments were mainly destined for the ports of the east coast, particularly Newcastle, Hull, Great Yarmouth, Colchester and Ipswich, although a minority were bound as far in the other direction as the ports of Cornwall and even Bristol and Chester which involved very long voyages indeed (Willan, 1938, pp. 203–7). The inland trade is less well documented than coastal commerce, but doubtless a similar range of commodities went by road to many towns in the Home Counties, the Midlands and beyond, and by river barge up the Thames and its tributaries. According to one recent estimate the carrying capacity of scheduled services by waggon and pack-horse to and from London more than doubled between the later 1630s and the early eighteenth century, and whilst the parts of the country nearest to the capital benefited most from this expansion it also involved an increased number of departures for more distant areas such as the South West, the West Midlands and Cheshire, and even the establishment of regular services to the far northern counties (Chartres, 1977 (2)).

That London's commerce was on an altogether different scale from that of any provincial city is reflected in the fact that not only were her merchants far more numerous, but that the richest of them accumulated fortunes which completely dwarfed those of the most successful businessmen elsewhere. Nearly two fifths of those elected as aldermen in the first quarter of the seventeenth century were worth over £20,000, and the wealth of a few like Sir John Spencer, Sir William Craven and Sir Baptist Hicks ran well into six figures. Nor were such huge accumulations built up only from overseas trade, for half of these men, including Craven and Hicks, were overwhelmingly concerned with domestic commerce: the latter indeed was the most successful shop-keeper of his age, and his main business was retailing sumptuous imported textiles to the wealthy from premises in Cheapside. In the provinces, on the other hand, fortunes of as much as £10,000 were extremely rare at any time before 1700, and seem to have been achieved only by a few of the most exceptionally successful Bristol merchants and West Country clothiers (Grassby, 1970. Lang, 1971; 1974).

Of course the number of merchants and wholesalers was never large in relation to the size of the population, even in London. However the amount of employment created by their offices and store-rooms, and by the commercial facilities that existed to serve them, which most certainly included many of the city's inns as well as impressive institutions such as the Royal Exchange and the great markets for cloth and leather at Blackwell Hall and Leadenhall respectively, was much more considerable. Greater by far, however, was the employment provided by shipping and the provision of port services, and by the later seventeenth century this had increased to truly enormous proportions, especially since, as London grew, her own needs generated a vast increase in incoming coastwise shipments of food-stuffs, building materials, raw materials for her industries and above all coal, of which imports rose fifteen fold between the 1580s and the first decade of the eighteenth century (Coleman, 1975, pp. 46–7).[12] Shipping owned in London rose from a mere 12,300 tons in 1582, to 35,300 tons in 1629, and to about 150,000 tons by 1686. There was some reduction in the size of crews during these years but even so the number of seamen required must have risen ten fold or more, and cannot have been less than 12,000 by the last of these dates (Davis, 1962, pp. 25, 33–5, 58–60). Tens of thousands more people were involved in repairing, maintaining and supplying these ships, and in providing lighterage, quayside, warehouse and all the other shore based services needed for the loading, unloading, moving and storage of their cargoes and those of the many ships owned in other English ports and abroad which also came to London. By the end of the seventeenth century shipping with a carrying capacity of over 300,000 tons cleared London yearly for foreign ports, and the volume of goods arriving and departing coastwise was certainly much greater: over 100,000 tons of coal alone had to be unloaded every year by the 1600s, and over 400,000 tons by the 1690s (Davis, 1962, p. 26. Nef, 1932, II, p. 381).

In the later sixteenth century the main factor behind the expansion of port employment in London was probably the rapid growth of the coal trade and coastal shipping in general, whilst in the later seventeenth century it was the growth of England's share in the international carrying trade and commerce with the trans-Atlantic colonies and northern Europe. (See below II, Ch. 9 sec. v.) Between 1664 and 1686 the number of vessels clearing London for North America and the West Indies rose from 88 to 247, and for Norway and the Baltic from 48 to 176. The great European war which began in 1689 brought the growth of trade and shipping to a halt for a generation, but its almost continuous expansion during the previous thirty or so years was probably the most important single factor in the continued growth in the population of London during a period when that of the country as a whole was no longer growing. Altogether, it has been suggested, shipping and the port may have employed as much as one quarter of London's work force by 1700 (Davis, 1962, pp. 15–19, 390). If the definition of port employment is extended to include the building of ships, which continued to flourish on the

[12] See also belwo II, Ch. 8 sec. vii.

Thames in the second half of the seventeenth century even though it declined elsewhere, and also industries which processed imported raw materials such as tanning, timber sawing and sugar-refining then it may be that even this figure is an underestimate. The proportion of the population whose employment depended indirectly on the port was, of course, very much greater still, for all those who worked there and their families had to be supplied with goods and services, and when the multiplier effects of the expansion of London's commerce are borne in mind, there can be little doubt that it acted as the leading sector in the city's phenomenal growth.

The sixteenth and seventeenth centuries, which saw the culmination of the process whereby London drew to itself so much of the foreign trade of the kingdom, also saw the final stages of its evolution into a capital city in a modern sense. The Tudor sovereigns liked to spend the summer months visiting their various country residences, but from Henry VIII's time onwards they remained more firmly based at Whitehall or St James's than the kings of the later Middle Ages had ever been, so that for most of the year the royal household was in residence there. This was an enormous organization which, when the private servants of the more senior officials are included, in the 1630s numbered 2500 persons or more, many of whom had families of their own, so that in total it was as large as a major provincial town, even before the numerous would-be courtiers, petitioners and hangers-on, who were attracted by its presence, are counted (Alymer, 1961, p. 27). Besides the household there were the administrative and financial departments of government. These had long been located at Westminster, but their number and complexity had been greatly increased by the so-called Tudor 'revolution in government', as had the size of the army of bureaucrats and clerks who operated them. The country's judicial system was also already centralized there well before 1500, but the development of the various prerogative courts from the later fifteenth century onwards, and even more the enormous increase in the amount of litigation being undertaken after the middle of the sixteenth century, meant that the tide of visitors who came to London in connection with their law-suits rose far higher than it had ever done before. According to Professor Stone, between 1550 and 1625 the number of suits heard annually by the courts of King's Bench and Common Pleas may have increased two fold and six fold respectively, and the number brought before the courts of Star Chamber and Requests multiplied no less than ten fold (Stone, 1965, p. 240).

An increase in the volume of legal business necessarily called forth an increase in the number of lawyers, and in consequence in the number of students attending the Inns of Court. However in such a litigious age the

advantages of possessing some legal knowledge were so great, especially
to landowners, since so much of the litigation concerned the title to
property, that large numbers of them sent their eldest son to one of the
Inns, even though they were not destined for any form of legal practice.
The Inns thus developed the reputation, and indeed the function, of
England's third university. By the 1610s total attendance at any one time
must have approached a thousand, and once again it is worth remember-
ing that this made them a more populous community than many market
towns (Stone, 1964). Another aspect of London's development as a
national capital was the increasing frequency and duration of the
meetings of parliament from the 1530s onwards, and every session
brought almost the entire peerage and upwards of 500 members of the
gentry, with their servants, up from the country weeks or months on
end. Even in the later sixteenth century parliaments were still occasional
rather than annual, and in the first forty years of the seventeenth there
were up to eleven years at a stretch without one, but from 1640 onwards
there were few years when some kind of an assembly was not sitting.

Westminster, where the impact of these developments was mainly
concentrated, was administratively, and at the beginning of our period,
still physically a separate entity. By the mid seventeenth century its own
growth, and the westwards expansion of the suburbs of London proper,
had created a single urban area, but it is essential to an understanding of
the development of what had by 1700 become the largest city in western
Europe to appreciate that in a very real sense it came about as the fusion
of two cities,[13] very different in their origins and nature. But if the main
force behind the growth of London in the limited sense was commerce,
and that behind the growth of Westminster was the presence of the court,
the bureaucracy, the lawyers and parliament, both derived further
impetus from the attractive power which the united metropolis increasingly exerted for the wealthy from all over the kingdom. This was partly
because it was the centre of the money market, where large loans could
most easily be raised or good security found for funds available for
investment; because the best doctors were to be found there; and some of
the best, or at least, by the seventeenth century, the most fashionable
schools, notably Westminster and St Paul's. But above all the attraction
of London was a social one. The presence of the court, of the leading
figures in Church and state, of so much legal and mercantile wealth, of
so many shops, inns and theatres – there were six or seven presenting

---

[13] Indeed of three cities if the largely industrial suburb of Southwark be included. This, too, was
physically separated from London proper, by the river Thames, and to a large extent retained a
separate identity symbolized by the fact that it was for centuries referred to as 'the Borough'
(Johnson, 1969, esp. chs. 7 and 10). Compare Maps 5a and 5b on pp. 206 and 207.

plays and other productions simultaneously in the early seventeenth century (Gurr, 1970, pp. 82–7) – ensured that the company was infinitely more stimulating, and the variety of the diversions and entertainments was infinitely greater than those available in even the largest provincial towns.

For those who could afford it, therefore, there was no adequate substitute for a visit to London. Particularly from about 1580 onwards the aristocracy and the richer gentry, and their families, came in increasing numbers and for longer periods, to escape the tedium of a winter in the country, to enjoy the pleasures of the only really large city in the kingdom and perhaps to find a marriage partner for a son or daughter. By the 1630s possibly as many as a hundred peers and several hundreds of the gentry owned or leased London houses, and if the much larger number of landowners who stayed in inns or took lodgings is considered, the seasonal influx must have run into many hundreds of families which, when wives, grown up children and servants are included, must have totalled several thousand individuals. Some indeed settled permanently, either because they had lost the taste for country life altogether or, in the case of poorly endowed younger sons and others whose financial resources did not match their inherited position in society, because by doing so they could escape the social pressures which forced them to maintain a way of life they could not afford. Incomes derived from estates in the provinces were thus spent in the capital, with important consequences for employment in the latter. So large was the influx to London that the government became seriously concerned, partly for political reasons, partly because overcrowding increased the risk of both fire and plague in the metropolis and partly because of the adverse consequences, real or imagined, for rural society.[14] It repeatedly expressed its disapproval in the early part of the seventeenth century, and in the 1630s Charles I made a serious effort to oblige landowners to go back to their homes in the counties and to stay there. Official attitudes, however, had no lasting effect on London's social rôle, which continued to gain strength throughout the seventeenth century as the fashionable housing developments in Covent Garden and its vicinity before the Civil War, and after the Restoration St James's Square and the first streets of

---

[14] Some of these consequences undoubtedly were real enough. The activities of dealers who supplied the London markets forced up prices in the areas from which they drew produce, to the advantage of producers, but to the detriment of provincial consumers, and in years of dearth they greatly worsened the food supply situation there. And in the mid and later seventeenth century continuing immigration to London contributed to the shortage of labour in some districts. In other cases, however, contemporaries blamed the growth of London for developments which were brought about by quite different forces.

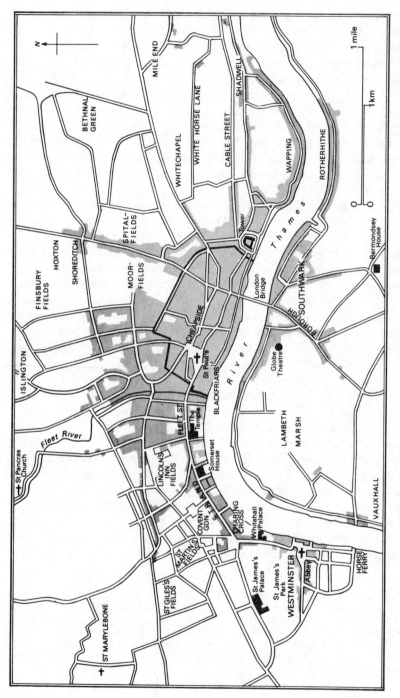

Map 5a London. Approximate built up area, *c.* 1600. (After: Brett-James, 1935, map facing p. 78.)

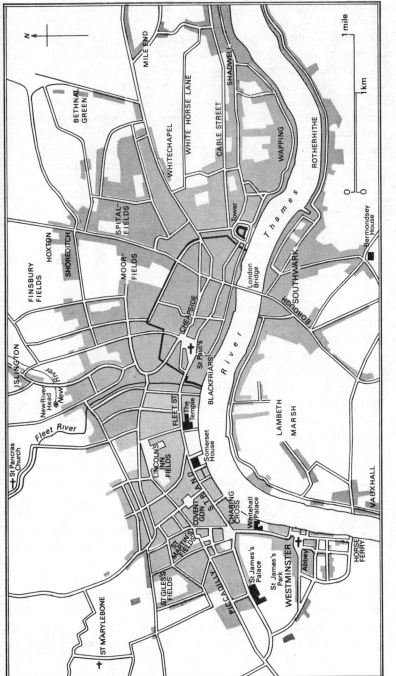

Map 5b London. Approximate built up area, *c.* 1700. (After Brett-James, 1935, map facing p. 494.)

what later became the West End, bear witness (Fisher, 1948. Stone, 1965, pp. 385–98).

The great number of people who came to London as permanent residents or temporary visitors naturally provided livelihoods for a vast host of others. The supply of essential goods and services maintained a growing army of craftsmen and retailers who, unlike most of those in the smaller and medium sized provincial towns, and many of those even in the larger ones, depended for their custom almost exclusively on those who were at least temporarily resident in the city, rather than on country people coming in for a weekly visit. The expansion of this sector of London's economy is suggested by the establishment during the course of the seventeenth century of no less than sixteen new markets in its rapidly spreading suburbs (Clark and Slack, 1972, p. 36. McGrath, 1948, ch. VIII). There is almost no statistical information yet available to indicate the relative importance of the various industrial and service occupations represented in the capital in this period, but there were several in which the demand for labour grew exceptionally fast and which probably came to be more important than they were elsewhere. Hostelry and catering was one of these, and the hundreds of inns, alehouses, cookshops, and by the later seventeenth century, coffee houses, must have employed thousands of people. Secondly the continuous spread of the built-up area (illustrated by Maps 5a and 5b) which continued despite repeated government proclamations against further building between 1580 and the 1660s, together with piecemeal redevelopment of the older parts of the city, created an enormous building industry. By the early seventeenth century the western, northern and north eastern suburbs were ringed with brickworks and tile kilns; and construction, like the port, must have absorbed a large number of the unskilled workers who drifted into the capital in ever increasing numbers. This was particularly so during the last third of the century when the gigantic task of first clearing and then totally rebuilding the area, formerly covered by some 13,200 houses and eighty-seven parish churches, devastated by fire in 1666, was shortly followed by a series of building booms which pushed the urban sprawl as far as Piccadilly in one direction, and Mile End and Poplar in the other (Brett-James, 1935, chs. III, IV, XV, XVI. Reddaway, 1940, *passim*).

London proper probably did not have a larger proportion of wealthy and comfortably-off residents than the main provincial towns, although Westminster may have done, but the well-to-do of the capital were both wealthier and far more numerous absolutely, and the presence of so many affluent residents and visitors certainly generated a great demand for domestic servants. The really rich families in either mercantile or court circles might well maintain a dozen servants or more, most of them women, whilst even a modestly prosperous tradesman was likely to have at least one or two. It was primarily for this reason that, at least in the inner areas, women significantly outnumbered men – in 1695 there were fewer than ninety of the latter to every hundred of the former – and there can be little doubt that service was the largest single source of employment for female immigrants from the provinces (Glass, 1969; 1972). For the same reason there was also an almost insatiable market for luxury commodities, so that their manufacture and supply was certainly expanding with exceptional rapidity from the later sixteenth century onwards. The number of mercers, for instance, was reported to have risen ten fold in the second half of that century (Stone, 1965, pp. 585–6). Most of London's luxury trades were found elsewhere on a smaller scale, but in a number of cases her craftsmen had a monopoly or near monopoly and supplied a national market. Particularly when a new luxury industry was to be established, the advantages of a location in or in close proximity to London were overwhelming. Thus from its first introduction to England in 1568 the manufacture of high quality Venetian style crystal glass, used for table ware and decorative objects, remained confined to the capital at least until the second half of the seventeenth century (Godfrey, 1975, Part I). Silk weaving, watch-making and coach-building were also industries which first grew up in London towards the end of the sixteenth century, and long remained confined there, whilst a hundred years later the printing of calicoes imported from India provides yet another example.

Of course carrying on manufacture in the capital involved certain disadvantages, in particular the high cost of labour and to a lesser extent of certain overheads such as rent, and there were also the restrictive regulations which city and gild authorities still attempted to enforce, sometimes with considerable vigour. However the first two of these drawbacks could be mitigated, and the third largely if not always wholly evaded, by conducting operations in the suburbs rather than in the city itself. On the outskirts, there was a ready labour supply furnished by the constant arrival of new immigrants from the country, more space and less likelihood of official interference. There was thus a long term drift of manufacturing activity to the periphery of the metropolis, accelerated by the destruction of so much of the central area in the fire of 1666, but which, in the case of some industries, was already largely complete by the beginning of the seventeenth century. For instance it was reported in 1619 that there were 3000 leather-workers outside the city walls mostly in Bermondsey, Southwark and Lambeth, and only forty remaining within them (Unwin, 1904, p. 128). However, dear labour was not of great account in the luxury industries, where wages made up only a small part of total costs. This was not the case with industries producing more mundane consumer goods, but proximity to the customer was always advantageous, and since poor transport facilities provided protection against provincial competition most of them were able to pass on higher costs in the form of higher prices, and thus continued to flourish. Nevertheless some industries were poorly represented in the capital. As early as the mid sixteenth century, and probably earlier still, most of London's flour was milled in the market towns of the Home Counties whence the bulk of her grain requirements were drawn, presumably because of competition for the few available water-power sites in and around the city. London had no malting facilities, and the manufacture of woollen cloth, which in the Middle Ages had been an industry of major importance, had collapsed almost completely before 1600, although textile finishing industries survived and indeed expanded considerably in the seventeenth century. Cloth-making was a highly labour intensive industry in which labour costs mattered greatly, and during the last decades of the period a number of other industries where the same was true began a migration to the provinces as the organizing entrepreneurs sought to reduce their wage bills. The making of hosiery thus moved to Nottinghamshire and adjacent counties, shoe-making to Northampton and silk throwing to North Essex (Fisher, 1935; 1971. Plummer, 1972, pp. 8–9). These, however, were exceptions. Throughout the period London was not only the greatest commercial city in the kingdom, it was also the greatest industrial producer: the scale of its industries was however primarily a result of its vast size and rapid growth, and only secondarily a cause of them.

The stream of immigrants attracted to London by all this economic activity flowed in from every part of England. We have noticed above that even the larger provincial towns recruited the bulk of theirs from quite limited hinterlands (see above sec. iv of this chapter), but London drew on the country as a whole. Most of the new-comers, among whom women seem to have been quite as numerous as men, arrived early in life in their teens or early twenties. The records of apprenticeships, and of people admitted to the freedom of the city after successfully completing an apprenticeship, only cover those whose families were well enough off to give their sons a start in life, but they show clearly that a high proportion of such immigrants came from surprisingly distant counties. In the early 1550s, for instance, over half of those admitted as freemen came from the North, and the North and North West Midlands, and whilst the relative importance of immigrants from the highland zone certainly declined as the period wore on, particularly in the seventeenth century, even in 1690 only just over a quarter of new freemen originating from outside London itself were from the Home Counties (Ramsay, 1978, Smith, 1973. Glass, 1969. Wareing, 1980).[15] Those sufficiently well-to-do to obtain an apprenticeship, even with a humble artisan gild, were however only a minority. Where all the others came from is not certain, but it is likely that many of them too were from far afield. Especially for the period before 1640, although decreasingly thereafter, there is some evidence that those driven to the towns by poverty, because there was neither land nor work for them in the countryside, tended to end up further from home than those going in a deliberate attempt to better themselves (Clark, 1972; 1979).

The scale of this movement of people to London was enormous. By the end of the period net immigration may have averaged 8–10,000 a year, but since there was a considerable return flow back to the country towns and rural areas, the actual number of new arrivals was much greater (Wrigley, 1967). In relation to the size of the existing city, however, immigration was at its most important in the later sixteenth and early seventeenth centuries, and particularly at this period there is no doubt that it caused acute social problems. The extremely rapid growth of the city made it inevitable that large areas of bad housing should develop in the spreading suburbs, such as Whitechapel, Wapping and Shoreditch to the East, and St Giles to the West. There was serious overcrowding in some areas, Westminster for instance, where some people lived five or six to a room. This was made worse by the efforts of the government to stem the growth of the capital by prohibiting the erection of new buildings, even though these were largely unavailing. Elsewhere pressure on space was less acute, but the dwellings were flimsy,[16] often single-storied, sometimes mere sheds and so tightly packed together that they were built as many as fifty to the acre, whilst entire communities grew up without any amenities whatsoever. As late as the 1660s the 40,000 people of the emergent East End were without a single market of their own (Power, 1972; 1978 (1) and (2)). Besides not only did people come to London faster than adequate accommodation could be provided, they also came faster than was warranted by the expansion of old forms of economic activity and the emergence of new ones. Extensive unemployment and under-employment, with their concomitants of crime and prostitution, were thus inevitable. In any event, much of what employment was available for the new arrivals, in the form of casual labour, domestic

[15] There was, however, an increase in the proportion deriving from London itself.
[16] In the riverine suburb of Shadwell in the mid seventeenth century nearly 90 per cent of houses were of only one or two stories, and less than one in ten was built of brick (Power, 1978 (2)).

service and apprenticeships with petty employers all too likely to fail or to cut back their labour force in times of economic stringency, was of a precarious and often temporary nature. The conditions of life in the rapidly growing city thus made it difficult for immigrants to find a secure and settled place in urban society, and ensured that many of them would fail to do so (Beier, 1978).

There was, therefore, another and darker side to the growth of London in the sixteenth and seventeenth centuries, which manifested itself both in the desperate poverty of large sections of the population and the terrible living conditions found in many districts. As we have noticed in an earlier chapter this combination provided ideal conditions for the spread of plague, which was always most destructive in the poorest and most congested parts of the city. (See above pp. 20–21.) The enormous mortality of the major epidemics of 1563, 1593, 1603, 1625, 1636 and 1665 cannot be gainsaid, yet in other respects some recent writers have probably over-stated the severity of London's social problems at this time, and underestimated the ability of the authorities to cope with them and to maintain order. Certainly as far as the City proper is concerned, and probably for the suburbs too, comparisons with the shanty towns of the present day 'third world' involve considerable exaggeration. It is true that the institutions created around the middle of the sixteenth century to provide for those unable, on account of poverty, illness, old age or extreme youth, to look after themselves were totally inadequate by the early seventeenth. Yet, even so, few Londoners ever starved, nor did anarchy rule the streets. Although the inner city parishes were generally better off than those lying on the periphery, even in 1650 rich and poor were not entirely segregated into distinct quarters of the town, although by 1700 they were fast coming to be. This ensured that in virtually every part of London reasonably large sums of money were forthcoming to deal with destitution, both from private charitable giving by the rich and from the community as a whole by means of the statutory poor rates (Pearl, 1979). Unrelieved want there undoubtedly was, but there was never any general breakdown, either in the relief of the poor or of social control, and law and order were well maintained in normal circumstances. It is true that there were sometimes food riots in the sixteenth century; and on several occasions from the mid seventeenth onwards, during the political crisis of 1640–2 and on the occasion of the Sacheverell affair in 1710, for instance, unruly mobs terrorized the capital. But it is clear that, at least in the seventeenth century, the mobs were not composed of the rootless poor driven to violence by material deprivation. Rather they seem to have been apprentices, journeymen and small masters acting partly in response to political and religious motives, and partly to deliberate manipulation by their betters (Holmes, 1976. Rogers, 1978).

The growth of London was one of the most striking and important of the changes which occurred within English society and the English economy between 1500 and 1700. By the standards of contemporary Europe London at the end of the Middle Ages was very much a city of the second rank, in no way comparable in size to Paris, Rome, Naples or Milan. Two hundred years later it was larger than all those places, the largest city in Europe, except for Constantinople (Corfield, 1976). Such a development could not but have profound effects on other aspects of national life, and indeed these were as apparent in the political and cultural spheres as they were in the economic and social. The limited extent of provincial urbanization was one such consequence we have already considered. (See above secs. i–iv of this chapter, *passim*.) Another, because of the chronic and substantial surplus of burials over baptisms, was to depress the rate of population growth, and in the middle and later seventeenth century to make a considerable contribution to the decline in national population which occurred at that time. We have also seen in Chapter 3 that the commercialization of agriculture received considerable impetus from the growth in demand for food-stuffs from London, and we shall see later that the development of coal mining in the North East owed even more to the capital. (See above pp. 68–9 and below II, Ch. 8 sec. vii.) Transport and communication facilities, in the form of a greatly enlarged fleet of coasting vessels, improvements to the navigability of some rivers, an expanded net-work of inland carrying services and a public postal system, were created primarily to serve London, but brought benefits to the country as a whole. Banking and other financial services and institutions were likewise called into being by the needs of the capital, but came to serve a national clientele. Moreover, since London was so much bigger than any provincial city, life there differed not merely in degree but in kind from that which could be experienced anywhere else, and this in turn gave rise to different values and modes of behaviour. In so far as these extended to patterns of consumption and attitudes to work, remuneration and leisure, they had considerable economic significance. London was not the only source of change in these respects, nor were residence in the capital and imitation of those who had been there the only channels whereby such new ways spread through society, but there is little doubt that they were among the most important (Wrigley, 1967. Fisher, 1971).[17]

---

[17] See also below II, Ch. 8 sec. iv.

7

SOCIETY AND THE POOR

i *The emergence of poverty as a problem*

In any pre-industrial society the great majority of the population is inevitably poor, and so it was in England in the sixteenth and seventeenth centuries. Nevertheless at the beginning of the period relatively few were entirely devoid of the means to keep body and soul together. Really desperate and chronic poverty tended to be the experience only of certain well defined categories of people, notably those disabled from working by illness, injury or old age; widows with dependent children; and orphans with no parent to care for them. Moreover in rural society the prevalence of customary arrangements to cater for such groups ensured that, as long as most families had land and livestock, most even of them were provided for more or less adequately. Family farmers who could no longer work their own fields normally made them over to a son or son-in-law, or if necessary a non-relative, in return for house-room and their subsistence as long as they lived. And it was almost universal for widows to retain part, or even all, of their late husband's holding until they died or remarried, or at the very least until their eldest son came of age, after which he would be obliged to support his mother. Serious harvest failure, outbreaks of animal disease or the levying of taxation by the crown might reduce households which normally managed well enough to dire straits, but otherwise destitution was only likely to befall members of that small minority of families dependent largely upon wages for their livelihood, and who had little else to turn to if deprived of their employment for whatever reason. The number of those at risk in any one place was not, therefore, very great, for many of those who appear in the records as landless in the early part of the period were in reality waiting to inherit a paternal holding. Most communities were thus able to support their own poor without undue strain, out of funds collected at the parish church, by intermittent acts of personal charity and by permitting those in need to beg on a regular basis (Hoskins, 1957, pp. 75–6, 189, 201–2. Faith, 1966. Spufford, 1974, pp. 88–90, 112–18, 162–4).

In the towns, especially the larger ones, serious poverty was encountered more often. This was partly because urban economies were more susceptible to disruption than were those of villages in which most people produced their own food. Thus in the short run high grain prices in urban markets could quickly reduce the demand for many types of services and manufactured goods; plague could disrupt normal trading arrangements, deprive families of their bread-winner and cause unemployment as the well-to-do sought refuge in flight; whilst any place which produced cloth for export was vulnerable to fluctuations in overseas trade, which were frequent and sometimes exceedingly violent. In the longer run the decline of an important industry, as happened at Coventry in the late fifteenth and early sixteenth centuries, or the loss of overseas trade which befell Bristol from the 1500s onwards and Southampton after about 1520, could bring about a shrinkage of economic opportunities and a chronic shortage of employment which undermined the prosperity of every section of the community (Phythian-Adams, 1978; 1979, esp. ch. 2). Poverty was also more prevalent because wage earners made up a much larger segment of society, and urban wage earners were in general more completely dependent on their wages than were rural ones. Wealth and income in the towns was distributed exceedingly unevenly, so that even the self employed craftsmen and petty traders made up a minority of the population, and the genuinely well-to-do merchants, shop-keepers and industrial producers formed a tiny group, although they invariably owned a disproportionately large share of the wealth. Thus the subsidy assessments of the 1520s show that at both Exeter and Coventry the richest 7 per cent of the population liable to tax owned approaching two-thirds of the taxable wealth, and at York more than half. By contrast in most places wage earners owning almost no property of any kind made up almost half the taxable population: 38 per cent at York, 40 per cent at Norwich and 46 per cent at Exeter, for instance. However when account is taken of those whose earnings were too small or too infrequent for them to be taxed at all, and those unable to earn anything, not to mention the omissions and inaccuracies inevitable in records drawn up in connection with taxation, then there can be little doubt that at least two thirds of the adult population may be regarded as belonging to the labouring classes (Hoskins, 1956. MacCaffrey, 1958, p. 250. Pound, 1966. Palliser, 1979, pp. 135-8). Direct comparisons of urban social structures at different dates are a hazardous exercise, because the sources of evidence are themselves not directly comparable, but it is clear that a roughly similar situation prevailed throughout the period. Thus the Hearth Tax returns of the 1660s and 1670s show that households with only one or two hearths, whose members must surely have been mostly labourers, journeymen and the like, or their widows, made up 76 per cent of the total at both Newcastle and Exeter, and 69.5 per cent at Leicester (Howell, 1967, pp. 12, 352. Hoskins, 1935, pp. 118–19. *V.C.H. Leics.* IV, p. 156). In smaller towns there was usually a somewhat more egalitarian social structure, but even there the majority of the inhabitants were employees of a relatively affluent minority.

Nevertheless the distribution of income was certainly less uneven in 1500 than it was to be later on, for the wage earners were materially better off at the beginning of the period than their successors were subsequently to become. Real wages were high enough to keep even the labourers above subsistence level, provided that they remained in employment, and many skilled journeymen were probably able to live in very modest comfort. Besides, a large section of the wage earning class, at Coventry in 1523 amounting to almost a quarter (24.8 per cent) of the town's entire population, were employed as in-servants, all of whose basic needs for both shelter and food were provided by their employers (Phelps Brown and Hopkins, 1981, ch. 2. Phythian-Adams, 1979, pp. 132–4, 204). And for those who, owing to misfortune or old age, were unable to support themselves, the towns were much more abundantly supplied with charitable institutions than the countryside. Some of the old medieval 'hospitals' had ceased to function by 1500, although many still continued: York had no fewer than twenty-two, some very small, but the largest housing sixty aged and bed-ridden persons in 1535 (Palliser, 1979, pp. 221–2). Many of the greatest monasteries too were urban, and although the full extent of their alms-giving is unknown it was certainly greater than was officially recognized at the time of their dissolution in the 1530s (Woodward, 1966, pp. 21–3). There was a greater concentration of wealthy residents in the towns than in any rural area, and in the early sixteenth century the day to day relief of the poor was still regarded as a christian duty incumbent upon all according to their means. The gilds had their almshouses and endowments for the support of members who had fallen on evil days, and the municipal authorities usually had some funds from which to provide periodic doles of money, food or fuel for the most needy.

As long as their economies remained reasonably prosperous and their populations grew only slowly, most towns did not therefore find that the support of their poor posed unduly serious problems. However, as the sixteenth century wore on an increasing number of urban authorities came to have cause for grave concern. As the rural population began to grow, and the economic and social structure of the villages in the mixed farming areas began to come under strain, many of those for whom there was neither land nor work in the places of their birth naturally gravitated

Table VI *Purchasing power of wage
rate of building craftsman in S.
England, 1500–1719*

Index numbers 1451–75 = 100

1500–09	96.5
1510–19	90.6
1520–29	68.4
1530–39	67.0
1540–49	60.0
1550–59	50.6
1560–69	62.0
1570–79	60.7
1580–89	56.7
1590–99	44.1
1600–09	42.5
1610–19	38.2
1620–29	42.9
1630–39	40.2
1640–49	45.1
1650–59	47.5
1660–69	46.7
1670–79	49.1
1680–89	54.1
1690–99	51.3
1700–09	59.1
1710–19	57.1

Source: Wrigley and Schofield, 1981,
Appendix 9 Table 2.

towards the towns (Clark, 1972). Some of them indeed found regular
employment when they arrived, but by flooding the labour market they
prevented money wages from rising by as much as did prices, so that the
real wages of all categories of urban workers steadily declined and
continued to do so until about 1620. As Table VI and Figure 4 show,
those of skilled workers in the building trades had, by the second decade
of the seventeenth century, fallen to only about 38 per cent what they had
been in the late fifteenth century. It is true that real earnings almost
certainly fell by less than did wage rates, as people worked longer hours
and took less time off in order to try to maintain the purchasing power of
what they received.[1] Nevertheless it became increasingly difficult for

[1] The provision by employers of meals for those employed (in effect partial payment in kind) also did
something to mitigate the extent to which falling real wage rates affected actual living standards.

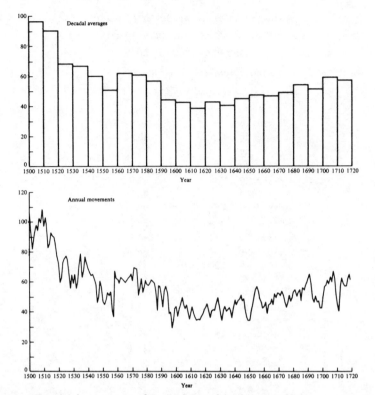

Figure 4 Purchasing power of wage rate of building craftsman, 1500–1719. Index numbers 1451–75 = 100. (Source: Wrigley and Schofield, 1981, Appendix 9 Table 2.)

wage earners to support large families, and virtually impossible for them to provide themselves with any sort of reserve by means of saving, so rendering them ever more vulnerable to misfortune.[2] Certainly many of those listed in late sixteenth century urban 'censuses' of the poor, such as that taken in Norwich in 1570, were in fact in employment, but simply not earning sufficient to maintain their dependants (Pound, 1962). In the case of Coventry it has been suggested that at the beginning of the period perhaps one fifth of the town's inhabitants were living on the poverty line (Phythian-Adams, 1979, p. 134), potentially liable to become destitute if

---

[2] The extent of urban poverty must also have been exacerbated by the long term decline in the proportion of town populations employed as servants who lived in their masters' homes. Compared with the 24.8 per cent found at Coventry in 1523, in a large sample of rural and urban communities over the period 1574–1821, but of which few antedate the mid seventeenth century, the average was only 13.4 per cent (Phythian-Adams, 1979, p. 204. Laslett and Wall, 1972, pp. 130–1, 151–2).

anything went wrong and almost certain to fall into dire distress in old age. But from the middle of the sixteenth century onwards almost the whole of the urban wage earning population was in this situation, that is 60 or 70 per cent of the total, and anything up to one fifth or even a quarter of the people in a large town might simultaneously be in need of relief if times were hard (Clark and Slack, 1976, p. 121). At Worcester in 1556, for instance, 700 people were being relieved, and a year later the number had risen to 1000 in a city whose total population was probably around 5000 (Dyer, 1973, pp. 166–7).

Besides, many of the new-comers to the towns did not find proper employment and they soon swamped the local charitable facilities,[3] whose existence seems often to have exacerbated rather than alleviated the situation by attracting people who would otherwise have gone elsewhere. In other words, as a result of what was happening in the countryside, the population of many urban centres was expanding more rapidly than the rather limited growth of economic opportunities warranted. The result was the development of a highly visible sub-stratum to urban society, living in cellars, divided tenements and hastily erected cottages, and surviving by begging, prostitution and crime. Already in the 1510s London and York were finding it necessary to enact regulations against unwelcome immigrants, and by the middle decades of the century not only these places but a number of other large provincial centres had been driven to take more comprehensive action. They undertook counts of their poor, established licensing schemes which permitted those incapable of earning a living to beg and attempted to drive away other beggars by threatening savage punishments and sometimes carrying them out. Some, like Bristol (1522), Canterbury (1552) and Norwich (1557) established municipal corn stocks in order to be able to provide the poor with food at moderate prices in times of dearth and thus prevent wage earners from becoming destitute in years of poor harvest. Some also followed the example of London, which between 1544 and 1557 established five great 'hospitals' (St Thomas's and St Bartholomew's for the sick and aged, Christ's for orphan children, Bridewell for the able bodied poor, and Bedlam for the insane), in creating institutions to which particular catagories of poor could be consigned. And when the numbers of poor people whom the munici-pality felt it incumbent upon them to relieve became too great to be supported by a combination of charitable endowments and voluntary alms-giving, even when the latter was encouraged and organized by the authorities, then compulsory levies were decreed, notably in London

---

[3] These had, in any event, been reduced by the Dissolution of the Monasteries.

(1547), Norwich (1549). Ipswich and Colchester (1557) and York (1561). However, in many even of the largest towns, Worcester for instance, such poor rates long remained a highly unusual expedient, resorted to only in the direst emergencies (Leonard, 1900, ch. III. Pound, 171 (1), ch. 5. Palliser, 1979, p. 275. Dyer, 1973, p. 167–8).

Throughout the period poverty acute enough to be of concern to those in authority remained mainly an urban matter, but gradually it ceased to be almost exclusively such. The mixed farming areas in effect exported much of their natural increase in population, and the employment problem it caused, in part to the towns and in part to neighbouring forest and pastoral industrial districts. But the concentration of landholding into fewer hands which occurred in the former, and the growth of a class of landless farm labourers (see above Ch. 3 sec. vii), meant that the traditional means of supporting those unable to work for a living ceased to be available for a growing number of families. Besides wage rates in the countryside were also declining steeply,[4] and by the 1610s those of agricultural labourers were down to 44 per cent of what they had been in the later fifteenth century (*A.H.E.W.* IV, 1967, p. 865). The enclosure of common land deprived the poor in many villages of an important resource, for the ability to maintain just one or two animals, a cow and a pig perhaps, could mean for some the difference between a precarious economic independence and wretched destitution. Similarly the increased emphasis on private rights of property, as opposed to communal ownership of resources, which accompanied the rise of commercial farming, meant that a whole range of practices which had once helped the least fortunate members of the community to scrape their subsistence – use of the commons by those technically without common rights, gleaning in the fields after harvest, or gathering fuel from the hedgerows and coppices for instance – came to be regarded with an increasingly evil eye by the gentry and larger farmers (Thompson, 1976). The support of the aged and infirm, of widows and orphaned children, known collectively to contemporaries as 'the impotent poor', thus came to pose the same problem that it had always done in urban areas. And the same was true in those mainly pastoral districts where rural industry grew to the point where considerable numbers were coming to rely upon wages for their livelihood. In almost every community for which evidence is available such people, amongst whom those too young to fend for themselves invariably made up the largest single group, comprised about 4 or 5 per cent of the total population and their numbers increased *pari passu* with the growth of the latter.

---

[4] This, however, may have been considerably less important a cause of poverty in the countryside than in the towns because, in general, rural wage earners were less fully dependent upon their money wages.

Another way in which developments in the countryside produced acute poverty was the increasing economic insecurity which affected both the family farmers in the mixed farming districts as the size of holdings diminished and rents and fines were forced upwards, and the smallholders in the pastoral districts where dependence upon industrial employment placed entire communities at the mercy of fluctuations in demand for their products. (See also above Ch. 3 secs. vii and viii.) The disruption of exports by war in 1528, for instance, quickly produced distress in Suffolk as merchants ceased to buy cloth and employment in consequence dwindled, whilst in another depression a century later (1629) the Essex justices informed the Council that the livelihood of 30,000 weavers and spinners in their county alone was threatened unless some remedy could be found (Leonard, 1900, pp. 47–9. Supple, 1959, pp. 103–4). Harvest failures, moreover, had even more serious consequences. In the first place the rural industrial proletariat, like the poor of the towns, found it difficult to buy food to subsist upon, for throughout the period movements in money wages both in the long and in the short term seem to have been determined by the supply and demand for labour, not by the cost of living. Wages did not, therefore, rise when bread increased in price, and indeed many wage earners would have found themselves with less work or none at all, for when basic food-stuffs became unusually expensive the amount of employment invariably diminished. But further many of the small family farmers, even in the mixed farming zones let alone in the pastoral ones, found themselves unable both to pay their rents and to feed their families.

In normal circumstances real destitution in the villages and small market towns was confined largely, if not exclusively, to the impotent. Periodically, however, when things went seriously wrong with the economy it emerged on a much larger scale, engulfing thousands of families which had thitherto been able to support themselves, however poorly. A proportion of the most desperate would be propelled onto the roads leading to the larger towns, suddenly swelling the constant trickle of rural–urban migrants to a steady stream. Every community which lay upon an important road would quickly become aware of their passage and of the increased flow of tramps and vagrants drifting from one town to the next in a vain search for more hopeful prospects. Some of these people, a high proportion of whom were young men in their late teens or early twenties, wandered very long distances from their homes. Most of those arrested at Exeter in 1565, for instance, came from the counties of the South West, but the group included individuals from as far away as Worcestershire, Berkshire, London and Berwick; and 22 per cent of a large sample of early and mid seventeenth century vagrants were picked up more than a hundred miles from their place of origin (Beier, 1974.

Slack, 1974. MacCaffrey, 1958, pp. 95–6). Usually they travelled in ones and twos, and doubtless were more to be pitied than anything else, but occasionally they formed themselves into larger gangs which begged and threatened their way from village to village, battening on families scarcely better off than themselves. The fear and hatred they then inspired perhaps[5] still echoes down the centuries in the old rhyme, 'Hark! Hark! The dogs do bark, the beggars are coming to town.'

If there were poor harvests only in one part of the country, or if trade depression struck on its own, then only limited districts might be affected by the crisis. But if the harvests failed throughout the realm, and especially if they did so when overseas trade was depressed, or during war-time when the periodic demobilization of forces repeatedly threw back onto the labour market thousands of men who had lost their place in civilian society, then the problem of the able bodied poor and vagrancy would become a national one of terrifying proportions. It did so, for instance, in the early and again in the late 1520s, in the mid 1540s, the mid and later 1590s, the early 1620s, 1629–31, the late 1640s and in 1661–2. Fearful of disorder the central government would be driven to take action.[6] Above all it would intervene in the grain trade to try to ensure that London and the other main towns were adequately supplied with food. It would bring pressure to bear upon exporters to continue to buy cloth, even though temporarily they were unable to sell it, in order to maintain industrial employment at the highest level possible. It would also strive to secure the enforcement of existing laws for the relief of distress and the suppression of vagrancy. Finally the next meeting of parliament would discuss, either at the suggestion of ministers or on its own initiative, whether fresh legislation were needed to deal with the crisis or, if the crisis were already passed, to be available for the future. Not all the national Poor Laws of the period thus emerged in the aftermath of a major crisis, but many of them did, including that of 1531 which was the first major statute devoted to the subject, the notorious Act directed against vagrants passed in 1547, the famous codification Acts of 1597 and 1601 and the Act of Settlement of 1662.

ii *The search for solutions*

Even in the early part of the sixteenth century there were perceptive individuals, like Sir Thomas More, who appreciated well enough that many of the able bodied people who were without employment and on

---

[5] Or perhaps not: another, very different origin has also been suggested for this. See I. and P. Opie (eds.) *Oxford Dictionary of Nursery Rhymes*, pp. 152–3.
[6] For a full discussion of government intervention in economic and social affairs, see below II, Ch. 10.

the roads, or begging in the towns, had not adopted that way of life out of choice. And indeed modern investigation bears out that most of those arrested as vagrants were honest, had formerly been employed as labourers, as servants or in the notoriously unstable cloth industry and were genuinely looking for work. Thus amongst those stopped at Salisbury in the 1620s was one John Hopkins, who, in the words of the city register, 'confesses he is apprentice to Robert Studdocke of Froome Selwood, Som., Weaver. He ran away from his master.' Another was 'Thomas Dadorne alias Trowe, Weaver', who was returned after punishment to Reading 'where he last dwelt many years', whilst a third was William Butler, 'wandering and begging, terming himself a glassman, having no passport' (Slack, 1975). Some undoubtedly did commit crimes as they travelled, but only a small minority were professional criminals and most of those who stole were driven to it by necessity. It has been noted elsewhere that there was a great deal of geographical mobility amongst the lower orders of society in this period (see above Ch. 1 sec. vi and Ch. 6 sec. iv), and the distinction between the man or woman who moved from job to job but succeeded in remaining in more or less continuous employment and the one stigmatized as an undesirable as a result of a vagrancy prosecution was not necessarily a clear one. It might be a matter of no more than the unexpected termination of employment, caused for instance by the death of the employer, or the heightened zeal of the local J.P.s at a time of political tension, which turned the first into the second (Beier, 1974).

The attitude of most articulate contemporaries to the able bodied unemployed had, however, been moulded by the generations of relative labour scarcity which had succeeded the fourteenth century plagues, and it was therefore widely accepted that if someone was without a job it was their own fault. Such voluntary idleness was viewed as a moral offence, harmful to the perpetrator, and one from which he or she must be deterred. But it was also an offence against society, for it was taken for granted that every individual had an allotted rôle, which was determined by the circumstances of their birth and which they had no business to abandon, and that of the lower orders was to perform manual labour. The support of the impotent poor by the giving of alms was a christian duty, enjoined by Church and state alike, and as their numbers grew and casual charity ceased to be adequate to relieve them, local authorities first in London (1533) and then in the country at large (1536) were instructed to collect all offerings intended for the poor and to supervise their distribution. To give to those who *could* work, on the other hand, was no act of charity and indeed was strictly forbidden by statute in 1531. Thus one Elizabethan preacher told his congregation, 'as for our rogues and vagabonds, I exclude them out of the role and number of poor men, commended by the spirit of God . . . who because they do not labour they should not eat' (Slack, 1972, p. 165). For such people punishment was generally considered to be the appropriate remedy, combined with a forcible return to their place of origin if they had strayed away from home, for no local community was willing to support paupers from any other district. The whipping of able bodied vagrants was prescribed by local ordinances in one town after another in the early and mid sixteenth century; and in a long series of enactments parliament prescribed it, or yet more savage punishments including branding, ear-boring and even death for persistent offenders.

Early parliamentary legislation on the subject of the poor does not, however, seem to have been widely enforced, and some of it, such as the Act of 1547 which ordained the highly impracticable expedient of enslavement for vagrants, was apparently scarcely enforced at all (Davies, 1966). Certainly not many vagrants were actually hanged, though some were on the strength of the Act of 1572 which was part of a drive against the floating and rootless members of society conducted by a nervous government in the aftermath of the Revolt of the Northern Earls (1569). There were other periods when for similar reasons the government showed particular concern about vagrants, for instance during the Spanish war at the end of the century, but in many places for much of the time the treatment the majority of them actually received was apparently not by any means as brutal as the law permitted. At Norwich, for instance, not only were many of those ordered to depart spared a whipping, but they were given time to arrange their own departure and even money for their journey. Likewise a census of the poor in the town of Warwick in 1586 revealed seven able bodied adult beggars, but only one of them was ordered to be whipped. The laws enacted by parliament and the local regulations of the municipalities empowered magistrates to proceed against the able bodied unemployed with a barbarous ferocity, but they probably only made full use of their powers in response to instructions from the Council, or when they felt that the local situation was getting out of hand (Williams, 1979, pp. 211–12. Pound, 1976. *V.C.H. Warws.* VIII, pp. 509–10).

Besides as the sixteenth century wore on the gradual accretion of experience led to some alteration in attitudes. The Act of 1572[7] for the first time recognized that certain categories of people might be without employment involuntarily, and that of 1576 provided that parishes should lay in stocks of material upon which they could be set to work,

[7] For a brief account of the sixteenth century statutes concerning vagrancy and poor relief, see Pound, 1971 (1).

although not until the reiteration of this proviso in 1597, at a time of particularly acute economic crisis, was it widely complied with. Nor, once the crisis had passed, was the provision of work long continued in most places, and in the early seventeenth century it was usually laid on only when economic conditions deteriorated again, and then just for short periods. However, the apprenticing of pauper children, an expedient which had long been common in the towns and which was finally incorporated into the national Poor Law in 1597, became general practice, since for a small sum paid to a master by way of premium a parish could rid itself of responsibility for the child's keep. The training such apprentices received was, however, frequently minimal and in practice they simply provided struggling craftsmen in low grade occupations with extremely cheap labour (Oxley, 1974, pp. 73–7).

Some towns and counties established permanent work-houses into which the able bodied poor could be gathered, and a few places, notably Norwich in the early 1570s, Salisbury in 1623 and London in 1649, attempted to set up comprehensive schemes of employment provision involving both work-houses and the putting out of materials. However, even work-houses on their own, let alone the more elaborate programmes, required more competent management than local authorities could provide for any length of time. Partly for this reason the latter never succeeded in being fully self-financing and they tended to arouse opposition among other producers who feared their competition in limited markets. At any rate they all foundered sooner or later (Pound, 1962. Slack, 1972. Pearl, 1978). By the later seventeenth century attempts to provide work for the able bodied poor seem largely to have ceased, although there may have been more work-houses in operation than the sources reveal. In most places, however, in so far as the able bodied received relief at all (see also below p. 232), it was in the same from as that provided for those who could not work, that is small doles of money, allowances of fuel, payment of house rent and the like (Webb and Webb, 1927, pp. 159–62, 166–70. Oxley, 1974, p. 80). The dominant strand of contemporary opinion by this time was that the best way to set the poor to work was not by artificial schemes but by pursuing economic policies at a national level which would create an increased demand for labour in the economy as a whole. There was not, however, universal agreement about this, and at the very end of the period a new movement to establish work-houses was beginning to get under way, of which the first fruit was the establishment of the 'Corporation of the Poor' at Bristol in 1696[8]

---

[8] This Act in effect created a single authority for the administration of poor relief in the city as a whole, responsibility previously having been in the hands of each of nineteen parishes, and its main purpose was to concentrate sufficient resources to build a large work-house. Both aspects of the

(Wilson, 1959. Webb and Webb, 1927, pp. 100–20). However, as a
significant part of the system of poor relief work-houses belong to the
eighteenth century rather than the seventeenth.

With the passage of time the financing of poor relief came to pose an
increasingly acute problem. We have already noticed how some urban
authorities had, even in the mid sixteenth century, been obliged to resort
to compulsory levies to raise sufficient funds, and in a succession of Acts
passed during the third quarter of the century parliament gradually
moved in the direction of giving parishes everywhere the power to do
likewise. In 1552 it was ordained that collectors of alms should be
appointed in each parish, and that those who refused to contribute should
be censured by the ecclesiastical authorities. In 1563 contributions, but
of unspecified sums, were made compulsory; and finally the compulsory
poor rate was incorporated into the Act of 1572. It was not, however,
envisaged that the rate would be levied save in emergencies, nor is there
much evidence that it was levied at all in most country districts before the
very end of the century, though some villages and small market towns in
southern and eastern England were raising modest sums in this way by
the 1580s (Hampson, 1934, pp. 8–12. Emmison, 1953. Clark, 1977,
p. 239). In most places, however, enough money was available out of
ordinary parish revenues, or could be raised by organizing church ales
and other similar festivities, to make this unnecessary. And certainly well
into the next century private charity rather than compulsory local
taxation continued to provide the bulk of the resources which became
available for the relief of poverty.

This charity took many different forms. Every parish church had its
poor box to which everyone who attended contributed according to their
means. In the villages yeomen and husbandmen often helped their poorer
neighbours with small gifts in cash or kind and lent them tools and
equipment. The well-to-do often distributed money and surplus food to
the poor in their immediate neighbourhood on a regular basis and some
rich people fed dozens or even scores daily for years on end. Thus in 1596
Sir Thomas Egerton was distributing weekly alms to sixty-two people in
the London parish of St Dunstan's, whilst in the mid seventeenth
century the Kentish landowner Sir George Sondes opened his doors to at
least twenty every week. Both the urban elite and, although less often,
that of the countryside helped to prevent starvation in the years of worst
food shortage by buying grain and re-selling it below cost price, and in
hard winters they might do the same with fuel. Conscientious landowners

Bristol experiment were widely copied in the years immediately following (Webb and Webb, 1927,
pp. 116–20).

often had more servants in their households and home farms than they strictly needed; they grew certain crops, flax and woad for instance, and in pastoral areas grain, as much or more for the employment they provided as for the profit they brought in; and they sometimes invested money in setting up local industries for the same reason (Stone, 1965, pp. 47–9. Chalklin, 1965, pp. 210, 241–2. *A.H.E.W.* V Part ii, 1984 pp. 238–40). It was conventional for rich people to leave something in their wills for the local poor, whilst some of those whose charitable inclinations were stronger established funds from which an income would be available in future years to relieve the poor of particular parishes. Others founded almshouses to care for the elderly and infirm, or schools to provide education for pauper children, whilst others again provided capital for the payment of apprenticeship premiums or to furnish those who had completed an apprenticeship with enough money to commence business on their own account.

The only part of this flow of benevolence which can actually be measured is that which was forthcoming from donors after their deaths and was provided for in their wills, and W. K. Jordan has shown that there was a very great increase in the sums bequeathed, with urban merchants emerging as by far the most generous group of testators. In the ten counties which, together with London, made up his sample, he found that benefactions for secular purposes averaged about £50,862 per decade in the first half of the sixteenth century, but thereafter rose steeply to reach a peak of £382,397 in the 1610s after which they declined to much lower levels (Jordan, 1959, ch. VII and pp. 367–75. Bittle and Lane, 1976, p. 209). Unquestionably some places benefited enormously from this generosity. At Exeter, for instance, three sets of almshouses were established between 1567 and 1634, adding twenty-six places to the sixty-three available in older foundations; endowments producing income for general poor relief rose from £10 a year in 1588 to £86 a year in 1640; the total of the revolving fund for lending out to merchants for establishing their own business stood at £2800 by 1617; and two grammar schools were founded in the 1630s (MacCaffrey, 1958, pp. 104–10 and ch. 5). Moreover, whilst municipal and parish authorities at best concentrated on relieving the worst *symptoms* of poverty, and frequently devoted much of their energy to shifting the problem elsewhere by waging vigorous war against vagrants, as this example suggests the bequests of the charitable were increasingly devoted to attempts to reduce its incidence.

Nevertheless what general significance should be attached to Jordan's findings is a difficult question, for when allowance is made for the fall in the purchasing power of money much of the apparent increase in charitable giving turns out to be illusory. On the other hand, since a high proportion of the bequests were in the form of land intended to establish permanent endowments, the income from which must certainly have risen with the passing years, there can be little doubt that the total yield of the constantly multiplying number of endowed charities easily outpaced inflation. It may even have increased sufficiently in real terms to match the rise in total population that occurred between the early sixteenth and the early seventeenth centuries, whilst in the period of more stable prices and much less rapid demographic growth after about 1640 the real value per head of population of the funds available from endowed charities must have increased significantly. But there is a good deal of evidence that many of them were inefficiently or corruptly administered, which must have resulted in a great deal of leakage. Besides it is far from clear how large a proportion of total charitable 'transfer payments' they accounted for, and if they increased other forms of giving seem certainly to have declined. The expansive 'hospitality' of the very rich gradually went out of fashion after the mid sixteenth century, so that there were fewer left-overs to distribute. Changing values, the constantly reiterated prohibitions against casual alms-giving in municipal by-laws and parliamentary statutes which reflected these changes, and ultimately the institution of compulsory poor rates, undoubtedly reduced the readiness of people to toss a coin to a beggar in the street or to listen to the plea of an old woman at the back-door (Bittle and Lane, 1976. Hadwin, 1978. Coleman, 1978). Indeed a reduced readiness to provide immediate help to the needy on a person to person basis was apparently becoming a source of social tension in some neighbourhoods by the later sixteenth century. It may have provoked an increase in petty theft, especially of food-stuffs in times of particular hardship (Walter and Wrightson, 1976). It has also been suggested that the upsurge in prosecutions for witchcraft after about 1560 was in part the result of guilt felt on this account. In other words people who had breached the customary ethical code by a refusal of charity to a poor person came to believe that a subsequent misfortune represented the revenge which the latter had procured by magical means (Macfarlane, 1970, pp. 204–6. Thomas, 1971, pp. 552–69).

Moreover even if the total volume of funds for the relief and prevention of poverty forthcoming from charitable sources increased in real terms throughout most of the period, it did not increase enough, nor was the increase widely enough distributed in a geographical sense to meet the need of all localities. On the one hand, even at the end of the period, there were some unfortunate villages in every district which had never attracted any important benefactions, so that their poor suffered worse deprivations than elsewhere. On the other hand, there were places, mostly large towns, where the number of those actually or potentially in need of relief had multiplied so rapidly that even a large increase in charitable endowments was not sufficient to provide for them. Here compulsory rates came to play a major rôle in the financing of poor relief well before 1600, and during the seventeenth century easily surpassed charity in importance, although a local emergency, such as the need to relieve the victims of a fire or an epidemic, was still more likely to be met by a special appeal for voluntary offerings than an increase in rates. At Salisbury in the early part of the seventeenth century the rates provided twice as much for poor relief as did charity, whilst at Newcastle in its middle decades the local charities on their own could not begin to meet the demands of the city's notoriously numerous poor (Slack, 1972, p. 179. Howell, 1967, pp. 314–19). And in London, evidence from a number of parishes in the 1640s and 1650s indicates that, save in a very few of the most affluent ones, the poor rates were very much more important than private charity (Herlan, 1977 (1) and (2); 1978).

If the traditional sources of funds for poor relief had ceased, on their own, to provide sufficient money in many of the larger towns even in normal times by the later sixteenth century, in times of acute economic crisis they proved inadequate almost everywhere. This became particularly evident during the mid 1590s when a series of disastrous harvests sent food prices rocketing, and the combined effects of dearth, shrinking industrial employment as dear bread absorbed purchasing power normally devoted to manufactures, and epidemic disease, caused widespread distress which extended much further up the social scale than usual. There were outbreaks of disorder, mostly small scale and highly localized, but including one in Oxfordshire which was potentially more serious, and it became clear to those in authority everywhere that something would have to be done to avert catastrophic social breakdown. It was in this setting that the Poor Law of 1597, subsequently amended in 1601, was enacted by parliament. This was essentially a codification and clarification of existing legislation and introduced little that was new in principle, but it provided a firmer basis for the collection of compulsory rates and their use not only to succour the impotent poor but also to provide work for the able bodied (Pound, 1971 (1), pp. 54–5). However, the legislators continued to assume that in normal circumstances charity would provide sufficient funds, and there was no intention that rates should be levied in every parish every year. But from this time onwards, whenever the economy took a turn for the worse the expedient of levying a rate to meet the extra costs that would be incurred in providing relief lay ready to hand, and was adopted in a steadily increasing number of places, rural as well as urban.

In fact the extent to which the Poor Laws were enforced and the way in which poor relief was administered was almost entirely a matter of local initiative, or absence of it, each parish being responsible for its own poor subject to the supervision of the county justices. The only period when the central government made any consistent effort to ensure that the legislation was fully implemented was during Charles I's personal rule in the 1630s, and the pressure then exerted by the Council does not seem to have been particularly effective. In Warwickshire, for instance, and no doubt elsewhere, the justices were more active in dealing with poverty in the 1650s than they had been before 1640. Indeed, if anything accelerated the gradual creation of a coherent system of poor relief in accordance with the statutes of 1597 and 1601 and turned the levying of compulsory poor rates outside the larger towns from the exception to the norm, it was probably the unique circumstances of the 1640s. The Civil War caused acute, albeit relatively short-lived, economic and social dislocation in many areas, and was immediately followed by a series of very bad harvests which forced grain prices higher than ever before. These events combined to cause acute distress in the later part of the decade, at the very time when power in most counties had passed to a new ruling élite. These were still almost invariably landowners, but they were more Puritan in outlook than their predecessors and tended to be parish squires rather than county magnates, and they seem for these reasons to have been more conscious of the needs of the humblest members of society. In Cheshire, for instance, the post Civil War justices adopted a very much less punitive attitude to the homeless poor than was normal, frequently made real efforts to get them housed somewhere and maintained an exceedingly tight control over both the price of grain and the conduct of the grain trade (Beier, 1966. Morrill, 1974, pp. 248–51).

The substantial gentry who resumed control of the counties in 1660 did not in general show the same conscientious zeal as the 'godly magistracy' which had held sway in the aftermath of the Civil War, but by the last third of the century poor rates were apparently being levied on a regular basis, if not yet everywhere at least very widely. There was, moreover a long term tendency for the amounts levied to increase, and certainly complaints by farmers and their landlords about the financial burden involved become increasingly frequent from this time onwards. One estimate suggests that in the middle of the century about £250,000 was raised annually in this way, whilst by the end of it the figure was perhaps £700,000 (Taylor, 1969, p. 12). Since the price level was roughly stable in this part of the period this did indeed represent a real increase of nearly three fold.

To some extent the growing importance of the rates reflects a decline in other sources of income for poor relief towards the end of the period. Church ales, for instance, which in some country areas, perhaps many, had rendered rates unnecessary, came to be increasingly frowned on by the authorities as Puritanism spread its hold among the élite, and were slowly but surely being suppressed (Hill, 1964, pp. 425–7). But there was also a continuous increase in the extent of poverty needing relief. For reasons discussed elsewhere after the middle of the seventeenth century crises caused by bad harvests were not as acute as those of the 1590s, early 1620s, 1629–31 or the late 1640s, and there was a slow but continuous improvement in real wages. (See, for instance, above Ch. 4 sec vi.) Wage rates for building craftsmen were higher by one third in the 1680s than they had been in the 1610s (see Table VI and Figure 4 on pp. 217 and 218 above), and for building labourers the increase was greater still (Phelps Brown and Hopkins, 1981, chs. 1–2). Besides, the problem of the poor may have gradually become less acute during the mid and later seventeenth century in many of the smaller and medium sized urban centres. A reduced rate of population growth and the enforcement of 'settlement' legislation slowed down the inflow of rural migrants (see also below sec. iii of this chapter), whilst employment opportunities were improved both by the emergence of new forms of manufacture and by the expansion of service occupations which reflected the increasing importance of many towns as centres of social life for large rural hinterlands. (See above Ch. 6 sec. iii.) On the other hand in the largest places, including London where everything was on so much larger a scale than anywhere else and which contained nearly half the entire urban population in the later seventeenth century, conditions of life for the poor and the extent of poverty remained appalling. Both were also very bad in fast growing clothing and dockyard towns such as Manchester and Chatham (Clark and Slack, 1976, pp. 42–3, 124–5). Meanwhile in the countryside the continued growth in the number of landless labourers in the mixed farming areas, and above all of those dependent upon industrial employment in many pastoral ones, meant that an ever larger proportion of the rural population were wage earners. In 1695 Gregory King estimated that there were, in the country as a whole, 1,275,000 'labouring people and out servants' and a further 1,300,000 'cottagers and paupers'. And he implied that all of them, with some smaller groups at a comparable economic level, together comprising a little over half of all Englishmen, were at least potential candidates for poor relief (Thirsk and Cooper, 1972, pp. 780–1). Some recent research, however, suggests that the implication may be unduly pessimistic (Holmes, 1977. Lindert, 1980), and certainly the number who could actually be described as paupers at any one time was normally much lower: it was, for instance, apparently about one sixth both in the market town of Lichfield and in the Leicestershire village of Wigston Magna (Coleman, 1956, p 285. Hoskins, 1957, pp. 201–2).[9]

But where wage employment was industrial employment the fraction was always liable to increase suddenly whenever trading conditions deteriorated. By 1660 or so the woollen industry had completed the adjustments to changed market conditions which had been underway in the earlier part of the century, and the volume of employment it provided was no longer subject to such violent fluctuation. (See below II, Ch. 8 sec. iii.) However, it remained an unstable element in the economy, and as we shall see large scale use of domestic workers was no longer confined to woollens. (See below II, Ch. 8 secs. xi and xii.) In any industry organized in this way employers tended promptly to reduce the amount of raw material they put out at the first hint of any contraction in demand, thus obliging their work force to bear much of the burden of hard times. Industrial employment may have helped to prevent large sections of the rural population from sinking into chronic and abject poverty, but for large numbers it was an insecure source of income, and when it ceased temporarily to be available many of those left unemployed had to be relieved by their parishes. By 1700 it was already notorious that, leaving aside the larger towns, it was the principal manufacturing districts where the poor rates were highest.

In fact, however, both in the main towns and some areas of rural industry, even charity and regular levying of the poor rate could not provide enough to alleviate the distress of all who were in need. Most of whatever was available seems everywhere to have been directed towards the groups traditionally regarded as 'deserving', that is the aged, the infirm and those too young to support themselves. Able bodied paupers, whose needs were no less real and whose plight was for the most part equally unmerited, seem invariably to have received a very much smaller share, even though their numbers must usually have been considerably greater. In part this was because of the persistence of unsympathetic attitudes to able bodied paupers; in part because they were often so numerous that the financial implications of providing proper relief for them all were too frightening to be contemplated; and in part because many of them were unlicensed immigrants from other districts who were not eligible for statutory relief in any event. Nevertheless the increasing rate burden of the last third of the seventeenth century seems to indicate that parishes were beginning to find it impossible in practice to avoid supporting a growing number of able bodied poor, since in many places

---

[9] The proportion actually in receipt of relief was normally very much lower still.

the rise was much larger than can be accounted for in any other way. In one parish in the Isle of Thanet, for instance, the rates rose from £84 3s 6d in 1663 to £279 1s 2d in 1702 (Chalklin, 1965. p. 256).

iii The control of the poor

The support which parish authorities provided to those they relieved was never more than minimal. Cottage or tenement rents would be paid, sparing allowances of winter fuel provided and small sums of cash were doled out. Likewise orphans and foundlings were boarded out with some poor family as cheaply as possible, perhaps provided with a rudimentary education, and then apprenticed to a master who would be chosen, as often as not, because he was prepared to accept a lower premium than any other. Basic medical attention was usually provided for the seriously ill, for women in childbirth and for family bread-winners disabled from earning by an accident. Often the cash allowances paid to the adult poor were so small, no more than a few pence a week, that on their own they could not possibly have provided the recipient with a subsistence income, and they must have been intended as a supplement, whether to some form of partial or occasional employment or to the charity of relatives and neighbours (Hampson, 1934, ch. iv. Oxley, 1974, ch. 4. Herlan, 1977 (1) and (2); 1978). But meagre though poor relief was, once the system developed in outline during the latter part of the sixteenth century was actually in operation everywhere, it was sufficient, just, to prevent the poor dying from lack of food, even in the years of greatest shortage. The seriously deficient harvests of 1594–7 caused numerous deaths from starvation, especially in the North but also in scattered pockets throughout the Midlands and South. After the dearth of 1623, however, even in the North only isolated individuals such as the occasional tramp or deserted child ever seem to have starved (Appleby, 1978, ch. 9). Increases in agricultural output, improvements in distribution and a reduced rate of population growth were clearly the underlying factors in this development, but it was not only the better maintenance of food supplies which accounted for the end of deaths by starvation. After all, if relief had not been distributed many would have been unable to buy enough food even at normal prices.

Relief, however, was not afforded to the poor unconditionally, and both those who controlled parish funds and those who managed charitable endowments used their power to grant or withold it as a means of controlling the lower orders. Those receiving doles might, for instance, have to wear a pauper's badge, and indeed an Act of 1697 made this compulsory everywhere. They might, especially in the mid seventeenth century when the influence of Puritanism was at its height, be obliged to attend church, be forbidden to frequent alehouses, to keep bad company or cohabit with persons of the opposite sex, whilst for the parents of illegitimate babies there was the prospect of a public whipping. The inmates of hospitals and almshouses paid for the more comprehensive provision they received by even greater restrictions on their liberty. It was common for them to be obliged to wear a distinctive garb, to have to attend regular prayers and to be forbidden to marry on pain of expulsion. They were generally subject to a discipline imposed by the master or mistress of the institution against which in practice they had no appeal, and they might be kept as virtual prisoners. Thus the founder of one Wiltshire almshouse in the 1680s prescribed that its inmates should 'lodge within their own appartments... and not gad abroad in the day time' (Clay, 1978, p. 311). It was often those members of the élite who were most active in promoting the physical well-being of the poor who were most inclined to insist upon adherence to strict standards of behaviour, for the protestant conscience which dictated that it was an individual's duty to help the poor interpreted this as much in terms of moral as of material welfare. The far-reaching scheme for the relief of poverty in Salisbury in the 1620s promoted by a group of Puritan magistrates, for instance, involved a particularly extensive degree of regimentation for its intended beneficiaries (Slack, 1972).

Everywhere those who would not work, or whose mode of existence was interpreted by the authorities as tantamount to a refusal to work, were liable to incarceration in the Houses of Correction which were erected from the later sixteenth century onwards. But the most far-reaching form of social control involved in the administration of the Poor Laws was the restrictions placed upon the freedom of the poor to move about as they liked. Any wanderer of whom the authorities did not like the look could be prosecuted for vagrancy and upon conviction forcibly returned to his place of origin, and few parishes would willingly provide relief to outsiders unless obliged to do so by the justices. Besides, at least by the later sixteenth century, most towns had elaborate regulations against the erection of new tenements without licence, against the subdivision of houses and the taking in of lodgers, all intended to prevent unwanted immigrants from establishing themselves. Similarly in the countryside many manors, especially in the mixed farming areas where manorial control tended to remain more effective than elsewhere, had similar rules, and these were reinforced by an Act of Parliament of 1589 forbidding the building of new cottages unless at least four acres of land were attached to them (Styles, 1963–4). And everywhere the authorities waged intermittent war on unlicensed alehouses which fulfilled a vital function in making movement possible for poor people, since they provided travellers and new arrivals not only with refreshment but also with accommodation, information about employment possibilities, and so on (Clark, 1978).

Now in practice none of this prevented a great deal of internal population mobility, for neither national legislation nor local regulations were ever effectively enforced in any one locality save for short periods, and in some places, for instance in the suburbs of towns, in wood pasture districts and in many parts of the highland zone where manorial control was often weak, and indeed wherever the gentry were few and far between, they were almost entirely neglected. In fact, as we have seen in Chapter 3, the growth of squatter communities on common land was a marked feature of the economic development of many such areas from the later sixteenth century onwards. (See esp. above ch. 3 sec. viii.) Elsewhere, however, it was often made difficult, even for people who arrived with the best of intentions, to establish themselves properly, and the various laws and local regulations now under discussion may to some extent have exacerbated the vagrancy problem they were supposed to cure.

It is probably true that in normal circumstances people moving short distances, within the districts where they were known and able to give a good account of themselves, would be left alone to find the work they sought. But although the vagrancy laws were not turned against all to whom they could have been applied, they *were* used selectively against certain groups amongst the poor for whom the authorities felt a particular distaste, especially young men without family ties who had come from well outside the locality and who had been on the road for a long time. Such people personified the social disorder of which contemporaries were so afraid, and in times of political tension were regarded as potential carriers of sedition (Slack, 1974. Beier, 1974; 1978. Pound, 1976). Further pressure against the long distance migrant derived from the gradual evolution during the early and mid seventeenth century of the idea that everyone, not just vagrants, should have a place of 'settlement' which was legally bound to provide them with relief if need arose, and to which they could be returned if they fell into poverty and became a charge on the rates. This was finally enshrined in the 1662 Act of Settlement which empowered justices to order the removal of almost any poor, or not so poor, person to their place of origin if it appeared likely that they would become 'chargeable' in the future, even if they were completely self supporting at the time. The respectable could get round this obstacle to making a change in their place of residence by obtaining a certificate from the parish where they had a settlement promising to assume responsibility for them if need arose, but in practice such a system could only operate between parishes within a fairly short distance of one another. There was undoubtedly a considerable decrease in the extent of long distance migration by the poor during the course of the seventeenth century. In part this reflected fundamental economic changes: a slower rate of population growth, and an improvement in the economic opportunities available in the highland zone with the spread of rural industry and increasing specialization in livestock husbandry. In part it may also reflect more effective poor relief in rural areas as more and more parishes there resorted to compulsory rates to discharge their obligations under the Acts of 1597 and 1601. But in part also it represented partially successful control by the propertied groups in society of that section of the poor which they most feared (Styles, 1963–4. Clark, 1979).

BIBLIOGRAPHY

This is a list of all works cited in the text of this volume, together with others which the author has consciously drawn upon for ideas, arguments, factual information or inspiration. It is not a complete list of all those consulted during the preparation of this book, still less a comprehensive bibliography of English economic and social history in the period.

The Agrarian History of England and Wales IV *1500–1640*, ed. J. Thirsk (Cambridge, 1967).

The Agrarian History of England and Wales V *1640–1750*, ed. J. Thirsk (2 parts, Cambridge, 1984).

Airs, M. *The Making of the English Country House 1500–1640* (London, 1975).

Allan, D.G. 'The rising in the West, 1628–31', *Ec.H.R.* 2nd ser. V, No. 1 (1952).

Appleby, A.B. 'Nutrition and disease: the case of London, 1550–1700', *J.I.H.* VI, No. 1 (1975).

Appleby, A.B. *Famine in Tudor and Stuart England* (Liverpool, 1978).

Appleby, A.B. 'Grain prices and subsistence crises in England and France, 1590–1740', *J.E.H.* XXXIV, No. 4 (1979).

Ault, W.O. *Open Field Farming in Medieval England* (London, 1972).

Aylmer, G.E. *The King's Servants. The Civil Service of Charles I 1625–1642* (London, 1961).

Aylmer, G.E. 'The crisis of the aristocracy 1558–1641', *P. & P.* 32 (1965).

Baker, A.R.H. and R.A. Butlin *Studies of Field Systems in the British Isles* (Cambridge, 1973).

Bamford, F. (ed.) *A Royalist's Notebook. The Commonplace Book of Sir John Oglander of Nunwell* (London, 1936).

Beckett, J.V. 'English landownership in the later seventeenth and eighteenth centuries: the debate and the problems', *Ec.H.R.* 2nd ser. XXX, No. 4 (1977).

Beer, B.L. *Rebellion and Riot. Popular Disorder in England during the Reign of Edward VI* (Kent State University, 1982).

Beier, A.L. 'Poor relief in Warwickshire, 1630–1660', *P. & P.* 35 (1966).

Beier, A.L. 'Vagrants and the social order in Elizabethan England', *P. & P.* 64 (1974).

Beier, A.L. 'Social problems in Elizabethan England', *J.I.H.* IX, No. 2 (1978).

Bennett, M.K. 'British wheat yields per acre for seven centuries', *Economic Journal. Economic History Supplement* III (1935). Reprinted in Minchinton I.

Beresford, M. *The Lost Villages of England* (London, 1954).

Beresford, M. 'Habitation versus improvement: the debate on enclosure by agreement', in F.J. Fisher (ed.), *Essays in the Economic and Social History of Tudor and Early Stuart England* (Cambridge, 1961).

Bettey, J.H. 'Sheep, enclosures and watermeadows in Dorset', in M. Havinden (ed.), *Husbandry and Marketing in the South West, 1500–1800* (University of Exeter, 1973).

Bettey, J.H. 'The development of water meadows in Dorset during the seventeenth century', *Ag.H.R.* 25, Part I (1977) (1).

Bettey, J.H. 'Agriculture and rural society in Dorset, 1570–1670' (unpublished Ph.D. thesis, University of Bristol, 1977) (2).

Bittle, W.G. and R.T. Lane 'Inflation and philanthropy in England: a reassessment of W.K. Jordan's data', *Ec.H.R.* 2nd ser. XXIX, No. 2 (1976).

Blackwood, B.G. 'The economic state of the Lancashire gentry on the eve of the Civil War', *N.H.* XII (1976).

Blanchard, I. 'Population change, enclosure, and the early Tudor economy', *Ec.H.R.* 2nd ser. XXIII, No. 3 (1970).

Blum, J. 'The European village as community', *A.H.* XIV, No. 3 (1971).

Bonfield, L. 'Marriage settlements and the "rise of great estates": the demographic aspect', *Ec.H.R.* 2nd ser. XXXII, No. 4 (1979).

Bonfield, L. 'Marriage settlements, 1660–1740: the adoption of the strict settlement in Kent and Northamptonshire', in R.B. Outhwaite (ed.), *Marriage and Society* (London, 1981).

Bowden, P.J. *The Wool Trade in Tudor and Stuart England* (London, 1962).

Brenner, Y.S. 'The inflation of prices in early sixteenth century England', *Ec.H.R.* 2nd ser. XIV, No. 2 (1961). Reprinted in P.H. Ramsey (ed.), *The Price Revolution in Sixteenth Century England* (London, 1971).

Brenner, Y.S. 'The inflation of prices in England 1551–1650', *Ec.H.R.* 2nd ser. XV, No. 2 (1962).

Brett-James, N.G. *The Growth of Stuart London* (London, 1935).

Bridbury, A.R. 'Sixteenth century farming', *Ec.H.R.* 2nd ser. XXVII, No. 4 (1974).

Bridbury, A.R. 'English provincial towns in the later Middle Ages', *Ec.H.R.* 2nd ser. XXXIV, No. 1 (1981).

Broad, J.P.F. 'Sir Ralph Verney and his estates 1630–1696' (unpublished D.Phil. thesis, University of Oxford, 1973).

Broad, J.P.F. 'Alternate husbandry and permanent pasture in the Midlands, 1650–1800', *Ag.H.R.* 28, Part II (1980).

Butlin, R.A. 'The enclosure of open fields and the extinction of common rights in England *c.* 1600–1750: a review', in H.S.A. Fox and R.A. Butlin, *Change in the Countryside* (London, 1979).

Cambridge Economic History of Europe IV, ed. C.H. Wilson and E.E. Rich (Cambridge, 1967).

Campbell, M. *The English Yeoman* (New Haven, 1942).

Campbell, R.H. 'The Anglo-Scottish Union of 1707: the economic conse-quences', *Ec.H.R.* 2nd ser. XVI, No. 3 (1964).

Carus-Wilson, E.M. *Medieval Merchant Venturers* (London, 1954).

Carus-Wilson, E.M. *Essays in Economic History* (3 vols., London, 1954–1962).

Chalklin, C.W. *Seventeenth Century Kent* (London, 1965).

Chalklin, C.W. *The Provincial Towns of Georgian England* (London, 1974) (1).

Chalklin, C.W. 'The making of some new towns *c.* 1600–1720', in C.W. Chalklin and M.A. Havinden (eds.), *Rural Change and Urban Growth 1500–1800* (London, 1974) (2).

Challis, C.E. 'The debasement of the coinage, 1542–1551', *Ec.H.R.* 2nd ser. XX, No. 3 (1967).

Challis, C.E. 'The circulating medium and the movement of prices in mid-Tudor England', in P.H. Ramsey (ed.), *The Price Revolution in Sixteenth Century England* (London, 1971).

Challis, C.E. 'Spanish bullion and monetary inflation in England in the later sixteenth century', *J.E.Ec.H.* 4, No. 2 (1975).

Challis, C.E. *The Tudor Coinage* (Manchester, 1978).

Chambers, J.D. *Population, Economy, and Society in Pre-Industrial England* (Oxford, 1972).

Chartres, J.A. 'Markets and marketing in metropolitan western England', in M. Havinden (ed.), *Husbandry and Marketing in the South West 1500–1800* (Exeter, 1973).

Chartres, J.A. *Internal Trade in England 1500–1700* (London, 1977) (1).

Chartres, J.A. 'Road carrying in England in the seventeenth century: myth and reality', *Ec.H.R.* 2nd ser., XXX, No. 2 (1977) (2).

Chibnall, A.C. *Sherington. The Fiefs and Fields of a Buckinghamshire Village* (Cambridge, 1965).

Clark, P. 'The migrant in Kentish towns, 1580–1640', in P. Clark and P. Slack (eds.), *Crisis and Order in English Towns* (London, 1972).

Clark, P. (ed.) *The Early Modern Town* (London, 1976).

Clark, P. *English Provincial Society from the Reformation to the Revolution: Religion, Politics and Society in Kent 1500–1640* (Hassocks, 1977).

Clark, P. 'The alehouse and the alternative society', in D. Pennington and K. Thomas (eds.), *Puritans and Revolutionaries* (Oxford, 1978).

Clark, P. 'Migration in England during the late seventeenth and eighteenth centuries', *P. & P.* 83 (1979).

Clark, P. and P. Slack *Crisis and Order in English Towns* (London, 1972).

Clark, P. and P. Slack *English Towns in Transition 1500–1700* (Oxford, 1976).

Clarkson, L.A. *The Pre-Industrial Economy in England, 1500–1750* (London, 1971).

Clay, C. 'Marriage, inheritance and the rise of large estates in England, 1660–1815', *Ec.H.R.* 2nd ser. XXI, No. 3 (1968).

Clay, C. 'The price of freehold land in the later seventeenth and eighteenth centuries', *Ec.H.R.* 2nd ser. XXVII, No. 2 (1974).

Clay, C. *Public Finance and Private Wealth. The Career of Sir Stephen Fox 1627–1716* (Oxford, 1978).

Clay, C. 'Property settlements, financial provision for the family, and sale of land by the greater landowners 1660–1790', *J.B.S.* XXI, No. 1 (1981).

Cliffe, J.T. *The Yorkshire Gentry* (London, 1969).

Coleman, D.C. 'Naval dockyards under the later Stuarts', *Ec.H.R.* 2nd ser. VI, No. 2 (1953).

Coleman, D.C. 'Labour in the English economy of the seventeenth century', *Ec.H.R.* 2nd ser. VIII, No. 3 (1956). Reprinted in Carus-Wilson II.

Coleman, D.C. Review of W.K. Jordan's *Philanthropy in England*, *Ec.H.R.* 2nd ser. XIII, No. 1 (1960).

Coleman, D.C. *Sir John Banks. Baronet and Businessman* (Oxford, 1963).

Coleman, D.C. 'The "gentry" controversy and the aristocracy in crisis, 1558–1641', *History* LI (1966).

Coleman, D.C. *Industry in Tudor and Stuart England* (London, 1975).

Coleman, D.C. *The Economy of England 1450–1750* (Oxford, 1977).

Coleman, D.C. 'Philanthropy deflated: a comment', *Ec.H.R.* 2nd ser. XXXI, No. 1 (1978).

Cooper, J.P. 'The counting of manors', *Ec.H.R.* 2nd ser. VIII, No. 3 (1956).

Cooper, J.P. 'The social distribution of land and men in England, 1436–1700', *Ec.H.R.* 2nd ser. XX, No. 3 (1967). Reprinted in R. Floud and D.C. McCloskey (eds.), *Essays in Quantitative Economic History* (Oxford, 1974).

Cooper, J.P. 'Patterns of inheritance and settlement by great landowners from the fifteenth to the eighteenth centuries', in J. Goody, J. Thirsk and E.P. Thompson (eds.), *Family and Inheritance* (Cambridge, 1976).

Cooper, J.P. 'In search of agrarian capitalism', *P. & P.* 80 (1978).

Corfield, P. 'A provincial capital in the late seventeenth century: the case of Norwich', in P. Clark and P. Slack (eds.), *Crisis and Order in English Towns* (London, 1972). Reprinted in P. Clark (ed.), *The Early Modern Town* (London, 1976).

Corfield, P. 'Urban development in England and Wales in the sixteenth and seventeenth centuries', in D.C. Coleman and A.H. John (eds.), *Trade, Government, and the Economy in Pre-Industrial England* (London, 1976).

Cornwall, J. 'English country towns in the fifteen twenties', *Ec.H.R.* 2nd ser. XV, No. 1 (1962).

Cornwall, J. 'The early Tudor gentry', *Ec.H.R.* 2nd ser. XVII, No. 3 (1965).

Cornwall, J. 'English population in the early sixteenth century', *Ec.H.R.* 2nd ser. XXIII, No. 1 (1970).

Cornwall, J. 'The squire of Conisholme', in C.W. Chalklin and M.A. Havinden (eds.), *Rural Change and Urban Growth 1500–1800* (London, 1974).

Crofts, J. *Packhorse, Waggon and Post* (London, 1967).

Cullen, L.M. *Anglo–Irish trade 1660–1800* (Manchester, 1968).

Dahlman, C.J. *The Open Field System and Beyond* (Cambridge, 1980).

Darby, H.C. *The Draining of the Fens* (Cambridge, 1940).

Davies, C.S.L. 'Slavery and Protector Somerset: the Vagrancy Act of 1547', *Ec.H.R.* 2nd ser. XIX, No. 3 (1966).

Davies, C.S.L. 'Peasant revolt in England and France: a comparison', *Ag.H.R.* 21, Part II (1973).

Davies, M.G. 'Country gentry and payments to London, 1650–1714', *Ec.H.R.* 2nd ser. XXIV, No. 1 (1971).
Davis, R. 'English foreign trade 1660–1700', *Ec.H.R.* 2nd ser. VII, No. 2 (1954). Reprinted in Carus-Wilson II and in W.E. Minchinton (ed.) *The Growth of English Overseas Trade in the Seventeenth and Eighteenth Centuries* (London, 1969).
Davis, R. *The Rise of the English Shipping Industry* (London, 1962).
Defoe, D. *A Tour through England and Wales* (Everyman ed., 2 vols. London, 1928).
Dewar, M. (ed.) *A Discourse of the Commonweal of This Realm of England* (Charlottesville Va., 1969).
Dietz, F.C. *English Government Finance 1485–1558* (Urbana, 1921).
Dobson, R.B. 'Urban decline in late Medieval England', *T.R.H.S.* 5th ser. 27 (1977).
Doolittle, I.G. 'The effects of the plague on a provincial town in the sixteenth and seventeenth centuries', *Medical History* 19, No. 4 (1975).
Drake, M. 'An elementary exercise in parish register demography', *Ec.H.R.* 2nd ser. XIV, No. 3 (1962).
Du Boulay, F.R.H. 'Who were farming the English demesnes at the end of the Middle Ages?', *Ec.H.R.* 2nd ser. XVII, No. 3 (1965).
Dyer, A.D. *The City of Worcester in the Sixteenth Century* (Leicester, 1973).
Edelen, G. (ed.) *The Description of England by William Harrison* (Ithaca N.Y., 1968).
Emerson, W.R. 'The economic development of the estates of the Petre family in Essex in the sixteenth and seventeenth centuries' (unpublished D. Phil. thesis, University of Oxford, 1951).
Emmison, F.G. 'The care of the poor in Elizabethan Essex', *Essex Review* LXII (1953).
Everitt, A. *The Community of Kent and the Great Rebellion* (Leicester, 1966) (1).
Everitt, A. 'Social mobility in early modern England', *P. & P.* 33 (1966) (2).
Everitt, A. *Change in the Provinces* (Leicester, 1969) (1).
Everitt, A. *The Local Community and the Great Rebellion* (Historical Assoc., 1969) (2).
Everitt, A. 'The English urban inn, 1560–1760' in his *Perspectives in English Urban History* (London, 1973).
Faith, R.J. 'Peasant families and inheritance customs in medieval England', *Ag.H.R.* XIV, Part II (1966).
Farmer, D.L. 'Grain yields on the Winchester manors in the later Middle Ages', *Ec.H.R.* 2nd ser. XXX, No. 4 (1977).
Fenoaltea, S. 'Risk, transaction costs, and the organization of medieval agriculture', *Explorations in Economic History* 13, No. 2 (1976).
Ferris, J.P. 'The gentry of Dorset on the eve of the Civil War', *Genealogists' Magazine* 15, No. 3 (1965).
Finch, M.E. *The Wealth of Five Northamptonshire Families, 1540–1640* (Northants. Record Society, 1956).

Firth, C.H. and R.S. Rait *Acts and Ordinances of the Interregnum* (3 vols., London, 1911).
Fisher, F.J. 'The development of the London food market 1540–1640', *Ec.H.R.* v, No. 2 (1935). Reprinted in Carus-Wilson I.
Fisher, F.J. 'The development of London as a centre of conspicuous consumption in the sixteenth and seventeenth centuries', *T.R.H.S.* 4th ser. 30 (1948). Reprinted in Carus-Wilson II.
Fisher, F.J. 'Influenza and inflation in Tudor England', *Ec.H.R.* 2nd ser. XVIII, No. 1 (1965).
Fisher, F.J. 'The growth of London', in E.W. Ives (ed.), *The English Revolution 1600–1660* (London, 1968).
Fisher, F.J. 'London as an "engine of economic growth"', in J.S. Bromley and E.H. Kossmann (eds.), *Britain and The Netherlands* IV (London, 1971). Reprinted in P. Clark (ed.), *The Early Modern Town* (London, 1976).
Fletcher, A. *Tudor Rebellions* (London, 1968).
Fletcher, A. *The Outbreak of the English Civil War* (London, 1981).
Flinn, M.W. 'Plague in Europe and the Mediterranean countries', *J.E.Ec.H.* 8, No. 1 (1979).
Floud, R. and D. N. McCloskey *The Economic History of Britain since 1700* (2 vols., Cambridge, 1981).
Fowkes, D. 'Nottinghamshire parks in the eighteenth and nineteenth centuries', *Transactions of the Thoroton Society* LXXI (1967).
Fox, H.S.A. 'Outfield cultivation in Devon and Cornwall', in M.A. Havinden (ed.) *Husbandry and Marketing in the South West 1500–1800* (University of Exeter, 1973).
Gay, E.F. 'The Temples of Stowe and their debts', *H.L.Q.* II, No. 4 (1939).
Gay, E.F. 'Sir Richard Temple: The debt settlement and estate litigation, 1653–1675', *H.L.Q.* VI, No. 3 (1943).
Gemery, H.A. 'Emigration from the British Isles to the New World, 1630–1700', *R.E.H.* 5 (1980).
Gilboy, E.W. *Wages in Eighteenth Century England* (Cambridge, Mass., 1934).
Glass, D.V. 'Socio-economic status and occupations in the City of London at the end of the seventeenth century', in A.E.J. Hollaender and W. Kellaway, *Studies in London History* (London, 1969). Reprinted in P. Clark (ed.), *The Early Modern Town* (London, 1976).
Glass, D.V. 'Notes on the demography of London at the end of the seventeenth century', in D.V. Glass and R. Revelle (eds.), *Population and Social Change* (London, 1972).
Godfrey, E.S. *The Development of English Glassmaking 1560–1640* (Oxford, 1975).
Gottfried, R.S. 'Population, plague, and the sweating sickness: demographic movements in late fifteenth century England', *J.B.S.* XVII, No. 1 (1977).
Gottfried, R.S. *Epidemic Disease in Fifteenth Century England* (Leicester, 1978).
Gough, J.W. *The Rise of the Entrepreneur* (London, 1969).
Gould, J.D. 'Mr Beresford and the lost villages: a comment', *Ag.H.R.* 3, Part II (1955).

Gould, J.D. 'The price revolution reconsidered', *Ec.H.R.* 2nd ser. XVII, No. 2 (1964). Reprinted in P.H. Ramsey (ed.), *The Price Revolution in Sixteenth Century England* (London, 1971).

Gould, J.D. *The Great Debasement* (Oxford, 1970).

Grassby, R. 'The personal wealth of the business community in seventeenth century England', *Ec.H.R.* 2nd ser. XXIII, No. 2 (1970).

Gurr, A. *The Shakespearean Stage, 1574–1642* (Cambridge, 1970).

Habakkuk, H.J. 'English landownership 1680–1740', *Ec.H.R.* X, No. 1 (1940).

Habakkuk, H.J. 'Marriage settlements in the eighteenth century', *T.R.H.S.* 4th ser. XXXII (1950).

Habakkuk, H.J. 'The market for monastic property 1539–1603', *Ec.H.R.* 2nd ser. X, No. 3 (1958).

Habakkuk, H.J. 'The English land market in the eighteenth century', in J.S. Bromley and E.H. Kossman (eds.), *Britain and the Netherlands* I (London, 1960).

Habakkuk, H.J. 'Landowners and the Civil War', *Ec.H.R.* 2nd ser. XVIII, No. 1 (1965)(1).

Habakkuk, H.J. 'La disparition du paysan Anglais' *Annales: Economies, Sociétés, Civilizations* 20, No. 4 (1965) (2).

Habakkuk, H.J. 'The rise and fall of English landed families, 1600–1800' (three articles), *T.R.H.S.* 5th ser. 29–31 (1979, 1980 and 1981).

Hadwin, J.F. 'Deflating philanthropy', *Ec.H.R.* 2nd ser. XXXI, No. 1 (1978).

Hajnal, J. 'European marriage patterns in perspective', in D.V. Glass and D.E.C. Eversley, *Population in History* (London, 1965).

Hamilton, E.J. 'American treasure and Andalusian prices, 1503–1660', *Journal of Economic and Business History* I, No. 1 (1928). Reprinted in P.H. Ramsey (ed.), *The Price Revolution in Sixteenth Century England* (London, 1971).

Hampson, E.M. *The Treatment of Poverty in Cambridgeshire 1597–1834* (Cambridge, 1934).

Harris, L.E. *Vermuyden and the Fens* (London, 1953).

Harrison, C.J. 'Grain price analysis and harvest qualities, 1465–1634', *Ag.H.R.* 19, Part II (1971).

Hatcher, J. *Plague, Population and the English Economy 1348–1530* (London, 1977).

Havinden, M.A. 'Agricultural progress in open field Oxfordshire', *Ag.H.R.* 9, Part II (1961). Reprinted in Minchinton I.

Havinden, M.A. 'Lime as a means of agricultural improvement' in C.W. Chalklin and M.A. Havinden (eds.), *Rural Change and Urban Growth* (London, 1974).

Helleiner, F. 'The population of Europe from the Black Death to the eve of the vital revolution', in C. Wilson and E.E. Rich (eds.), *Cambridge Economic History of Europe* IV (Cambridge, 1967).

Herlan, R.W. 'Poor relief in the London parish of St Antholin's Budge Row, 1638–1664', *Guildhall Studies in History* II, No. 4 (1977)(1).

Herlan, R.W. 'Poor relief in the London parish of St Dunstan in the West', *Guildhall Studies in History* III, No. 1 (1977)(2).

Herlan, R.W. 'Poor relief in London during the English Revolution', *J.B.S.* XVIII, No. 2 (1978).

Hey, D.G. *An English Rural Community. Myddle under the Tudors and Stuarts* (Leicester, 1974).

Hexter, J.H. 'The English aristocracy: its crises and the English Revolution, 1558–1660', *J.B.S.* VIII, No. 1 (1968).

Hinton, R.W.K. *The Eastland Trade and the Commonweal* (Cambridge, 1959).

Hill, C. *Society and Puritanism in Pre-revolutionary England* (London, 1964).

Holderness, B.A. *Pre-Industrial England. Economy and Society, 1500–1750* (London, 1976)(1).

Holderness, B.A. 'Credit in English rural society before the nineteenth century', *Ag.H.R.* 24, Part II (1976)(2).

Hollingsworth, T.H. 'The demography of the British peerage', supplement to *Population Studies* XVII, No. 2 (1964).

Hollingsworth, T.H. *Historical Demography* (London, 1969).

Hollis, D. *Calendar of the Bristol Apprentice Book 1532–1565*, Part I (Bristol, 1949).

Holmes, C. *The Eastern Association and the Civil War* (Cambridge, 1974).

Holmes, G.S. 'The Sacheverell Riots', *P. & P.* 72 (1976).

Holmes, G.S. 'Gregory King and the social structure of pre-industrial England', *T.R.H.S.* 5th ser. 27 (1977).

Horsefield, S.K. *British Monetary Experiments* (Cambridge Mass., 1960).

Hoskins, W.G. *Industry, Trade and People in Exeter 1688–1800* (Manchester, 1935).

Hoskins, W.G. 'The reclamation of the waste in Devon, 1550–1800', in *Ec.H.R.* XIII (1943).

Hoskins, W.G. 'The Leicestershire farmer in the sixteenth century', in *Essays in Leicestershire History* (Liverpool, 1950).

Hoskins, W.G. 'The estates of the Caroline gentry' in W.G. Hoskins and H.R.P. Finberg (eds.), *Devonshire Studies* (London, 1952).

Hoskins, W.G. 'An Elizabethan provincial town: Leicester', in J.H. Plumb (ed.), *Studies in Social History* (London, 1955).

Hoskins, W.G. 'The English provincial towns in the early sixteenth century', *T.R.H.S.* 5th ser. 6 (1956). Reprinted in P. Clark (ed.), *The Early Modern Town* (London, 1976).

Hoskins, W.G. *The Midland Peasant* (London, 1957).

Hoskins, W.G. 'The Elizabethan merchants of Exeter', in S. Bindoff, J. Hurstfield and C.H. Williams (eds.), *Elizabethan Government and Society* (London, 1961). Reprinted in P. Clark (ed.), *The Early Modern Town* (London, 1976).

Hoskins, W.G. 'The Leicestershire farmer in the seventeenth century,' in his *Provincial England* (London, 1963).

Hoskins, W.G. 'Harvest fluctuations and English economic history, 1480–1619', *Ag.H.R.* 12, Part I (1964). Reprinted in Minchinton I.

Hoskins, W.G. 'Harvest fluctuations and English economic history, 1620–1759', *Ag.H.R.*16, Part I (1968).

Hoskins, W.G. *The Age of Plunder 1500–1547* (London, 1976).

Howell, R. *Newcastle-upon-Tyne and the Puritan Revolution* (Oxford, 1967).

Hull, F. 'Agriculture and rural society in Essex 1540–1640' (unpublished Ph.D. thesis, University of London, 1950).

John, A.H. 'The course of agricultural change, 1660–1760', in L.S. Pressnell (ed.), *Studies in the Industrial Revolution* (London, 1960). Reprinted in Minchinton I.

John, A.H. 'Aspects of English economic growth in the first half of the eighteenth century', *Economica* N.S. XXVIII (1961). Reprinted in Carus-Wilson II.

John, A.H. 'Agricultural productivity and economic growth in England 1700–1760', *J.E.H.* XXV, No. 1 (1965).

John, A.H. 'English agricultural improvement and grain exports, 1660–1765', in D.C. Coleman and A.H. John (eds.), *Trade, Government and Economy in Pre-Industrial England* (London, 1976).

Johnson, D.J. *Southwark and the City* (London, 1969).

Johnson, M.A. 'Buckinghamshire 1640–1660' (unpublished Ph.D. thesis, University College of Swansea, 1963).

Jones, E.L. 'Agriculture and economic growth in England 1660–1750: agricultural change', *J.E.H.* XXV, No. 1 (1965). Reprinted in Minchinton I.

Jones, E.L. *Agriculture and Economic Growth in England 1650–1815* (London, 1967).

Jordan, W.K. *Philanthropy in England, 1480–1660* (London, 1959).

Jordan, W.K. *Edward VI. The Young King* (London, 1968).

Kerridge, E. 'The movement of rent 1540–1640', *Ec.H.R.* 2nd ser. VI, No. 1 (1953). Reprinted in Carus-Wilson II.

Kerridge, E. 'The returns to the inquisitions of depopulation', *E.H.R.* 70 (1955).

Kerridge, E. *The Agricultural Revolution* (London, 1967).

Kerridge, E. *Agrarian Problems in the Sixteenth Century and After* (London, 1969) (1).

Kerridge, E. 'The agricultural revolution reconsidered', *A.H.* XLIII, No. 4 (1969) (2).

Kew, J. 'The disposal of the crown lands and the Devon land market, 1536–58', *Ag.H.R.* 18, Part II (1970).

Kussmaul, A. *Servants in Husbandry in Early Modern England* (Cambridge, 1981).

Lane, C. 'The development of pastures and meadows during the sixteenth and seventeenth centuries', *Ag.H.R.* 28, Part I (1980).

Lang, R.G. 'London's aldermen in business: 1600–1625', *The Guildhall Miscellany* III, No. 4 (1971).

Lang, R.G. 'The social origins and social aspirations of Jacobean London merchants', *Ec.H.R.* 2nd ser. XXVII, No. 1 (1974).

Laslett, P. *The World We Have Lost* (London, 1965).

Laslett, P. and R. Wall *Household and Family in Past Time* (Cambridge, 1972).

Leonard, E.M. *The Early History of English Poor Relief* (Cambridge, 1900).

Leonard, E.M. 'The inclosure of the common fields in the seventeenth century', *T.R.H.S.* N.S. XIX (1905). Reprinted in Carus-Wilson II.

Lindert, P.H. 'English occupations, 1670–1811', *J.E.H.* XL, No. 4 (1980).

MacCaffrey, W.T. *Exeter, 1540–1640* (Cambridge Mass., 1958).

Macfarlane, A. *Witchcraft in Tudor and Stuart England* (London, 1970).

Macfarlane, A. *The Origins of English Individualism* (Oxford, 1978).

Machin, R. 'The Great Rebuilding: a reassessment', *P. & P.* 77 (1977).

McCloskey, D.N. 'The persistence of English common fields' in W.N. Parker and E.L. Jones (eds.), *European Peasants and their Markets* (Princeton, 1975).

McCloskey, D.N. 'English open fields as behaviour towards risk', *R.E.H.* 1 (1976).

McGrath, P.V. 'The marketing of food, fodder and livestock in the London area in the seventeenth century' (unpublished M.A. thesis, University of London 1948).

McIntosh, M.K. 'The fall of a Tudor gentle family: the Cookes of Gidea Hall, Essex, 1579–1629', *H.L.Q.* XLI, No. 3 (1978).

Mendels, F.F. 'Proto-industrialization: the first phase of the industrialization process', *J.E.H.* XXXII, No. 1 (1972).

Minchinton, W.E. *Essays in Agrarian History* (2 vols, Newton Abbot, 1968).

Mingay, G.E. 'The size of farms in the eighteenth century', *Ec.H.R.* 2nd ser. XIV, No. 3 (1962).

Mingay, G.E. *English Landed Society in the Eighteenth Century* (London, 1963).

Mingay, G.E. 'Dr Kerridge's agricultural revolution: a comment', *A.H.* XLIII, No. 4 (1969)(1).

Mingay, G.E. Review of E. Kerridge's *The Agricultural Revolution*, *Ag.H.R.* 17, Part II (1969)(2).

Mingay, G.E. *The Gentry* (London, 1976).

Miskimin, H.A. 'Population growth and the price revolution in England', *J.E.Ec.H.* 4, No. 1 (1975).

Morgan, R. 'The root crop in English agriculture, 1650–1870' (unpublished Ph.D. thesis, University of Reading, 1978).

Morrill, J.S. *Cheshire 1630–1660. County Government and Society during the English Revolution* (Oxford, 1974).

Nef, J.U. *The Rise of the British Coal Industry* (2 vols., London, 1932).

Nef, J.U. 'Silver production in Central Europe' *Journal of Political Economy* XLIX (1941).

Opie, I. and P. Opie (eds.), *Oxford Dictionary of Nursery Rhymes* (Oxford, 1952).

Outhwaite, R.B. *Inflation in Tudor and Stuart England* (London, 1969).

Outhwaite, R.B. 'Who bought crown lands? The pattern of purchases 1589–1603', *B.I.H.R.* XLIV (1971).

Overton, M. 'Computer analysis of an inconsistent data source: the case of probate inventories', *Journal of Historical Geography* 3, No. 4 (1977).

Overton, M. 'Estimating crops yields from probate inventories', *J.E.H.* XXXIX, No. 2 (1979).

Overton, M. 'English probate inventories and the measurement of agricultural change', in A. Van Der Woude and A. Schuurman (eds.), *Probate Inventories* (Wageningen, 1980).

Oxley, G.W. *Poor Relief in England and Wales 1601–1834* (Newton Abbot, 1974).

Palliser, D.M. 'Epidemics in Tudor York', *N.H.* VIII (1973)(1).

Palliser, D.M. 'York under the Tudors: the trading life of the northern capital', in A. Everitt (ed.), *Perspectives in English Urban History* (London, 1973)(2).

Palliser, D.M. 'Dearth and disease in Staffordshire, 1540–1670', in C.W. Chalklin and M.A. Havinden (eds.), *Rural Change and Urban Growth* (London, 1974).

Palliser, D.M. 'A crisis of English towns? The case of York, 1460–1640', *N.H.* XIV (1978).

Palliser, D.M. *Tudor York* (Oxford, 1979).

Palliser, D.M. "Tawney's century:brave new world or Malthusian trap?', *Ec.H.R.* 2nd ser. XXXV, No. 3 (1982).

Parker, L.A. 'The agrarian revolution at Cotesbach 1501–1612', *Leicestershire Archaeological Society* XXIV (1948).

Patten, J. 'Village and town: an occupational study', *Ag.H.R.* 20, Part 1 (1972).

Pattern, J. *Rural–Urban Migration in Pre-Industrial England* (Research Paper No. 6, School of Geography, University of Oxford, 1973).

Patten, J. *English Towns 1500–1700* (Folkestone, 1978).

Pearl, V. 'Puritans and poor relief. The London workhouse, 1649–1660', in D. Pennington and K. Thomas (eds.), *Puritans and Revolutionaries* (Oxford, 1978).

Pearl, V. 'Change and stability in seventeenth century London', *London Journal* 5, No. 1 (1979).

Pelling, M. and C. Webster 'Medical practitioners', in C. Webster (ed.), *Health, Medicine and Mortality in the Sixteenth Century* (Cambridge, 1979).

Pettit, P.A.J. *The Royal Forests of Northamptonshire* (Northants. Record Society, 1968).

Phelps Brown, H. and S.V. Hopkins *A Perspective of Wages and Prices* (London, 1981).

Phythian-Adams, C. 'Urban decay in late medieval England', in P. Abrams and E.A. Wrigley (eds.), *Towns in Societies* (Cambridge, 1978).

Phythian-Adams, C. *The Desolation of a City. Coventry and the Urban Crisis of the late Middle Ages* (Cambridge, 1979).

The Plague Reconsidered. A New Look at its Origins and Effects in 16th and 17th Century England (supplement to *Local Population Studies*, 1977).

Plummer, A. *The London Weavers' Company* (London, 1972).

Pollard, S. and D.W. Crossley *The Wealth of Britain 1066–1966* (London, 1969).

Pound, J.F. 'An Elizabethan census of the poor', *U.B.H.J.* VIII (1962).

Pound, J.F. 'The social and trade structure of Norwich 1525–1575', *P. & P.* 34 (1966). Reprinted in P. Clark (ed.), *The Early Modern Town* (London, 1976).

Pound, J.F. *Poverty and Vagrancy in Tudor England* (London, 1971)(1).
Pound, J.F. *The Norwich Census of the Poor 1570* (Norfolk Record Society, 1971)(2).
Pound, J.F. 'Debate. Vagrants and the social order in Elizabethan England', *P. & P.* 71 (1976).
Power, M. 'East London housing in the seventeenth century', in P. Clark and P. Slack (eds.), *Crisis and Order in English Towns* (London, 1972).
Power, M. 'The East and West in early modern London', in E.W. Ives, R.J. Knecht and J.J. Scarisbrick (eds.), *Wealth and Power in Tudor England* (London, 1978)(1).
Power, M. 'Shadwell. The development of a London suburban community in the seventeenth century', *London Journal* 4, No. 1 (1978)(2).
Prince, H. *Parks in England* (Shalfleet Manor I.O.W., 1967).
Raach, J.H. *A Directory of English Country Physicians* (London, 1962).
Ramsay, G.D. 'The recruitment and fortunes of some London freemen in the mid sixteenth century', *Ec.H.R.* 2nd ser. XXXI, No. 4 (1978).
Ramsey, P.H. (ed.) *The Price Revolution in Sixteenth Century England* (London, 1971).
Reddaway, T.F. *The Rebuilding of London after the Great Fire* (London, 1940).
Roberts, R.S. 'The personnel and practice of medicine in Tudor and Stuart England. Part I. The provinces', *Medical History* VI (1962).
Rogers, N. 'Popular protest in early Hannoverian London', *P. & P.* 79 (1978).
Scarisbrick, J.J. 'Cardinal Wolsey and the common weal', in E.W. Ives, R.J. Knecht and J.J. Scarisbrick (eds.), *Wealth and Power in Tudor England* (London, 1978).
Schofield, R.S. 'The geographical distribution of wealth in England, 1334–1649', *Ec.H.R.* 2nd ser. XVIII, No. 3 (1965). Reprinted in R. Floud (ed.), *Essays in Quantitative Economic History* (Oxford, 1974).
Schofield, R. and E.A. Wrigley 'Infant and child mortality in England in the late Tudor and early Stuart period', in C. Webster (ed.), *Health, Medicine and Mortality in the Sixteenth Century* (Cambridge, 1979).
Schumpeter, E.B. *English Overseas Trade Statistics 1697–1808* (Oxford, 1960).
Sheail, J. 'The distribution of taxable population and wealth in England during the early sixteenth century', *Transactions of the Institute of British Geographers* 55 (1972).
Shrewsbury, J.F.D. *A History of the Bubonic Plague in the British Isles* (Cambridge, 1970).
Simon, B. *Education in Leicestershire 1540–1940* (Leicester, 1968).
Simpson, A. *The Wealth of the Gentry 1540–1640* (Chicago and Cambridge, 1961).
Skipp, V. 'Economic and social change in the Forest of Arden, 1530–1649', in J. Thirsk (ed.), *Land, Church, and People* (British Agricultural History Society, Reading, 1970).
Skipp, V. *Crisis and Development. An Ecological Case Study of the Forest of Arden 1570–1674* (Cambridge, 1978).

Slack, P. 'Poverty and politics in Salisbury, 1597–1666', in P. Clark and P. Slack (eds.), *Crisis and Order in English Towns 1500–1700* (London, 1972).
Slack, P. 'Vagrants and vagrancy in England 1598–1664', *Ec.H.R.* 2nd. ser. XXVII, No. 3 (1974).
Slack, P. *Poverty in Early Stuart Wiltshire* (Wiltshire Record Society, 1975).
Slack, P. 'Mortality crises and epidemic disease in England 1485–1610', in C. Webster (ed.), *Health, Medicine and Mortality in the Sixteenth Century* (Cambridge, 1979).
Slack, P. 'The disappearance of plague', *Ec.H.R.* 2nd ser. XXXIV, No. 3 (1981).
Slater, G. *The English Peasantry and the Enclosure of the Common Fields* (London, 1907).
Slicher Van Bath, B.H. *Yield Ratios, 1810–1820* (Wageningen, 1963 (1).
Slicher Van Bath, B.H. *The Agrarian History of Western Europe* (London, 1963)(2).
Smith, R.M. 'Some reflections on the evidence for the origins of the "European marriage pattern" in England', in C. Harris (ed.), *The Sociology of the Family* (Keele, 1979).
Smith, S.R. 'The social and geographical origin of the London apprentices 1630–1660', *The Guildhall Miscellany* IV, No. 2 (1973).
Spufford, M. 'The schooling of the peasantry in Cambridgeshire, 1575–1700', in J. Thirsk (ed.), *Land, Church and People* (British Agricultural History Society, Reading 1970).
Spufford, M. *Contrasting Communities* (Cambridge, 1974).
Stone, L. 'The educational revolution in England, 1560–1640', *P. & P.* 28 (1964).
Stone, L. *The Crisis of the Aristocracy, 1558–1641* (Oxford, 1965).
Stone, L. 'Social mobility in England, 1500–1700', *P. & P.* 33 (1966).
Stone, L. and J.C.F. Stone 'Country houses and their owners in Hertfordshire 1540–1879' in W.O. Aydelotte, A.G. Bogue and R.W. Fogel (eds.), *Dimensions of Quantitative Research in History* (Princeton, 1972).
Styles, P. 'The evolution of the law of settlement', *U.B.H.J.* IX (1963–4).
Supple, B.E. *Commercial Crisis and Change in England, 1600–1642* (Cambridge, 1959).
Sutherland, I. 'When was the Great Plague? Mortality in London, 1563 to 1665' in D.V. Glass and R. Revelle (eds.), *Population and Social Change* (London, 1972).
Tate, W.E. *The English Village Community and the Enclosure Movements* (London, 1967).
Tawney, A.J. and R.H. Tawney 'An occupational census of the seventeenth century', *Ec.H.R.* V, No. 1 (1934).
Tawney, R.H. *The Agrarian Problem in the Sixteenth Century* (London, 1912).
Tawney, R.H. 'The rise of the gentry, 1558–1640', *Ec.H.R.* XI, No. 1 (1941). Reprinted in Carus-Wilson 1.
Tawney, R.H. 'The rise of the gentry: a postscript', *Ec.H.R.* 2nd ser. VII, No. 1 (1954).

Taylor, G. *The Problem of Poverty 1660–1834* (London, 1969).
Thirsk, J. *English Peasant Farming* (London, 1957).
Thirsk, J. 'Industries in the countryside', in F.J. Fisher (ed.), *Essays in the Economic and Social History of Tudor and Early Stuart England* (Cambridge, 1961).
Thirsk, J. 'Seventeenth century agriculture and social change', in J. Thirsk (ed.), *Land, Church, and People* (British Agricultural History Society, Reading, 1970).
Thirsk, J. 'New crops and their diffusion: tobacco growing in seventeenth century England', in C.W. Chalklin and M.A. Havinden (eds.), *Rural Change and Urban Growth* (London, 1974).
Thirsk, J. *Economic Policy and Projects* (Oxford, 1978).
Thirsk, J. and J.P. Cooper *Seventeenth Century Economic Documents* (Oxford, 1972).
Thomas, K. *Religion and the Decline of Magic* (London, 1971).
Thompson, E.P. 'The grid of inheritance: a comment', in J. Goody, J. Thirsk, and E.P. Thompson (eds.), *Family and Inheritance* (Cambridge, 1976).
Thompson, F.M.L. 'The social distribution of landed property in England since the sixteenth century', *Ec.H.R.* 2nd ser. XIX, No. 3 (1966).
Thorner, D. 'Peasant economy as a category in economic history', in T. Shanin (ed.), *Peasants and Peasant Societies* (London, 1971).
Thorner, D., D.T.B. Kerblay and R.E.F. Smith (eds.) *A.V. Chayanov on the Theory of Peasant Economy* (Homewood Ill., 1966).
Thrupp, S. 'The problem of replacement rates in the late medieval English population', *Ec.H.R.* 2nd ser. XVIII, No. 1 (1965).
Trevor-Roper, H.R. 'The gentry 1540–1640', *Ec.H.R.* Supplement No. 1 (1953).
Tudor Economic Documents, eds. R.H. Tawney and E. Power (3 vols., London, 1924).
Tupling, G.H. *The Economic History of Rossendale* (Chetham Society, 1927).
Unwin, G. *Industrial Organization in the Sixteenth and Seventeenth Centuries* (Oxford, 1904).
Van Bath, *see* Slicher Van Bath.
Victoria County History of Leicestershire II, eds. W.G. Hoskins and R.A. McKinley (London, 1954).
Victoria County History of Leicestershire III, eds. W.G. Hoskins and R.A. McKinley (London, 1955).
Victoria County History of Leicestershire IV, ed. R.A. McKinley (London, 1958).
Victoria County History of Oxfordshire X, ed. R.B. Pugh (London, 1972).
Victoria County History of Warwickshire VIII, ed. W.B. Stephens (London, 1969).
Victoria County History of Yorkshire. The City of York, ed. P.M. Tillott (London, 1961).
Walter, J. and K. Wrightson 'Dearth and the social order', *P. & P.* 71 (1976).
Wareing, J. 'Changes in the geographical distribution of the recruitment of

apprentices to the London companies 1486–1750', *Journal of Historical Geography* 6, No. 3 (1980).

Webb, S. and B. Webb *English Local Government: English Poor Law History Part 1. The Old Poor Law* (London, 1927).

Westerfield, R.B. *Middlemen in English Business* (New Haven, 1915).

Willan, T.S. *River Navigation in England* (Oxford, 1936).

Willan, T.S. *The English Coasting Trade 1660–1750* (Manchester, 1938).

Willan, T.S. *The Inland Trade* (Manchester, 1976).

Willan, T.S. *Elizabethan Manchester* (Chetham Society, 1980).

Williams, P. *The Tudor Regime* (Oxford, 1979).

Wilson, C. 'Treasure and trade balances: the mercantilist problem', *Ec.H.R.* 2nd ser. II, No. 2 (1949).

Wilson, C. Review of W.K. Jordan's *Philanthropy in England, E.H.R.* 75 (1960).

Wilson, C. *England's Apprenticeship 1603–1763* (London, 1965).

Wilson, C. 'The other face of mercantilism', *T.R.H.S.* 5th ser. 9 (1959). Reprinted in D.C. Coleman (ed.), *Revisions in Mercantilism* (London, 1969).

Wilson, C. 'A letter to Professor McCloskey', *J.E.Ec.H.* 8, No. 1 (1979).

Wolffe, B.P. *The Royal Demesne in English History* (London, 1971).

Woodward, G.W.O. *The Dissolution of the Monasteries* (London, 1966).

Wrigley, E.A. 'Family limitation in pre-industrial England', *Ec.H.R.* 2nd ser. XIX, No. 1 (1966).

Wrigley, E.A. 'A simple model of London's importance . . . 1650–1750', *P. & P.* 37 (1967). Reprinted in E.A. Wrigley and P. Abrams (eds.), *Towns in Societies* (Cambridge, 1978).

Wrigley, E.A. and R.S. Schofield *The Population History of England 1541–1871. A Reconstruction* (London, 1981).

Yelling, J.A. *Common Field and Enclosure in England 1450–1850* (London, 1977).

Youings, J. *The Dissolution of the Monasteries* (London, 1971).

INDEX

Acclom family, of Moresby, Yorks., 89
agrarian laws, 79–80, 83, 84
agricultural depression: in later seventeenth
century, 91, 92–3, 95, 97, 123, 130, 162,
163; support of tenants by landlords in,
123–4
agricultural implements, 59, 63, 64, 119, 174
agricultural labourers, see labourers
agriculture: general, Chs. 3 and 4, *passim*;
increase in output of, 63, 104, 107, 138–9,
138n, 139–41, 233; productivity of, 31, 63,
107, 111, 112–16, 118, 123, 124, 126ff, 133,
135, 136, 137–8, 140–1, 162; increased
investment in, 118ff, 129–30; rate of return
on investment in improvements, 124;
increased specialization, 116–18; increased
variety of output, 139; extent of England's
self-sufficiency in products of, 102–6;
proportion of population employed in, 165;
importance of to economy, 102–3, 139–41;
techniques, backward nature of, 112–14;
techniques, improvement of, 104, 112, 118,
119, 125, 126ff, 130ff, 137–8, 141, 162;
literature concerning, 131; internal trade in
products of, 57, 68–9, 102–4, 166, 169,
173–7, 179, 183–4, 200–1, 202, 210, 213,
222, 230 (*see also* markets; marketing);
practised by townsmen, 172; *see also*
commercial farming; mixed farming;
pastoral farming; peasant farmers
ale, *see* brewing
alehouses, 186, 208, 234, 234–5
almshouses, 216, 227, 234
Alnwick, Northumb., 172
America, Spanish, silver from, 33, 35
American colonies: emigration to, 25; trade
with, 136, 200, 202
animal products, *see* livestock products
Antwerp, 199
apothecaries, 185
apprentices, 188, 189, 196, 210–11, 212

apprenticeship, 183, 192, 195; of pauper
children, 225, 233; provision of premiums
by charity, 227
arable farming, *see* mixed farming
arable land, estimated acreage of (1695), 136
Arden, Forest of, 117
aristocracy: demographic experience of, 20,
24; and rebellions, 77; as landowners, 142,
143 (Table); wealth and estates of, 36, 143,
155, 156; rise of new families into, 146;
and marriage portions, 148; and royal
largesse, 157n (*see also* office-holders); and
the Civil War, 159; conspicuous
expenditure by, 122, 149–50, 157; sales of
land by, 157; resort of to London, 204–5;
see also landed families; landed magnates;
landlords; landowners; landownership
armed forces: economic effects, of
mobilization of, 47–8, of demobilization of,
222; family farmers as back-bone of, 79
artificial grasses, 132–3, 134
Arundel, Sussex, 172
Ashby de la Zouch, Leics., 176
Ashton-under-Lyne, Lancs., 18
assembly rooms, 187
assizes, 184
astrologers, 185
Atlantic, sea lanes to, from London, 198
attorneys, 182–3, 184
Aubrey, John, 111
Audley End, Essex, 149
Austria, 33
Avon, R. (War.), 179, 181n
Avon, R. (Wilts.), 181n
Aylesford, Earls of, 164

Bacon, Sir Nicholas, 153
Backhouse, James, of Kirby Lonsdale,
Westm., 177
bakers, 179, 195
balance of payments, 35, 37

253

enclosure of forests in, 78; dairying in, 55; water meadows in, 129; grain from, 176
drainage: general, 63, 115, 118, 119, 120, 134; of the Fens, 78, 108, 110, 125
Drake, Sir Francis, 36
drapers, 177
dried fruits, 177, 179
drovers, 181
Durham, Co.: population of, 1; agriculture of, 55, 116; open fields in, 73n
Dutch republic, *see* Netherlands
dyeing, of cloth, 193
dyestuffs, cultivation of, 99, 102, 136, 227
dysentry, 8, 18

East Anglia: population of, 1, 28; agriculture of, 57, 116, 131, 133, 137-8; cloth industry of, 69, 199; towns of, 20, 171, 194; retail shops in, 177-8; *see also* Essex; Norfolk; Suffolk
East India Company, 37, 163, 199
Egerton, Sir Thomas, 153, 266
Ellesmere, Lord Chancellor, *see* Egerton, Sir Thomas
emigration, 25-6
employment: creation of to combat poverty, 225, 227
enclosure: of open fields, 56, 67, 70 and n, 71, 72-3, 75-6, 79-80, 84-5, 90, 114-5, 118, 121, 126, 128, 134-5, 152 (*see also* conversion); of open fields, temporary, 114-5, 128, 135; of common land, 69, 71, 73 and n, 76, 80, 81, 84, 100-1, 107, 122, 126, 127 (*see also* cultivated area, increases in; encroachments); in Midlands, 67, 75-6, 85, 117, 123, 134-5; and introduction of improved methods, 128, 133; popular hostility towards, 77-8, 80-1, 84-5; hostility of government towards, 78-80 (*see also* agrarian laws); commissions of enquiry, 76; change in attitudes towards, 79-81, 128; by agreement, 73, 75, 84-5, 128; by act of parliament, 73 and n, 97; costs and financing of, 80, 82, 120, 123-4, 125; increase in rent as result of, 81 and n; as motive for land purchase, 152, 163; as result, not cause of social change, 88; and growth of poverty, 220; *see also* engrossing
encroachments, 98, 100-1, 107
epidemics: demographic effects of, 6 and n, 7 and n, 10, 12-13, 14-15; and scarcity of food, 8, 9, 16, 17-18, 19 and n, 26; and towns, 13, 20-2, 165, 188-9, 205, 212; economic impact of, 44, 215, 229
equity of redemption, 125, 159
esquires, 156

Essex: mortality crisis in, 18; agriculture of, 118; open fields in, 73n; landed society in, 152, 155; cloth industry of, 194, 221; silk industry in, 210; towns of, 194
estate management, 67, 81-4, 85ff, 147, 164, 184 (*see also* landlords; leases; rents and fines)
Exeter: population of, 166; mortality crisis at, 18; price of grain at, 38; occupations at, 195-6; distribution of wealth at, 215-16; trade of, 178, 199, 200; distributive functions of, 179; as capital market, 183; vagrants at, 221; charitable bequests at, 227; schools in, 186
Exmoor, 107
export trade, 141, 199-200, 222 (*see also* cloth, exports of)

fairs, 173-4, 177
fallow crops, *see* hitch crops; turnips
fallowing: general, 64, 113, 126, 128, 132n; reduced frequency of, 132, 136, 137, family: in peasant society, 60, 64; landed *see* landed families
family farmers, *see* peasant farmers
family limitation, 11, 23
family reconstitution, 5 and n
famine, *see* starvation
Far East, trade with, 200
farm buildings: on peasant farms, 59, 63; construction of new, 82, 109, 120, 121, 124, 125
farms, size of, *see* holdings, size of
farmers, *see* commercial farmers; peasant farmers
farm implements, *see* agricultural implements
Farnham, Surrey, 169, 176
fashion, changes in, 106
Fens, the: general, 27, 56, 61, and n, 100, 136, 138; drainage of, 78, 108, 110, 125
Fermour family, 144
fertility, *see* population, birth rate of
fertilizer, 63, 113, 119, 127 (*see also* manure; marl)
fines, *see* rents and fines
fish, 102, 175, 179
fishing, 62
Fitzwilliam family, of Milton, 160
flax, 102, 136, 137, 227
flour milling 210
fodder crops, 53, 56, 111, 130-5, 139
food and drink trades, 179, 195, 208 (*see also* alehouses; inns)
forests, royal: settlement of, 2, 27-8; migration into, 100, 190; economies of, 56, 62, 117; disafforestation and enclosure of, 78, 109, 145; *see also* woodland